Spi: e of

Healthcare

Also by Simon Robinson

Agape: Moral Meaning and Pastoral Counselling
Case Histories in Business Ethics (ed. with Chris Megone)
Their Rights: Advanced Directives and Living Wills Explored (with Kevin
Kendrick)

Also by Kevin Kendrick

Ethical Counselling: A Workbook for Nurses (with Philip Burnard)
Advancing Nursing Practice in Cancer and Palliative Care (ed. with
David Clarke and Jean Flanagan)*

*published by Palgrave Macmillan

Spirituality and the Practice of Healthcare

SIMON ROBINSON,
KEVIN KENDRICK
AND
ALAN BROWN

palgrave
macmillan

First published 2003 by
PALGRAVE MACMILLAN
Houndmills, Basingstoke, Hampshire RG21 6XS and
175 Fifth Avenue, New York, N.Y. 10010
Companies and representatives throughout the world

PALGRAVE MACMILLAN is the global academic imprint of the Palgrave Macmillan division of St. Martin's Press, LLC and of Palgrave Macmillan Ltd. Macmillan® is a registered trademark in the United States, United Kingdom and other countries. Palgrave is a registered trademark in the European Union and other countries.

ISBN 0–333–77797–2

This book is printed on paper suitable for recycling and made from fully managed and sustained forest sources.

A catalogue record for this book is available from the British Library.

10   9   8   7   6   5   4   3   2   1
12   11   10   09   08   07   06   05   04   03

Typeset by Cambrian Typesetters, Frimley, Surrey
Printed and bound by J.W. Arrowsmith Ltd., Bristol

Contents

List of Boxes and Tables

Boxes

Tables

Preface

Writing this book has been itself something of a spiritual journey, involving loss and creation. It began in the year 1999 when Kevin Kendrick and I started to explore the overlaps between spirituality, ethics and healthcare. By 2001 we had the first draft ready of this book, and Jon Reed of Palgrave was helping us to chart the choppy water of inter-disciplinarity. By late 2001, Kevin had died in a tragic road accident. Kevin was a big man with a very big heart, and a great deal more to contribute to reflection on theory and the development of practice. Characteristically, he left behind many collaborative projects to be continued and completed. This book is the last one to which he contributed. I hope it is a fitting tribute to his memory.

Alan Brown stepped into the breach to help complete the text, contributing a rich and practical perspective to the narrative, whilst maintaining the enthusiasm of Kevin.

I am conscious that there are many people who helped us to reach this stage, not least long suffering colleagues, friends and family of all three of us. We thank them all. Several, however, stand out: Alan's sister Audrey, and Christopher, a constant guide, mentor and friend, Kevin's wife Pauline, and my wife Angie. This book is for them.

Simon Robinson, Leeds, 7 March, 2003

Acknowledgements

The publisher and authors would like to thank:

Jones and Bartlett Publishers, Sudbury, MA for permssion to reprint Marilyn Krysl, Midwife and Other Poems on Caring, 1989. www.jbpub.com

Faber and Faber, for permission to reproduce 'Aubade' from 'Collected Poems' by Philip Larkin

Full bibliographic information for all sources is given in the 'References' section at the end of each chapter.

Introduction

> When we arrived at Auschwitz, it was a bright, sunny day and a series of jet streams appeared in the sky. They may have been experimental V2 bombs, but I had not seen such a sight before, and for a while I believed that God himself would intervene. . . . Hope was to believe that evil would be destroyed, even though it looked invincible, with no evidence whatsoever of any forces of good . . . And there was faith. That God knew what was happening. That he let it happen and that it had purpose. Most of the time this was difficult. Too difficult.
>
> I knew then, and know now, that my survival had nothing to do with being different or better or more deserving. And one of my burdens, indeed an irrational sense of guilt ever since, has been precisely that I do not know why I survived. In all sorts of ways much of what I have tried to do and tried to be ever since has been to give some sense of meaning to that survival. (Gryn 2000, 248)

The search for meaning is a basic human need, and it is one that arises directly out of adversity. For Hugo Gryn the heart-rending experience of childhood in Auschwitz led to a search for meaning which veered through the conventional faith of organised religion to a spiritual awareness that was at its keenest when he knew there were no answers – that God would not rescue him. The search for meaning did not end there, indeed it fuelled the rest of his remarkable life.

That same search for meaning is evidenced in the earliest tribes whose well-being was dependent upon good hunting and good farming. They struggled to understand why the crops failed, their prey had moved from the tribal grounds, or an earthquake had destroyed their village: 'Why has this happened to us?' From such powerlessness it is a short step to link these events to figures of power – the gods or their messengers – who must be appeased in some way if the same is not to happen again. When death comes, and the gods can no longer be influenced, then that same need to find meaning emerges with stories and ideas about the afterlife. These explain how, even though we seem to have come to an end, there is still hope. With all that, the stories begin to say something about justice. Making sense of one's life and death experience has an ethical dimension, which is why so often when we care for those who are suffering, we hear the cry, 'This is not fair! Why should this happen to *me*?'

Finding meaning though is not just about explaining events, or trying to control an inhospitable universe or trying to find justice in the patterns of life. It is also, beneath all that, about our significance and value as human beings. Bravely and tenaciously humankind continues to assert its worth in a universe which seems to have no meaning, and which seems to say, therefore, that we are not significant – as a race or as individuals. Some would claim that we are at the centre of that universe, if only because we seem to be the only creatures that can develop self-awareness and hold conversations with ourselves. It did not feel like that for Gryn. On the contrary he felt abandoned, that no one or no thing had remained faithful to him or to his people, and that they, therefore, had no value. Much of his life in the camp was about trying to find that value, that sense of dignity.

In this book we propose that spirituality is precisely about this search for meaning, the search for perspective, understanding and value, a search which takes place at intellectual, emotional and physical levels for all of us. Most of us do not begin to take that search seriously until we face the adversity that challenges our belief systems, the beliefs and relationships that give meaning and value to our lives.

All of this applies especially to our experience of illness. The more serious the illness, the more dramatic the challenge to our sense of life meaning. Hence, we argue that attention to spirituality is central to healthcare. It is not a 'bolt-on' option but a central part of how we provide that care. It reminds us that health-care is not simply about the delivery of a service, but about a relationship in which the nurse, in collaboration with family and other colleagues, enables the patient to make sense of, to find meaning in, their illness. Enabling in this context simply means giving the patient permission to let go and articulate that meaning. It may simply be an affirmation of meaning that has been honed over years. It may be a moment of great change where awareness of limitations, not least mortality, comes through for the first time. It may be awareness that the meaning that has been there for years can no longer make sense of the experience. All of this has elements of map making about it, with the map being modified as the explorer is faced by the experience of the journey. Meaning may be articulated through the language of body or feeling rather than ideas. It may be that there is no means of articulation and the nurse simply has to give the other the space to be. It may, of course, be that the person simply refuses to take up the chance to think and feel her or his way to meaning.

Attention to spirituality will certainly lead to attitudes that support the healing process. In some situations where the psychological health of the person is affected it may lead to healing itself. In all this the nurse may be with the patient for a comparatively short time and, in any case, cannot be responsible for that person's life meaning. He/she is, however, in a privileged and critical position and can enable reflection at points where others would not have access. The nurse, in effect, becomes the 'skilled companion', who can accompany the patient on her spiritual journey.

All of this points to a dynamic view of spirituality and we attempt to develop the argument in the following way:

Chapter 1 charts a modern history of spirituality and what has led to a concern for spirituality in healthcare. Chapter 2 offers a working definition of spirituality in terms of: awareness and appreciation of the other, including the self; the capacity to respond; and the generating of life meaning from those relationships. Such meaning is holistic, involving awareness of the cognitive, affective and somatic elements of the self and others, and also based in a sense of value, both unconditional and responsive. This enables the person to feel that he/she is part of an other, person or group, and therefore that he/she belongs, and he/she is able to contribute to that other. In turn, this leads to the development of faith and hope. At its core is the experience and attitude of empathy and unconditional acceptance – a form of love.

It is essentially not problem solving, but rather about a life-long journey or quest and how we handle that journey. The vehicle of that journey is narrative, which enables the person to both articulate, reflect on, critique and develop or affirm the life meaning implicitly or explicitly held. The articulation of that narrative demands an accompanist.

Chapter 3 takes us into the world of suffering and illness and looks at attempts to find meaning. A reflection on suffering looks at the views of different theologians and philosophers. The conclusion is that, for the most part, these involve attempts to control the experience of suffering. Spirituality rather focuses on the meaning of the person, identity and purpose, in that suffering. It is this that sustains meaning and a sense of value, whatever the outcome of the suffering. This does not question the healing process but is rather a vital support for it. Chapter 4 examines and critiques recent approaches to spiritual assessment in healthcare. Chapter 5 focuses on the spirituality of the patient and carer in practice. It first looks at the spiritual journey or *process* and how the patient can begin to make sense of the illness experience. Then it analyses the *presence* of the nurse who accompanies the patient and how this facilitates the process.

The next four chapters focus on different aspects of spirituality and care. Chapter 6 looks at spirituality at different stages of life, focusing on childhood, childbirth and ageing. Chapter 7 examines the spirituality of death, dying and the experience of loss. This is an area most often associated with spiritual care not least because of the intense difficulties in finding life meaning in death. Chapter 8 looks at mental health and how spirituality relates to this. Chapter 9 reflects on spirituality and the learning disabled. It examines both what the learning disabled have to teach those around them about spirituality and how the carer can enable those with learning disabilities to attend to their own spirituality.

Chapter 10. The final chapter sums up the major conclusions of the book. It looks at the spirituality of the professional nurse and the nursing profession, including the professional virtues of nursing, and the ethos, training and care necessary for the nurse her- or himself to find and maintain spiritual meaning in her work. The role of the chaplain is also articulated, to see this in relation to the work of the nurse. The chapter concludes with the suggestion that the profession of nursing has much to contribute to a wider view of spirituality necessary for care.

This is a book on spirituality and healthcare. As such, it does not intend to be a detailed handbook about working with religions in the healthcare context. References are made to religious faiths at various points, as examples of spirituality. We would strongly recommend Henley and Schott's *Culture, Religion and Patient Care in a Multi-Ethnic Society* as a handbook for detailed examination of the different faiths and their relevance to treatment (1999).

The major focus of this book is on the nurse but all of its points are equally relevant to other branches of healthcare. A good deal of the focus has been on hospital work, but again any of the points can be applied to primary care.

The question of gender, and how to refer to the nurse and patient has exercised us greatly. We determined in the end to mix genders randomly, and would wish to assure the reader that there is no gender 'agenda'.

We do not begin to examine the question of spiritual healing and what its basis might be. We prefer, on occasions, to simply refer to spiritual techniques, such as prayer or meditation, that have been examined and proved to be fruitful in relation to conventional health-care approaches.

Above all we hope to give equal weight to reflection on the nature of spirituality and to the practical implications for care. However noble, fine or interesting the ideas, unless spirituality can be embodied in practice it is ultimately without meaning.

References

Gryn, H. (2000) *Chasing Shadows* (London: Viking).

Henley, A. and Schott, J. (1999) *Culture, Religion and Patient Care in a Multi-Ethnic Society* (London: Age Concern).

1

Spirituality: The Story so Far

This chapter sets the scene. It involves a brief review of developments in spirituality during the twentieth century, noting how it was dominated by the Christian Church in the West, giving the example of the Church of England, and how the postmodern era and the New Age movement led to a very different view. It then looks at a second crucial development, which has focused on spirituality and practice, picking up the stress on spirituality as a human, rather than a transcendent dimension. The chapter then focuses on the attempts of nursing and healthcare to integrate the new insights into spirituality into practice. Emerging from this are a number of tensions which we note have not been addressed either in the numerous books on spirituality and healthcare or in practice. These tensions involve the different professions and different views of spirituality within the professions. We end the chapter by noting the different elements which will need to be addressed if there is to be an effective attempt to include spirituality as part of holistic care, and a care which can involve all members of the healthcare and medical team.

Spirituality

In the western world the Christian Church has dominated spirituality, relating it directly and exclusively to religion. Spirituality was not a reflection on or development of the human spirit, whatever that might be, but rather a reflection on the Holy Spirit, the third 'person' of the Godhead, and attempts to develop that relationship. Hence, the term spirituality is often defined by the Christian Churches as the practice of worship and prayer which enables an awareness of the Holy Spirit (James 1968). Such spirituality was dominated by the clergy, part of whose task was 'spiritual direction', guiding the lay person into how he might develop his religious faith. In western society, where the church was the centre of learning and care, this led to

1

the church taking responsibility for healthcare and education and for any underlying spiritual meaning.

The Church of England within the twentieth century was slow to develop its understanding of what it meant by spirituality in relation to health and healing. The norm was to follow Prayer Book teaching, much of which is based on the notion of judgement. For example, in the Visitation to the Sick, we are told,

> Whatsoever your sickness is, know you certainly, that it is God's visitation . . . And . . . that if you truly repent of your sins, and bear your sickness patiently, it shall turn to your profit . . . From whom the Lord loveth he chasteneth. (Book of Common Prayer)

A number of clergy railed against this thinking, including Percy Dearmer, who started the Guild of Health in 1904, assisted by Conrad Noel. The Lambeth Conference of 1908 then considered its position on health and healing, setting up a committee to look at this in particular. The committee admitted that the growing interest in spiritual and mental healing could be the result of the Church's neglect to get across the full meaning of Christian theology. It was accepted that inherent within the ministrations of the Church to the sick, a disproportionate stress had been laid upon the preparation for death. It was also accepted that sickness had too often been regarded as a cross to be borne with passive resignation, whereas the proper approach would be to regard it as 'a weakness to be overcome by the power of the spirit'. This would today be seen as judgemental in terms of definitions of weak and strong, but it was an acknowledgment that restoration of harmony in mind and will, could often bring about the restoration of the harmony of the body.

The Church's ministry of healing was discussed again at the Lambeth Conference of 1920. Practical recommendations included a call for a fuller presentation of the Church's doctrine on true spirituality and for teaching on the efficacy of individual and corporate prayer, and the effects of Holy Communion. The most important element of the 1920 Committee's Report was that, for the first time, a Committee of a Lambeth Conference urged the 'recognition of the ministry of the gifts of healing in the Church, and that these should be exercised under due licence and authority'. The findings of the Committee were not published until 1924, but it went so far as to suggest the licensing of healers who were both orthodox in belief and willing to cooperate with the medical profession and the parochial clergy. It also endorsed the Church's ministry of healing, referring to unction and the laying on of hands, as having scriptural authority and being sacramental. During the late 1930s and early 1940s, William Temple, as Archbishop of Canterbury, worked to set up a group of interested parties which, in 1944, was to become the Churches' Council for Health and Healing. Temple's correspondence shows that he was unable to commit to paper quite what his understanding of spirituality was in relation to health and healing, except that he sincerely felt that those concerned were on the edge of something potentially very great. Unfortunately, he died before the Churches' Council really got under way.

There have been other forays by the Church of England to understand both its own position on health and healing and to give advice to others. The last was the publication of a report *Time to Heal* (Church of England 2000). It is ironic that at the very time that this rather long report was published, the Churches' Council was just about to meet its demise and the Guild of Health was to move out of its London headquarters because of dwindling numbers.

Anglican clergy have always held 'the cure of all souls', that is, responsibility for pastoral and spiritual care for all within the parish area. Despite the presence of other denominations it was accepted that even if you were not an active church member that each person was part of a system of care which gave shared meaning, value and purpose at times of personal development or crisis, not least through the rituals of baptism, wedding and funeral. But as Bruce (1995, 35) points out, it is not at all clear, even within the Christian traditions, what it means to be a member of a particular church or group.

Christian church membership (Protestant and Roman Catholic) fell during the last century from 7.4 million in 1900 (30 per cent of the adult population) to 5.6 million in 1990 (12 per cent of the adult population). There began a breakdown of what might be termed traditional spirituality with the emergence of the postmodern era and the New Age movement when a very different perspective on spirituality was ushered in.

The new spirituality

Scholars argue fiercely about whether we are in so-called postmodern times and, if so, how such a world might be characterised (Connor 1989). It is, however, possible to distinguish between postmodernity as a theory and the experience of the postmodern era. In the first of these, new ways of understanding language and social constructs are argued for. Baudrillard, for instance, sees the division between art and life as breaking down (Baudrillard 1983). There is no objective sense of reality and each person has to create their own reality and underlying life meaning. Whether or not we agree with such theory it is hard not to accept something of the postmodern *experience*, in which old certainties have broken down. Such an age is characterised by:

- An explosion of scientific and technological progress, making resources available that were undreamed of even fifty years ago. At the same time this leads to a stress on rights and choice, of which the Patient's Charter and other Government initiatives have played their part; and also to attitudes and value perspectives that are quite new. The feminist movement, for instance, would not have grown in the way that it did without the means to freedom, such as contraception.
- An increasing influence of theories which stress relativity, indeterminacy or chaos. These began with Freud and his stress on the unconscious, culminating in the postmodern thinkers such as Derrida (Reader 1997).
- Changing patterns of behaviour and institutions such as marriage and the family, caused partly by the increase in wealth and increased mobility, but also by changes in attitude towards the sanctity of marriage and the notion of securing a partnership for life.
- A greater development and awareness of cultural and religious diversity within society, caused by increased migration and global awareness.

All of this has lead to a breakdown of any sense of objective knowledge and, in particular, adherence to the so-called 'grand narratives' of the last century which had gone before. Grand narratives are those 'stories' which claim some universal truth (Lyotard 1979). They range from views about the person, characterised after the Enlightenment as an autonomous rational decision-maker, to views about the purpose of humanity, dominated in the West by the Christian ethic. Such grand narratives might exist in the minds of the great thinkers or they might give meaning and purpose to whole nations that help to sustain them through times of crisis. The grand narrative of the British Empire, for instance, gave meaning to the people of Britain and beyond, buttressing the initial acceptance of the sacrifice of so many in the First World War. In turn, beneath this was a Christian ethic that had been dominant in the West. We no longer buy into those narratives in quite the same way. So much of the cultural and economic underpinnings have gone. Major conflagrations such as the First World War raised questions about the underlying assumptions, leading eventually to a greater stress on individualism and the values of the free market. The grand narratives have been replaced by many different narratives, both local and national. There are still major narratives, including national loyalty, consumerism, the free market and the more communitarian views (with a stress on the importance on the development of community). However, these are either in competition or dialogue (Brueggemann 1997, 718ff.). None of these narratives are more acceptable than the other and there are no privileged interpreters of any meaning.

Spirituality in the West had been seen as directly expressed in the Christian narrative. Many do still view it in that way. However, with the breakdown of the acceptance of the grand narratives three things began to happen:

- The emergence of a spiritual vacuum. Spirituality had become so identified with the churches that if the churches were no longer a critical part of the life of the majority then it followed that for the majority there was no 'spiritual life', and nowhere to engage in spiritual practice or dialogue.
- The privatising of 'things spiritual'. If the public language of spirituality, as practised in the churches, was no longer accessible to the majority, then the world of the spirit was seen as something quite private. In one sense the privatising had already begun. The power structures of the churches tended to discourage reflection within churches, seeing the priest or minister as the 'expert' or 'guru' who had the orthodoxy and spoke for the community. The individual believer would often see his faith then as private. This was, however, reinforced by elements in the postmodern world, not least with the stress on individual taste and freedom.
- An attempt to reclaim the spiritual life in a way that anyone could be part of it. Here the postmodern era intersects with the New Age movement.

The New Age

The New Age movement, which began in the 1960s, is really a loose collection of many different movements and ideas which assert many different spiritualities. It generated a real sense of excitement and inspiration focused on the idea that each person can discover, control and develop her own spirituality in her own way. A common theme throughout the movement is asserting freedom from a view of spirituality that had been imposed by patriarchal institutions and authorities.

Other central themes include:

- Spirituality as acceptable, whatever the form, unless it harms another. Hence, there is a tolerance of a great range of spirituality. Indeed, all existence is seen as a manifestation of some greater Spirit. All religions are seen as an expression of this same reality.
- Everyone is free to choose his or her own spiritual path.
- Spirituality is to do with the 'other worldly', stressing the mystical and even magical. This seems a conscious attempt to locate spirituality in the numinous, that which is beyond and greater than oneself.
- Spirituality as largely anti-rational. Feelings and experience are paramount.
- All life is interconnected and human beings work together with the Spirit to create reality.
- At the source of all this is a form of cosmic love which enables all human beings to be responsible for themselves and for the environment.

Underlying much of this was a strong sense of the intrinsic goodness of humanity and a sense of a continued evolution towards spiritual enlightenment, both for the individual and the community. Whilst there is a sense of novelty about this movement it is also concerned to recapture something of the past. Hence, paganism, for example, claims a history extending back well before the Christian era (Perry 1992). They are also concerned to chart the connection between spirituality and well-being and health, leading to a proliferation of complementary therapies (Watt 1995). Hence, New Age elements have developed views on spirituality and medicine.

The New Age movement is not without criticisms. The optimism about human nature and society, for instance, has little sustained empirical support. Since the flowering of the movement, there have been many examples of conflict and disasters, in the Middle East, the Balkans, Southern Africa and so on, which do not indicate spiritual evolution. Secondly, the movement by definition lacks critical rigour. If all forms of spirituality are acceptable then there can be no common criteria for how to judge the claims and the worth of any particular spirituality. Thirdly, the movement is not as inclusive as it would claim. On the contrary, the majority of New Agers are, in fact, articulate, middle class and middle aged. They have no more success in connecting with the vast majority of the population than the main line faiths (Perry 1995).

Despite such criticisms the movement remains important to any understanding of spirituality in the West in recent years. Perry sums it up in this way, 'In general . . . it demonstrates a high degree of social and ecological awareness; it demonstrates a particularly useful attitude in understanding that life can be led as a self reflective process of growth and transformation; and liberates spirituality from the confines of religious dogma and empowers direct personal experience'. (Perry 1992, 36). In all this, it is fair to say that it offered a new paradigm for spirituality.

Spirituality of practice

A very different focus has attempted to locate spirituality not so much in the experience of the numinous as in the everyday experience of the person, as a member of different organisations, as a learner, as experiencing different crises. A recent report from the Leeds Church Institute has examined the spirituality of work organisations, focusing in particular on how members of these organisations relate their work to life meaning, and how the organisation of work might enable this (Randolph-Horn and Paslawska 2002). The spiritual dimension of professional activities has even been covered in areas such as engineering. Carter, for instance, locates 'spiritual qualities' at the centre of the skills and qualities needed by the professional engineer (Carter 1985).

However, applied spirituality has been focused most securely in education and healthcare. This is hardly surprising as the development of both areas has been intimately linked to the institution of the church. Only in the nineteenth century did the church begin to let go of responsibility for education, passing it on to the state. In healthcare, the title Sister, which still largely exists today, is a throwback to the sisterhoods which developed in the 19th century. Titles such as Almoner, which disappeared in favour of social workers in the late 1960s, represented a link between almsgiving, the church and the much earlier infirmarian brothers within religious houses.

However, the focus of spirituality in both areas has become wider than simply the religious. Spirituality is not something which is brought *to* the practice of learning or caring but something which is bound up in it, with spiritual meaning emerging from reflection upon the experience and the practice. Hence, there is a great deal of research into practical spirituality (George *et al.* 2000).

Education has, furthermore, had the concern for spirituality and spiritual development enshrined in legalisation and codes. The 1988 Education Reform Act, for instance, requires schools to promote 'the spiritual, moral, cultural, mental and physical development of pupils' (Alves 1991). The 1944 Education Act extends the idea to the community:

> and it shall be the duty of the local education authority for every area, as far as their powers extend, to contribute to the spiritual, moral, mental and phys-ical development of the community by securing that efficient education . . . be available to meet the needs of the population of their area.' (HM Government 1944, 4)

However, not far beneath this concern for the spiritual there are tensions. In the midst of the postmodern era, religion, and in particular the Christian religion, still wants to be involved in defining the spiritual dimensions of practice. Beck (1999, 153 ff.) charts the way in which reli-gious thinkers have been involved in the developments of spirituality in the curriculum and suggests that part of this involvement is an attempt to smuggle in a very particular view of spirituality, once more connected to a formal religious view. Such an approach tends to identify spiritual-ity with religion, and argues that spirituality is the basis of moral mean-ing and behaviour. The argument, however, simply assumes clear connections between spirituality, religion and morality. Hence, it does not provide any way in which different approaches to spirituality can be included in any educational process. Often this comes down to an attempt to include different *religious* approaches, thus once more moving away from an examination of what sense spirituality might have for the majority of people who are not involved in organised religion.

In a very different way, other researchers, such as Peter Doble and Chris Meehan at the University of Leeds, are looking to develop a spirituality in education that would be essentially school centred, with staff and pupils developing a reflective spiritual framework for their school (Meehan 1999).

Despite support in legislation for the development of spirituality in education then, what it means and how it can be practised in this context is still very much a matter of debate.

Spirituality and healthcare

Like education, there are strong drivers which encourage focus on spirituality in healthcare. Also, like education, there are underlying tensions. These reflect once more the complexity of the term spirituality but also the concerns of the different stakeholders in this area. The four key ones are chaplains, nurses, doctors and patient or family, and we will briefly examine the debate from their different perspectives.

Healthcare chaplaincy

The chaplain's identity is based around spiritual care and therefore he has a real interest in trying to define what is meant and to work closely with others. For some, the question is about delivery of spiritual care in a postmodern health service. For others, there is the key question of integrity. How does the chaplain provide effective person-centred spiritual care for patients and staff, without losing his identity as a member of his faith community? Many chaplains seem to be questioning their own identity and authority, resulting in a rush towards contained professionalisation and registration. This is linked to monitored continuing professional development programmes under the auspices of the College of Health Care Chaplains and the Hospital Chaplaincies Council, with the plea for chaplains to be included on the list of recognised professions within the health service, from which they are currently excluded.

The role of the chaplain has, for the most part, been filled by ordained members of particular churches. The very term and role of chaplain is fundamentally a Christian one, with the chaplain attached to the place of worship, the chapel. In one sense, then, there is a public expectation that the chaplain will come to his task with all the moral and spiritual meaning of the church. This may cause some, including healthcare and medical staff, to be unsure of the motivation of the chaplain. The implication for some is that the chaplain is there to care for the patient in an instrumental way, to care for her in order, ultimately, to convert her to the way of the church. Behind this is the fear that the chaplain cannot be both patient centred and God or church centred.

Pattison (2001) goes further and argues that modern healthcare chaplaincy is in danger of 'dumbing down the Spirit'. He argues that the Christian tradition is centred in the Holy Spirit. As such it is essentially charismatic. The Holy Spirit is not a being who can be controlled or used, but is essentially independent and autonomous. The effects of the Spirit are not confined to the individual but are very much about the building up of the spiritual community. Both these points, therefore, demand a view of spirituality that is not individual centred or consumerist in the sense of the person being able to select what spirituality she might want. Rather the growth and development of spirituality demands growth in community and in response to the other, not least the Holy Spirit. Hence, Pattison writes of the Spirit taking initiatives which we must be ready to respond to. Pattison suggests that this is a very difficult tradition to follow, precisely because it is not possible to control the Spirit, and that it is very tempting for modern chaplains to move away from this distinctive view of Christian spirituality into what he sees as 'a more generalised and less specific language about spirituality that is more sanitised and acceptable in the modern world' (Pattison 2001, 37). Hence, there is the danger of a loss of integrity. Pattison concludes that the chaplain cannot be a 'spiritual broker'. He cannot be all things to all people. He must share the wisdom and tradition of his community and, with that, deepen any understanding of spirituality in healthcare.

Pattison's concern for integrity of the Christian chaplain is, however, limited and limiting. Firstly, he fails to see the complexity of modern spirituality, which as noted above is far more than 'pick and mix'. Secondly, he ignores the fact that there are many different views of the Christian spiritual narrative (Robinson 2001). Thirdly, he fails to see the need for dialogue in spiritual reflection and, with that, the importance of listening as much as sharing any particular narrative (Drane 2001). Fourthly, he fails to acknowledge that healthcare begins with the patient, his needs and autonomy, and not with the articulation of any religious narrative. Hence, whilst the chaplain may have his own spiritual base within a religious tradition he cannot by definition impose that on the patient. This does not mean a 'dumbing down' of spirituality. On the contrary, it means attention to the patient to enable him to develop and own his own spirituality, as something developing in relation to his significant life experience and in relation to his experience of the illness. Of course, the patient may not want to own or develop a spirituality. He may simply hold to a spirituality to take him through the experience of illness. He may hope for an affirmation of a spirituality which has been important. He may look to a development of spirituality and a change. Giving attention to any of these responses as part of healthcare is very different from buying in to some unthinking spirituality, as Pattison's view implies. Hence, it focuses on the person and his experience, enabling him to take responsibility for making sense of this in relation to his social networks.

In the light of this the chaplain is indeed a spiritual broker who focuses on the spiritual need of the patient and helps him make sense of the situation. He can offer:

- An enabling role, allowing the patient to reflect on his own spirituality. Lyall argues that a key part of any pastoral and spiritual care is precisely to enable the person to reflect on practice and the meaning of that practice (Lyall 2001).
- A great reservoir of cultural meaning. As we shall see in more detail below, many people who experience suffering turn to rituals and practice which is as much a part of culture as it is about religious observance. Parents of a dying baby, for instance, often look to the rite of baptism, whether they believe in that faith or not. It is most often the Christian chaplain who can mediate that, precisely because of the church's historical position culturally.
- An awareness of other faiths and perspectives that he should be uniquely placed to work with and relate to. Hence, he is in a unique position to coordinate a response to religious spiritual need.
- His own tradition and the community of faith of which he is a part, which he can offer to those of his own faith. As we shall see, even this might not be straightforward. Many patients with an apparently secure religious faith find the experience of illness a time of spiritual challenge, leading to growth and change.

This is a 'both and' model of the chaplain, as someone who is concerned for a wider view of spirituality as well as the religious rights of particular groups. None of this questions the integrity of the chaplain. On the contrary, if integrity can be defined as being true to and in dialogue with the different members of one's relational network, this is precisely what this model enables the chaplain to be.

If the chaplain is to be a part of the healthcare team and offer these different approaches to spirituality then there needs to be developed a common framework of spirituality which is essentially practice and person centred. Without this, dialogue and collaborative practice are not possible.

The nursing profession

In the past two decades there has developed a real sense of ownership by the nursing profession of the concept and practice of spirituality and spiritual care, leading to many publications. There are several reasons for this. Firstly, a good deal of the history of nursing is based in some understanding of spirituality (Bradshaw 1994). Secondly, the concern for holistic care evidenced in recent years inevitably seeks to include all aspects of care. The development of nursing models of care from the 1970s onwards has often included the need to address what might be termed sensitive issues, including patient spirituality and sexuality. This stress on care very much differentiates the nursing profession from the medical profession, and its emphasis on cure. Thirdly, the nurse, in general, spends more time with the patient than other healthcare professionals, and thus can actually get to know the patient better than the doctor or chaplain. Hence, some nurses argue that they are in the best position to be aware of and respond to the spiritual needs of the patient (O'Brien 1998).

This concern for spiritual care is embodied in a number of Professional Codes or educational recommendations. One recommends that nurses should be able to 'Undertake and document a comprehensive, systematic and accurate nursing assessment of physiological, social and spiritual needs of patients, clients and communities' (UKCC 2000, 13). The American Association of Colleges of Nursing takes this a stage further. The nurse should be able to 'Comprehend the meaning of human spirituality in order to recognise the relationship of beliefs to culture, behaviour, health and healing . . . and to plan and implement this care' (AACN 1986, 5). Such professional codes are reinforced by the revised Patient's Charter which assures the patient that, 'NHS staff will respect your privacy and dignity. They will be sensitive to and respect your religious, spiritual and cultural needs at all times' (DoH 2001, 29).

Like the concern within education, then, spirituality is enshrined in official health-related documents. As in education, references to spirituality are both generalised and unclear. There are no guidelines on how these aims might be achieved. Moreover, within the different references there seem to be different emphases. The UKCC code looks very much to fully formed spiritual beliefs. The remaining two look to something less consumer orientated and more complex. The Patient's Charter can distinguish religious from spiritual needs, though does not say what the distinction is. In some ways, the most interesting is the AACN code. This looks to the way in which beliefs, not simply religious ones, relate to different aspects of the patient's life meaning and experience. Intriguing though this is, however, there are again no indications of how such comprehension might be achieved.

The lack of precise guidance in terms of spirituality and practice is made even more difficult given that there are some very different theories and models of nursing. Some see spirituality as implicit in the nursing response (Rogers 1980, Roy 1980). Others see spirituality as explicit (Parse 1981, Watson 1985, Neuman 1995). Explicit attention to spirituality in turn takes many different forms:

• An uncritical association of spirituality with religion (O'Brien 1998).
• The view that the Christian religion especially has something to offer (Bradshaw 1994).
• Attempts to create an objective view of spirituality. This in turn can move into attempts to medicalise spirituality and develop methods of assessment of spiritual need and distress (McSherry 2000).

It is perhaps not surprising that the actual practice of spiritual care is very variable (Oldnall 1996). The very different approaches and the lack of clear direction about the nature of spirituality also reveal a lack of clear aims and objectives in nurse training. This is perhaps not surprising given the generic nature of the use of the term nurse for very different types of people who undergo training for very different types of nursing: general, mental health, learning disability, children's, and the specialities of midwifery and health visiting. There is also quite a significant issue of the nurse or nurse lecturer being comfortable with their own spirituality and having some understanding of it. For to have a personal recognition that we are spiritual beings opens up the possibilities for an encounter with another about their own spirituality. In addition, there is little evidence of the nursing and chaplaincy professions beginning to bring together their different perspectives. A recent book on spirituality in the healthcare context, for instance, focused on healthcare chaplaincy with only one contribution from a nurse (Orchard 2001).

Oldnall and others consider the possible reasons for the lack of attention to spirituality in practice. Firstly, it could simply be that there is less and less time to give attention to the idea of spiritual care. This needs time and, with the reduction in the number of nurses and the increase in patient throughput, there is not the time. Along with this could be a reluctance to focus on spirituality precisely because it gives the impression of having to develop yet another skill.

Secondly, Oldnall suggests that most nurses see spiritual needs in terms of religion and therefore simply refer what they perceive as spiritual needs to the chaplain (Oldnall 1996) or, as has been common practice, merely chart in nursing records under the heading spirituality the patient's religion, and in cases where the patient is not quite sure, chart Church of England. There are major questions too about boundary definitions and maintenance. For some nurses they may see the need of the patient more in terms of psychological need and will therefore refer any problems to the counsellor or psychiatrist, the bereavement department in the hospital, or to a community group. Behind this are questions as to how the nurse can begin to distinguish between factors such as spiritual distress and anxiety or depression. The question of professionalisation also emerges here. In one sense the counsellor is seen as the one who is qualified to deal with such problems. It is not always clear, for instance, what the qualification of the chaplain is. It is easy in all this to lose any sense of what spirituality actually is.

The medical profession

The response of the medical profession to the question of spirituality has been variable. In one respect it has been quite the opposite of the nursing profession. There have been few writings on the subject in general medicine, although as far back as 1936 William Temple promoted the development of a National Council for Pastoral and Medical Co-operation, with a view to promoting conferences on the subject of psychology, spirituality and medicine. Although this Council was supported by many senior churchmen and medical staff, it never really got off the ground. More recent exceptions have been in the areas of care of the dying and cardiology (Thoresen and Hoffman Goldberg 1998, Cobb 2001). There has also been great interest in the use of spiritual techniques. Often this has been in the part that prayer or meditation might play in actually affecting therapeutic outcomes (Koenig 1997).

Concern for spirituality has also led to major development in mental health, especially in the USA. Part of this has been in the development of so called 'positive psychology' by Martin Seligman (Gillham 2000). This movement has focused on the development of positive personal qualities, especially what have been characterised in philosophy and religion as the virtues. Such qualities have included hope and faith, and the capacity to forgive. In all cases, the writers have looked to establish on an empirical basis how the development of such qualities actually affect therapeutic outcomes, in general as well as psychological medicine (Miller 1999).

All of this deepens and develops aspects of spirituality that have not been touched upon in most nursing literature but which do have some overlap with chaplaincy work. The stress on forgiveness, for instance, as a critical aspect of therapy links in to the traditional concept and practice of pastoral care (Worthington 1998). However, there is little dialogue between the medical profession and chaplaincy or nursing. Some space is found for spirituality in medical education, especially in optional Special Study Modules at the University of Leeds, but this is not taken seriously enough to be mentioned in the core curriculum.

The patient

The spirituality of the patient is at the centre of healthcare. It has generated a considerable amount of research, examining attitudes and therapeutic outcomes. However, similar tensions to those above exist in this area. As research in spirituality of work shows the ordinary person is not clear themselves about the meaning of spirituality (Randolph-Horn and Paslawska 2002). This can lead to some patients ignoring questions about spirituality, or trying to say what they think the health worker wants to hear. Researches into patient spirituality range from examination of a generic view of patient spirituality (Ross 1995, Ross 1997), to work on the efficacy of formal religious acts such as prayer (Koenig 1997). All of these are relevant to spirituality, but again can lead to confusion for the patient about what spirituality actually is. All of this is compounded by a lack of clarity and confidence amongst health workers.

It is precisely because of this that any attempt to get to grips with spirituality and healthcare must be patient focused. Hence, much of this book will concentrate on the life meaning which is challenged or which emerges from the experience of the patient.

Conclusion

Spirituality through the late twentieth century broke free of the simple identification with religion. This has helped us to see that whilst any religion is an embodiment of spirituality no single religion can sum up all spirituality. Spirituality is something much broader than religion. The major distinctions can be summed up in Box 1.1.

Box 1.1   Distinctions between spirituality and religion

- Religion is focused in social institutions. As such, it is concerned to maintain the boundaries of that institution, not least through defining orthodoxy and orthopraxy. Spirituality has no concern for boundaries, indeed it moves beyond them in the search for meaning.
- Religion has tended to be prescriptive with meaning transmitted through doctrine and the stories of the community. Spirituality is more about discovery of meaning in the context of the person.
- Whilst religion may provide an important motivational and disciplined framework for spiritual development it is not necessary for it. As we noted above, the New Age points to the possibility of self-directed spirituality.
- Religions are founded upon experience of and faith in the divine – the transcendent other. Spirituality finds significant meaning in a much broader way, including experience of and faith in other people and the environment.

A key part of the broadening of spirituality has been the attempt to focus concerns in education and healthcare in practice. Nonetheless, tension still remains in the healthcare professions and it is not surprising that spiritual care as a practice is not well established. Part of this problem involves definition of the term, part of it involves lack of clarity with regard to professional boundaries, and part of it involves the inevitable lack of trust where there is no shared framework for discussion or practice.

Certain things are necessary, then, if all the enthusiasm for this subject is to be creatively released and monitored in practice:

- A working definition of spirituality that all parties can recognise, accept and 'buy into' with integrity.
- A definition of spirituality that is practical, that is one that can set out achievable and significant goals in the context of the therapeutic relationship.
- A framework for discussion such that different traditions of spirituality can be respected and continue to be in dialogue. This enables common elements of different spiritualities to be recognised and

held together with an awareness and appreciation of different spiritual perspectives.

- Clear indication of how spiritual care might be practised in different contexts of healthcare.
- Some indication not simply of the spirituality of the patient but also of the professional health worker.
- Some indication of training needs in terms of spirituality.

It is to the first of these that we turn in the next chapter.

Questions and exercises

1. The aim of any guided work at the end of this chapter is to set a benchmark against which you can chart the development of your reflections throughout the book.
2. Before moving into a working definition of spirituality, brainstorm what the term spirituality means to you and what you believe is *your* spirituality. Would you strongly associate spirituality with religion?
3. At this stage also make a note of the practice of spirituality in your workplace. Is it ever explicitly referred to by the care team. If so, by whom? Does your work involve spiritual care? If so, in what way?

References

American Association of Colleges of Nursing (AACN) (1986) *Essentials of College and University Education for Nursing* (Washington: AACN).

Alves, C. (1991) 'Just a matter of words? The religious education debate in the House of Lords', *British Journal of Religious Education*, **13**, 3.

Avis, P. (1989) *Eros and the Sacred* (London: SPCK).

Baudrillard, J. (1983) *Simulations* (New York: Semiotext).

Beck, J. (1999) ' "Spiritual and Moral Development" and Religious Education', in A. Thatcher (ed.) *Spirituality and the Curriculum* (London: Cassel).

Bradshaw, A. (1994) *Lighting the Lamp; The Spiritual Dimension of Nursing Care* (London: Scutari Press).

Brueggemann, W. (1997) *Theology of the Old Testament* (Nashville: Abingdon).

Bruce, S. (1995) *Religion in Modern Britain* (Oxford: Oxford University Press).

Carter, R. (1985) 'A taxonomy of objectives for professional education', *Studies in Higher Education*, **10**, 2, 135–49.

Cobb, M. (2001) *The Dying Soul* (Buckingham: Open University Press).

Connor, S. (1989) *The Post Modern Culture* (Oxford: Blackwell).

Church of England (2000) *A Time to Heal: A Contribution Towards the Ministry of Healing* (London: Church House Publishing).

Department of Health (DoH) (2001) *Your Guide to the NHS* (London: Department of Health).

Drane, J. (2001) *Unknown Gods, Declining Churches, and the Spiritual Search of Contemporary Culture* (London: SCM).

George, L., Larson, D., Koenig, H. and McCullough, M. (Spring 2000) 'Spirituality and Health: What we Know, What we need to Know', in *Journal of Social and Clinical Psychology*, **19**, 1, 102–16.

Gillham, J. (2000) (ed.) *The Science of Optimism and Hope* (Radnor: Templeton Foundation Press).

HM Government (England and Wales) (1944) *Education Act 1944* (London: HMSO).

ICN (2000) *Code of Ethics for Nurses* (Geneva: ICN).

James, E. (1968) (ed.) *Spirituality for Today* (London: SCM).

Koenig, H. (1997) *Is Religion Good for your Health? The Effects of Religion on Physical and Mental Health* (New York: Howarth Press).

Lyall, D. (2001) *The Integrity of Pastoral Care* (London: SPCK).

Lyotard, J-F. (1979) *The Postmodern Condition* (Manchester: Manchester University Press).

McSherry, W. (2000) *Making Sense of Spirituality in Nursing Practice* (Edinburgh: Churchill Livingstone).

Meehan, C. (1999) *'Spiritual Development' and 'Developing Spirituality' in Relation to the Distinctiveness of Catholic Sixth Form Schools.* Unpublished PhD thesis (University of Leeds).

Miller, W. (1999) (ed.) *Integrating Spirituality into Treatment* (Washington DC: American Psychological Association).

Neuman, B. (1995) *The Neuman Systems Model* 3rd edn., Norwalk: Appleton and Lange).

O'Brien, M. (1998) *Spirituality in Nursing* (Boston: Jones and Bartlett).

Oldnall, A. (1996) 'A critical analysis of nursing: meeting the spiritual needs of the patient' *Journal of Advanced Nursing*, **23**, 138–44.

Orchard, H. (2001) (ed.) *Spirituality in Heath Care Contexts* (London: Jessica Kingsley).

Parse, R. (1981) *Man-Living-Health: A Theory of Nursing* (New York: John Wiley and Sons).

Pattison, S. (2001) 'Dumbing down the Spirit' in H. Orchard (ed.) *Spirituality in Health Care Contexts* (London: Jessica Kingsley).

Perry, M. (1992) *Gods Within* (London: SPCK).

Perry, M. (1995) 'Idealism and Drift', in J. Watt (ed.) *The Church, Medicine and the New Age* (London: The Churches' Council for Health and Healing).

Randolph-Horn, D. and Paslawska, K. (2002) *Spirituality at Work* (Leeds: Leeds Church Institute).

Reader, J. (1997) *Beyond All Reason* (Cardiff: Aureus).

Robinson, S. (2001) *Agape , Moral Meaning and Pastoral Counselling* (Cardiff: Aureus).

Rogers, M. (1980) 'Nursing: A Science of Unitary Man', in J. Riehl and C. Roy (eds) *Conceptual Models for Nursing Practice*, 2nd edn. (New York: Appleton-Century-Croft).

Ross, L. (1995) 'The spiritual dimension: its importance to patients' health, well being and quality of life and its implications for nursing practice' *International Journal of Nursing Studies*, **32**, 5, 457–68.

Ross, L. (1997) 'Elderly patients' perceptions of their spiritual needs and care: a pilot study' Journal of Advanced Nursing, **26**, 710–15.

Roy, C. (1980) 'The Roy Adaptation Model', in J. Riehl and C. Roy (eds) *Conceptual Models for Nursing Practice*, 2nd edn. (New York: Appleton-Century-Croft).

Thoresen, C. and Hoffman Goldberg, J. (1998) 'Coronary Heart Disease: A Psycho-social Perspective', in S. Roth-Roemer, S. Kurpius Robinson and C. Carmin (eds) *The Emerging Role of Counseling Psychology in Health Care* (New York: Norton) 94–136.

UKCC (United Kingdom Central Council for Nursing, Midwifery and Health Visiting) (2000) *Requirements for Pre-registration Nursing Programmes* (London: UKCC).

Watson, J. (1985) *Nursing: Human Science and Human Care* (Norwalk: Appleton-Century-Croft).

Watt, J. (1995) (ed.), *The Church Medicine and the New Age* (London: The Churches' Council for Health and Healing).

Worthington, E. (1998) *Dimensions of Forgiveness* (Radnor: Templeton Foundation Press).

2

Spirituality:
A Working Definition

In hospital the days were busy; the nights frightening. I remember vividly one night in particular. I lay in bed, in a state of extreme anxiety, sweating profusely, having wakened in terror from a nightmare about fighting with death. When I stretched out my hand for reassurance that I was still alive, the night nurse brusquely placed it back on my stomach and told me firmly to go back to sleep. Contrary to my previous experience of nurses, she appeared to perceive her task solely in terms of monitoring the machines, supplying the drugs which, if I was lucky, might keep me alive. And I was grateful for the vigilance. But my spirit needed keeping alive too; I needed to be literally in contact with the pulse of a living being. I felt isolated from the rest of humanity in my fight to stay alive. As I lay there, too terrified to fall asleep in case I had another nightmare, I felt something furry brushing against my cheek. It was the teddy bear Andrew had brought back from Canada for me. It symbolised the love and prayers of all those who were concerned for me. I was too ill to be ashamed of getting comfort by cuddling a child's toy; at that moment the teddy was all I had. But touching him was sufficient to calm me down and enabled me to get some revitalising sleep. Next morning the hospital chaplain responded to my outstretched hand. He took it and grasped it gently but firmly. I felt safe with him around. We talked a little – it's difficult through an oxygen mask. But holding my hand in his was his most significant contribution to my recovery. I felt connected in some mysterious way to a person who was close to God and so able to be a channel through which his life sustaining force could flow to me. (Lyall 1997)

Margaret Lyall had experienced a pulmonary embolism and as she lay there in a state of disorientation, feeling close to death, attending to her *spirit* mattered to her. There are different views as to what the spirit might be including a transcendental or essential dimension of life (Reed 1987, Highfield 1992), a force or energy (Sims 1994, Boyd 1995, King and Dein 1998), and life meaning and purpose (Hiatt 1986, Doyle 1992, Joseph 1998). However, rather than involving distinct models, all of these indicate important aspects of the human spirit which as described was central to Lyall's recovery. In this chapter we will first look at the meaning of spirit and then develop a threefold definition of spirituality. We will then look behind this definition to the dynamic of spirituality, what it is that enables an awareness of the other to develop. This will focus on empathy and unconditional care. Finally, we will examine spirituality as a continual process, centred on the articulation of narrative and reflection on meaning.

Spirit

The term spirit comes from the Latin *spiritus* (Hebrew *ruach,* Greek *pneuma*), meaning breath, wind, and even life principle. It is that which is vital to and animates the self. As such the spirit is not primarily about ideas but about lived experience, something which brings together both values and skills. Hence, the spirit is evidenced not so much in doctrines but in action and attitude, through being embodied. Doctrines, understandings of what that spirit is, may be developed not least to help maintain that spirit, but they are not the spirit as such. This view of the spirit has a strong sense of holism – involving the integration of affective, cognitive and physical elements, and making it impossible to isolate the spiritual from the physical. The spirit is a dynamic reality that expresses itself in the body. This can apply also to groups. Hence, it is possible to speak of team or company spirit, revealed in the way that members of the team are integrated and work together to express purpose and achieve tasks.

The holistic view of the spirit is well supported by empirical evidence that charts the relationship between feelings, thoughts, the body and the social and physical environment (Swinton 2001, 16–17). Importantly, the term spirit refers to both the sense of life (that which animates), the identity (that which particularly characterises the person or group), and the qualities of that person or group. By definition it is something which is to be admired, and which is of significant meaning and value.

This holistic view of the spirit contrasts sharply with the more dualistic view of the spirit as quite separate from the body. This arose from the philosophy of Plato and ultimately led to the view that the 'spirit' was that which was incorruptible, hence immortal, and of the highest value, and the body was that which was corrupting and corruptible, and of the least value (Edwards 1999, 86-9). Whilst such dualism has been very influential and continues in many popular ways of thinking it has little in empirical terms to support it. Moreover, it tends to lead to a fragmentation of human experience.

At another level, for Margaret, the spirit was about something beyond the self. It was difficult to hold onto her spirit without reaching out beyond the self and being aware of the *other*, be that another person including all her family and faith community, or God's presence mediated by an other person. Some writers on the spirit have tried to locate it purely in the transcendent, that which is beyond the self. However, clearly for Margaret it could not simply be contained there. An awareness of the other was critical to awareness of her spirit as she experienced the fear that threatened to overwhelm her sense of self. This points to an interactive relationship between the self and the other out of which emerges the spirit, and an awareness of the spirit. Reed tries to focus on this relationship by distinguishing between the soul (the holistic essence of the person) and the spirit, that which is beyond the person and which the person responds to (Reed 1998). In openness to the other, and in dialogue with the other, the person develops the awareness of his essential self. On the grounds that distinguishing the soul and spirit can be confusing we prefer to see the spirit as the holistic and experiential essence of the self which is discovered in and through relating to the 'other'.

Many writers have suggested that the spirit might be seen as a power or force which is at the heart of personal growth, allowing the person to transcend the self and thus learn, and in some way integrate personal experience (Goddard 1995). There is no doubt that a developing sense of power was at the centre of Margaret Lyall's experience. However, such power was something which emerged *from* the relationships that she was aware of, and which were so important to her. These relationships enabled her to be more aware of her essential self, reducing anxiety and increasing a sense of well-being, and thus empowering her. The spirit was not a power or energy in itself. In such contexts, Swinton (2001, 15) argues that the concept of power or energy is used in a metaphorical way. To speak of the spirit as 'like a force' or involving force is quite different from the idea of the spirit as energy itself.

The spirit is also strongly connected to the development of significant meaning. Ellison (1983, 331) describes the connection in this way. 'It is the *spirit* of human beings which enables and motivates us to search for meaning and purpose in life, to seek the supernatural or some meaning which transcends us, to wonder about our origins and our identities, to require morality and equity.'

In another sense the spirit itself is discovered in and through the reflection on and development of value and meaning. Hence, Margaret's locating of her spirit in the midst of her fear and confusion was very much about holding on to that which was of ultimate value for her. As she later articulated her story, first with the chaplain and then in her book, she was able to deepen her awareness of all that made up her essential self and what this meant to her.

What is spirituality?

Spirituality is about the practice and outworking of the spirit and the ways in which it is developed, with its different aspects and relationships connected, sustained, and understood. As we shall see, this may involve the spirituality of any individual or that which is developed in and through the disciplines and practices of a group. It is often a combination of both. Essentially, then, spirituality is relation and action centred, and about making connections with these different aspects of life. It is possible to refer to spirituality as an academic discipline, involving systematic research that reflects upon such practice and the meanings that may emerge from that. Spirituality, however, cannot be simply an academic discipline, precisely because reflection is holistic and embodied, involving more than simply intellectual understanding and awareness.

A working definition of spirituality then involves three parts and is summed up in Box 2.1.

Box 2.1   Spirituality

- Developing awareness and appreciation of the other (including the self, the other person, the group, the environment and, where applicable, deity).
- Developing the capacity to respond to the other. This involves putting spirituality into practice, embodying spirituality, and thus the continued relationship with the other.
- Developing ultimate life meaning based upon all aspects of awareness and appreciation of and response to the other.

We will examine each part of this definition.

Awareness and appreciation of the other

The other is that which is beyond the self and in this category can be included: the self, the other person, the group, the environment and the divine. Each of these might be deemed to be of ultimate value and could be the ground of the person's faith.

The self

It is reasonable to speak of the self as other (Riceour 1992). In one sense the self is indeed simply one amongst others and so is an other to someone else. In another sense we can speak of the person moving beyond the self. The psychological distance achieved enables the person to begin to see her self and so begin to actually see the self as other. Hence, we can speak of self-transcendence. This self-transcendence enables, firstly, some awareness of the whole person, thoughts, feelings, physical experience, practice, and relationships. For Margaret, this involved bringing together her physical pain and weakness, her affective pain – with fear and loneliness, and the cognitive and affective side of her which was 'fed' by an awareness of her relationship to the significant person and groups in her life. It did not magically take away the pain and fear which threatened to engulf her but did allow her to transcend that and to feel that as part of her whole self.

Secondly, there was an awareness of the self as both same and different. Difference is about the uniqueness of the person, essential for the particular identity of the self. However, the self cannot be understood if it is completely different. Indeed, complete difference makes the self a stranger, someone who has no point of contact, who is not identified with. Equally, if the self is simply the same as others, located purely as one of many, with no distance from the group, there is the danger of a loss of identity. Margaret locked into both of these aspects. The presence of an other, albeit a teddy, reminded her of her community, the people that she belonged to, hence the sameness. Her roles within those communities demonstrated her difference, a difference that was viewed not simply in terms of the nature of the self but of the action and contribution which that self makes.

Thirdly, awareness of the self involves awareness of the limitations of the self. Holistic awareness of the different aspects of the self can thus never lead to or point to wholeness, in the sense of completeness. For Margaret the ultimate limitation that she was aware of was her mortality. As she focused on that she was increasingly aware she was interdependent not independent. In practice this inevitably means acceptance in certain contexts of dependence without any sense of shame, beautifully summed up in the sight of Margaret clutching the teddy. All of this leads gradually to an appreciation of the self, as both limited but also creative, as interdependent but also dependent. The self is revealed as essentially ambiguous, the same as others but different.

Awareness of the self leads to the capacity to develop dialogue with the self, something which distinguishes human experience from other species (van der Ven 1998, 108ff). This openness to the self is the basis of healthy self criticism necessary for spiritual growth. Clearly, this awareness of the self involves a reflection on the interior of the self. It can, however, be only half the story of self awareness, since the self and its narrative is developed in relation to others.

The self is a physical, embodied (somatic) being, as well as one of emotion and intellect. This somatic awareness includes an awareness of sexuality, the person's sexual identity and being. This area is a good example of the way in which historically there has been a fragmentation of the person. The spirit was often seen as not simply distinct from but antipathetic to the body and thus to sexuality. Sexuality is by definition ambiguous, both a wonderful experience and expression of the embodied person and also something fraught with risk and moral challenge.

The easiest way to handle this culturally was often to simply separate the spirit (good) from the sexual (bad). As Avis notes, the result was to devalue the physical and sexual and thus to retreat from real awareness of the self and other in all its ambiguity and risk (Avis 1989). Spirituality rather involves the integration of sexuality with the self and looks to find meaning in relationships which include this (Helminiak 1998).

Interpersonal relationships
Awareness of the other person, like awareness of the self, involves recognition of difference and sameness. For the other to be simply different means that there is no point of common humanity through which to relate to them. Hence, the person who is seen purely as different is often literally dehumanised, seen as enemy as well as stranger. This is the spiritual dynamic at the heart of racism, expressed ultimately in the Holocaust (Bauman 1989).

Equally, to see the other as purely the same can lead to loss of identity, that which makes the other unique. As Kahlil Gibran notes of marriage this demands distance and space between the two,

Fill each other's cup but drink not from one cup.
Give one another of your bread but eat not from the same loaf.
Sing and dance together and be joyous, but let each one of you be alone, even
as the strings of a lute are alone though they quiver with the same music.
(Gibran 1995, 5)

This means that the spirituality of the interpersonal relationship
must be dynamic. The sameness that is recognised in the other
provides the basis for trust and collaboration, it enables the person to
see the other. The difference provides the basis for continued learning, disclosure, and discovery.

The personal and interpersonal are then connected in this context.
It is not possible to be aware of the holistic and distinctive nature of
the self without developing awareness of the other. Equally it is not
possible to see the other without seeing something of the self in the
other (Buber 1937).

The greater group

Beyond the one-to-one relationship is corporate or cultural spirituality. For Margaret the corporate identity of the family and the church
provided her with both a sense of belonging and security, and also a
sense of active participation and contribution. Once more this
provides the dimensions of sameness and difference. Such a dimension
is part of what it means to be human, hence as Mbiti writes in the
context of African spirituality, 'A person cannot detach himself from
the religion of his group, for to do so is to be severed from his roots,
his foundation, his context of security, his kinship and the entire
group of those who make him aware of his own existence' (Mbiti
1990, 2).

This element in society is increasingly lost under the stress of
consumerism and individualism which tend to stress the contract
nature of groups, that is groups formed from individual choice and
with no historical or moral claim on the person outside of a mutually agreed contract. Groups, as a result, can easily become instrumental, simply used by the person for her own ends.

Increased awareness of any group reveals complexity and ambiguity.
Every group, for instance, has both community elements (ways in which
the members relate and support), and institutional elements (ways in
which the group manages, orders and maintains itself). The institutional
element is often seen as the enemy of community, with bureaucracy
replacing relationships, creating distance between individuals or sub

groups, or defending the group from the outside. Nonetheless, the institution is necessary for the continued running of the group.

Each will have narratives that try to articulate the purpose and values of the groups and rules and regulations for the maintenance of order. Each group, in different ways, takes on a life or character of its own, expressed through narrative and practice. Each group will also have very different sub groups that relate in different ways to the whole group. Each group will also relate in different ways beyond itself, possibly even have a purpose which is greater than it own particular good or the good of its members. Hence, it is possible to speak of the spirituality of the group.

For Margaret there was also a reminder that she was part of, and had faith in, several groups. Multiple group membership might be thought to militate against the corporate spirituality of Mbiti. However, in fact we are inevitably members of more than one group, including:

- given family;
- chosen family, developed through partnerships entered into;
- school and higher or further education;
- local community;
- work;
- interest groups;
- faith groups.

One group may be more central than others, with the person placing more faith in it, yet all are part of the meaning structures of the person. Moreover, being a member of more than one group can help to clarify both the wider meaning of the group or groups, and the identity of the person. Johannes van der Ven refers to intertextuality, the dialogue which the self develops with the narratives or texts of all the different groups and through which personal moral and spiritual meaning is developed (van der Ven 1998, 258 ff.). In other words there is rarely one narrative alone that provides life meaning. Life meaning arises out of the different narratives in dialogue. This is stressed in the work of Kelly who is able to reflect not only upon the spirituality centred around different groups but also of a nation itself, in his case Australia (Kelly 1990).

The environment
The term transcendent can be applied to all the above categories, moving beyond the self, aware of that which is beyond the self, the

person or the group. The term, however, is most often used with the last two categories, those of the wider environment and the divine. The environment has a wide definition, from the physical and social environment which surrounds us each day, to the environment that is created through art, to nature itself. The environment, of course, can be so vast that the sense of otherness is overwhelming. Standing at the foot of the Bridal Veil Falls at Niagra, for instance, it is difficult not to feel a part of the greater whole, a literally breath-taking experience, which can lead to a momentary loss of the sense of the self as separate. However, there are boundaries there, not least for safety, and without boundaries and thus a knowledge of the self compared to the other, there could be no actual conscious awareness of the other.

Awareness of the environment as another presence is not simply about difference. The spirituality of the Lakota native Americans, for instance, perceives the environment in terms of its own familiar social networks of belonging. Hence, a Lakotan can pray, 'for all my relatives', including, animals, birds, plants, water, rocks and so on (Lartey 1997, 121 ff.). In the same way, St. Francis of Assisi was able to refer to, 'dear mother earth' or 'brother sun and sister moon'.

Once again a genuine awareness of the environment reveals ambiguities and complexities. Humans depend upon the environment for sustenance, and it depends upon human kind for protection and responsible stewardship. At the heart of this is an interconnectedness that sees humans existing as part of the environment and affecting it whatever they do (McFague 1997). It can also be very threatening, not least when out of control. Hence, Rudolf Otto pinpoints the ambivalent response of fascination and fear (Otto 1923).

Deity

For many, the divine is the epitome of the transcendent. Any deity tends to be seen as totally other, with the idea of him or her as all powerful, perfect and so on. This sense of otherness informs common views of the concepts holy or sacred, meaning 'set apart'. For Margaret, however, the critical point about her faith object, the ground of her being, was that she be able to relate to him directly. She could not begin to understand him or be aware of him as simply the transcendent being. Indeed, by definition such a being is alien, and cannot be understood. Characteristically, the more that the otherness of the divine is stressed the more he/she is seen as a figure to be feared, and thus to be placated with sacrifices and the like. It is critical then to see the sameness in any divinity as well as the difference. This is expressed well in the Hebrew *imago deo* doctrine – that man was made in the image of God (Genesis 5:1). It is also expressed in Christian spirituality through the idea of God becoming man in Christ. The human face of God is the way in which the presence of God can be expressed, making that which is the experience of God immanent, and lifting the relationship from the tyrannical God who is to be feared to one who identifies with his people. It is precisely that imminence that Margaret needed by her bedside, and which could only be communicated through the *presence* of a person.

There are, of course, many different expressions of the spirituality of the divine, but all seek some sense of the divine in the present 'known' experience, and all have some sense of the complexity of the divine. Ascribing human qualities to the divine has, of course, been common in many religions, from Ancient Greece to Hinduism.

Summing up so far
Even at this stage it is clear that spirituality in this view is essentially relational and reflective. It cannot be static, or simply be a set of meanings forced upon experience. Moreover, it is well suited to the idea of a postmodern time, precisely because it recognises that anyone's spirituality may involve relationships with many different groups. Hence, by its very nature spirituality is not likely to depend on a meta-narrative, one story that gives meaning to experience.

In slightly different ways, in each of these areas, awareness involves knowledge of:

- the holistic other, involving cognitive, affective and somatic elements and as connected to and affecting a network of others;
- the other as both same and different, and hence ambiguous;
- the interdependence of the different others;
- the nature of the other as always emerging, as always learning and therefore never totally knowable;
- the other as involving both imminence, awareness of the self, and transcendence, a movement beyond the self.

The capacity to respond to the other

Response to the other is essentially about the articulation of spirituality in practice. It involves roles that express something of the relationship to others, and the contribution towards these relationships.

The working out of these roles involves the expression of the uniqueness of the person and their particular part in any relationship.

The response to the other can be seen in terms of *vocation* (calling), or response to the *calling*, or needs, of the other and in terms of placing *trust* in the other. The idea of vocation has tended to be either restricted to particular purpose or professions or in practice to the Christian spirituality, with God calling the Christian. However, in terms of a broader human spirituality all the different others 'call' the person in some ways. The environment calls the person or group to be aware of the complexities and interconnectedness and to respond with responsible stewardship. The group calls the person or other groups to be aware and to respond to need with a particular contribution. The other person calls for response as her needs are disclosed. McFadyen argues that such a call is the basis of personhood (McFadyen 1990). Any calling, of course, has to be tested, and as shall be seen below, it also involves negotiation about how responsibility is to be shared.

The response to the other may be one of accepting need *for* the other in some way. We need the environment for our continued existence and different groups for social and physical well-being. Acknowledging that need, and the way in which the other fulfils it, enables us to begin to trust the other. Placing trust in the other is a clear response to that person, group or environment.

The response of the person to the other then becomes an embodiment of spirituality, life meaning in action. In this sense the response is another aspect of transcendence, with action going beyond the self. The embodiment may be individual or collaborative. Importantly, the embodiment of this spirituality is in itself a working out of the life meaning, not simply the applying of a set meaning to the situation. Indeed, it is not possible to fully understand any life meaning other than in and through the practical testing and outworking of it (Riceour 1992).

Developing life meaning

Developing life meaning is often identified purely with the development of doctrines – belief systems that set out something about the nature of life and its different aspects. However, life meaning in the light of the holistic and community perspective cannot be simply confined to conceptual beliefs. It is rather located in and understood in two major ways:

- *holistic meaning.* This involves whole person awareness.
- *value-based meaning.* Meaning here is discovered in the value the person recognises in herself and others. Such value is based on both a sense of unconditional acceptance from the other and a sense of the worth and contribution to the other and the wider community, a sense of purpose.

Holistic meaning
Knowledge and awareness involves four levels of meaning: cognitive (to do with ideas about the world), affective (to do with emotions), somatic (to do with 'body language', including tactile communication) and interpersonal. This can involve awareness of all of these aspects of the other and how these affect each other. Once again this cannot be a complete awareness. In most situations the person reflects and discovers different aspects of the self that may have been previously not recognised or accepted. Such awareness is mediated through one or more of the routes of knowledge. In Margaret's case the somatic knowledge – provided by touching the teddy – was able to mediate the interpersonal knowledge and affective knowledge which gave her a sense of security. Later, cognitive meaning was worked through as she articulated her story to the chaplain, enabling feelings and beliefs to come together. The experience was not made sense of simply in terms of doctrinal truths but rather in terms of how she retained her holistic identity in the light of the intense feelings of fear, loneliness, isolation and desolation.

Such an holistic knowledge involves the development of integration and ultimately of *integrity*. Solomon suggests that integrity involves several different virtues which come together to form a 'coherent character' and identity. It involves:

- *Making connections* between: the different aspects of the self (cognitive affective physical); the self and practice. This leads to a holistic way of thinking and the development of cognitive, affective and somatic knowledge.
- *Consistency of character* between the self and its values and practice; past present and future; and between different situations and contexts. The response may not be the same in every context but will remain consistent with the identity of the person. Implied in this is the idea of being true to the self.
- *Honesty.* This involves a high degree of transparency, so that the self can be open to the other, including the self.

- *Responsibility.* This involves taking responsibility for meaning and value. If the person simply accepted the views and meaning of the other then there could be no separate identity, and no genuine attempt to relate the different aspects of experience. This demands responsibility both for thinking through meaning and for putting that meaning into practice. In the light of the interconnectedness of human experience it also demands both responsibility for the self *and* others (Solomon 1992, 168).

Human limitations make it impossible to have 'complete' integrity. Hence, integrity is best seen as a continual process, with the person discovering more about the different connections and how they affect each other. Central to this is the capacity to reflect and so to enable self criticism and learning. Though there can never be wholeness in the sense of completeness, it is possible to speak of being at one with the self, something enabled by self acceptance.

Meaning and value

Life meaning is attached to value. It is not simply about interesting ideas but rather meaning which is central to the life project and reflects the value of the person and her identity. Indeed the formation of an identity that connects to these factors provides the ground of value.

At one level this is about the acceptance of the self as valuable in herself. This demands acceptance based on unconditional value, an inclusiveness that emerges from an awareness of the other as part of common humanity. This is ultimately the basis of *faith*. Faith is developed in response to that which gives value to life. Hence, Fowler defines faith in two ways:

> (1) the foundational dynamic of trust and loyalty underlying selfhood and relationships. In this sense faith is a human universal, a generic quality of human beings;
> (2) a holistic way of knowing, in which persons shape their relationships with the self, others and the world in the light of and apprehension of and by transcendence. (Fowler 1990, 394 ff.)

Fowler refers to two other views of faith that are specifically religious: the response to the gift of salvation; and obedient assent to revealed truth.

Faith, in its generic sense, is very much belief *in* an other. This may involve any of the others noted above, or ideas related to them.

Clearly such faith will vary from complete trust in the other to partial or working trust. The latter can build faith on the other whilst being aware of its limitations.

   Such belief directly affects practice. This is in contrast to belief *that* or belief *about*. It is possible, for instance to believe in the concept of God, or *that* God exists, without making the belief *in* him the basis of life. Fowler argues that faith develops through discernible stages. Each of these stages is about the development of the self and the relationship of the person to the different others (see Chapter 6).

   The second basis of value that provides significant meaning is to do with purpose. As the person responds to the other so her instrumental value is articulated. She is of value because she has a purpose in relation to others. All of this provides a view of reality that is not just 'given' but also created, and this begins to generate *hope*. Hope has often been associated with some quasi mystical concept based upon future promises. Hence, some expressions of spirituality see hope as based upon the promise of life after death (Edwards 1999). The problem with this approach is the danger of forming hope around a concept. This may satisfy cognitive knowledge but can have little to say to affective understanding, not least where the person is suffering pain or anxiety. Margaret Lyall's anxiety was not going to be dispelled by doctrine. She needed the presence of a person and a sense of her spirit, in relation to others, to enable meaning that was relevant to her experience.

   For Margaret hope was not found in future promise but rather in the acceptance of the other, both the immediate acceptance of the carers and the presence of the community, and in the gradual confirmation of the capacity to respond based upon her previous relationships. Acceptance is critical. It says to the person that they, as a person, are not without hope. This contrasts with the experience of some people who in their early life have received the message that they are in fact 'hope less', or can only have hope on certain conditions, such as pleasing parents.

   The capacity to respond is also critical for hope in that it provides the possibility of a continued meaningful engagement with the other. Response might be long term and complex or short term and limited. This might include even simply the capacity to hold another's hand and squeeze back. At the other extreme, awareness of the other and the capacity to respond in collaborative practice literally opens up many possibilities which further enable the person to envision the future. Hope in this sense becomes the capacity to envision the future positively, however brief that may be, and whatever the awareness of the response may be. Such an envisioning itself provides a further level of life meaning (Robinson 1998).

The articulation of meaning in practice may lead either to the confirmation of previous meaning (and perhaps a deepening of the meaning) or to discovery of new meaning that will lead to change in values and practice. In Margaret's case this involved the reflection on her previous narrative and the reinforcement of a well worked out life meaning. For others, this may involve reflecting on practice for the first time and examining underlying assumptions of which they were not fully aware.

In the light of this, response to the other leads to a creation of meaning in and beyond the self, not least in the way in which the person can begin to create meaning in collaboration with others. In this respect, the embodiment of spirituality is one which is an extension of integrity – summed up in the Judeo-Christian concept of *shalom*. This is often translated as peace. However, it is not just the absence of conflict or aggression but rather the creation of right relationships. If integrity is about being true to the self and at one with the self then shalom is about being true to and being at one with the other. This is not about a simplistic acceptance of the other, but rather about relating to the other in all her ambiguity. It is concerned as much for justice as for peace. It aims to create relationships that face the reality of the other but also create reality through reconciliation and collaboration. Hence, it is difficult to confine spirituality to the personal realm, reaching out to society and even politics (Selby 1983).

The development of meaning in spirituality, then, is focused on holistic, existential and value meaning which relates to the different relationships. In particular, it focuses on the development of *faith* in the other and *hope* which is generated through significant purpose and function leading to reconciliation and possibly forgiveness (*shalom*).

One element in this is about finding meaning through transcendence. Hence, Reed sums up spirituality as 'the human propensity to find meaning in and through self transcendence; it is evident in perspective and behaviours that express a sense of relatedness to a transcendent dimension, or to something greater than the self and may or may not include formal religious practice' (Reed 1998, 50).

The dynamics of the spirit

As noted above, the dynamic of awareness is not passive or fixed. It involves transcending the self, enabling a perspective on the self and dialogue with the self. It involves an awareness of the other as transcending the self yet also part of the self, both different and the same. With that sense of the other comes often the sense of the holiness, sacredness or specialness of the other. This has often been associated with experience of the divine but is not exclusive to it. Similar experiences can be discovered with the environment and also with other people or groups. Spirituality also involves a transcendence of the self in and through the embodiment of the response to the other, a response which may include the other, in a further response to some greater other, such as the environment (Aldridge 2000, 38). Central to this dynamic and the resultant development of meaning are *empathy* and *unconditional acceptance*. The first can be seen as a skill or capacity, the second as an attitude. Both of these operate in the context of a continual process.

Empathy

Scheler defines empathy as 'a genuine reaching out and entry into the other person and his individual situation, a true and authentic transcendence of the one's self' (quoted in Campbell 1984, 77). The idea of moving beyond the self has its problems, not least because it assumes fixed boundaries to the self that are being transcended. It is better expressed as a movement beyond the concerns of and for the self, and with this an expansion or reaching out of the self. This involves moving away from the things that cause the person to attend in an exclusive way to the self, such as fears or guilt, and which block any openness to the other. It also involves not taking the self and self concerns too seriously. Hence, Scheler writes of abandoning 'personal dignity'. Empathy, then, fosters an attitude of humility, humour and playfulness, developing a wry openness and appreciation of the ambiguity of the human condition.

With humour is also wonder and awe, precisely because the openness to the other is constantly revealing something new, and because, as Berryman suggests of children, transcendence involves living 'at the limit of their experience' (Berryman 1985). Myers argues that this is the case in spirituality of all ages (Myers 1997).

Hence, Phenix argues that 'human consciousness is rooted in transcendence, and that the analysis of all human consciousness discloses the reality of transcendence as a fundamental presupposition of the human condition' (Phenix 1964). Michael Jacobs suggests then that spirituality is precisely found in the 'margins', the places between each other (Jacobs 1998).

We would further argue that such transcendence is not static but is a continual to-ing and fro-ing between the self and the other, each time learning a bit more about the self and the other and the self reflected in the other. This is also an awareness which is not self-conscious but rather one which is 'unmindful' of 'individual spirituality' allowing 'the instinctive life to look after itself'. This simple letting go of the self is contrasted with a self-conscious concern for the other, where the calculated concern itself tends to dominate. This may be compared with the classical pianist whose technique can actually get in the way of the music. The pianist who is really aware of the spirit of the music allows the music to shine through naturally. This reaching out to the other applies in all the categories set out above. Hence, Scheler bemoans the way in which an awareness of nature has been increasingly lost (Campbell 1984, 78).

As empathy reaches out so the person becomes more open to the other and in turn the other begins to disclose more of himself. What is being disclosed will doubtless involve incongruities, ambiguities and contradictions, and mismatches in perception. Empathy, then, is a way of seeing the other that goes beyond surface impressions. Data about the self and the other emerges over time, reflecting an awareness that involves continual growth and learning. Empathy may well confirm data well known in an established relationship. However, because the person is continually emerging in relation to the changing world, new aspects of him are revealed. Facts and truth become 'a creation of the relationship itself, a continuous coming into being of possibilities requiring further exploration' (Margulies 1989, 12). This involves mutual disclosure, discovering the self as well as the other, through the essentially 'dialectal quality of finding and creating meaning' (Margulies 1989).

Margulies notes four components of empathy which involve holistic awareness:

- *Conceptual empathy*, stressing cognitive understanding of the other;
- *Self experiential empathy*, referring to memories, affects and associations which are stirred in the listener, thus causing her to identify with the experience of the other;
- *Imaginative/imitative empathy*, involving imagining oneself into a model of the other's experience;
- *Resonant empathy*, the experience of 'affective contagion', where the listener feels the feelings of the other (Margulis 1989, 19).

All these components are important in developing and communicating empathy. The first two in particular provide ways of deepening understanding of the other. The last two connect to second level empathy, where the listener hears not only the story but the feelings behind the story.

The dynamic of empathy is essentially one of risk. To see the other, the person has to reach out. He cannot stay in the safety of the narrow self and thus has to lose that security. Hence, for empathy to flourish there must be courage to reach out, imagination to see the possibility beyond the self, and above all acceptance of the person.

Unconditional acceptance

Like empathy, unconditional acceptance is fundamental to therapeutic and religious and non-religious traditions (Outka 1972, Rogers 1983, Bauman 1993, Robinson 2001). It is well summed up by the Greek word *agape*, a form of love. Robinson notes that this involves not simply a way of relating but also a way of knowing and of empowering (Robinson 2001).

A way of relating. Agape is an acceptance of the self and other which sets no conditions. All are equally valuable. This love is very different from *eros* – the more romantic love which is based upon the attraction of the other, and which is therefore conditional upon such attraction. Agape is faithful to the other whatever the response.

A way of knowing. Agape is critical to the dynamic of empathy. The truth about the other, in particular about the other person, will not be disclosed, not least to the self, without an awareness of being accepted. Weil can thus argue that 'love sees what is invisible' (quoted in Gaita 2000, xvi), in others and in the self. Invisibility of the true nature of others is often created by our own stereotypes and judgements. Equally, the person can only begin to see her self, including difficulties and flaws, once she feels accepted (van Deusen Hunsinger 1995). In this sense, then, truth and acceptance come together.

Because of this, it is precisely agape which enables the ambiguity of the other to be held together – to see the other in all her ambiguity and still remain committed to her. Hence, *faithfulness* (fidelity) and *honesty* (veracity) operate closely together. Agape enables the other to be seen both as the same – part of common humanity, but also as quite unique. Indeed, as Gaita argues, the common humanity of the other person, and therefore any sense of the universal, is only known through the awareness of the particular other, something revealed as they develop and craft their own story (Gaita 2000, xxix).

A way of empowering. Importantly then agape does not attempt to manipulate or control but precisely gives the other freedom to develop awareness of the self and others, and the freedom to respond. Hence, as W.H. Vanstone notes, this involves giving power to the other. 'The power which love gives to the other is the power to determine the issue of love – its completion or frustration, its triumph or tragedy. This is the vulnerability of authentic love . . .' (Vanstone 1977, 67).

Spirituality may relate to the narratives and traditions of history but ultimately it can only be achieved through the person freely working out her own meaning in relation to others.

In all of this, agape is essential to the awareness of the self and other. Because of human limitation such awareness is difficult without the perspective of another in any case. The Johari Window (Box 2.2) demonstrates well how difficult it is to see the whole person. In this, the person is represented as a window with four panes: one known by the person and no one else, one by the person and others, one known only by others and one known to none – either the self or others.

Box 2.2 The Johari Window

Known to the person	Unknown to the person
Known by others	*Known by others*
Known to the person	Unknown to the person
Not known by others	*Not known by others*

Source: Adapted from Armstrong *et al.* 1999, 103.

Agape then holds together the ambiguities in the other and still enables growth. As Schlauch notes it holds together several aspects in itself:

• *Doubting and believing.* Agape does not simply involve a naïve belief in the other but rather believes in and tests the other out. Both are important in enabling the truth.
• *Separation and connection.* The other cannot be seen if she is too close. In that perspective it is hard to see the other as uniquely the other.

Agape holds together both perspectives. Hence agape is essentially a practical love that is drawn so far into the other that it loses perspective.
• *Understanding and explanation.* Agape enables an existential understanding of the other, and also a more 'objective' explanation of the other (Schlauch 1990).

The dynamic of spirituality then is both enabled by and enables the growth of faith, hope, empathy and unconditional acceptance. The idea of love noted here should be distinguished from romantic love or one that becomes over involved. On the contrary, this is a form of moderated practical love that requires distance to see and enable the other.

The spiritual journey

The dynamic of spirituality, seen as the development of awareness and meaning, involves a reflective, relational process. In the history of different spiritual traditions, this process is often seen as a journey or quest. There is no arriving, only travelling and the constant searching, learning and development. At the same time the dynamic of spiritual awareness, empathy and love, requires a companion on the journey, someone to enable the reflective cycle.

This state of continual journeying is inevitable in a relational view of spirituality. The person can never know the other fully, and in any case is faced by many challenges to life meaning that are posed by experience, not least the immense challenges of illness. The process can be best seen as a recurring learning cycle involving several phases, similar to Kolb's learning circle (cf. Kolb 1984).

• *Articulation* of narrative in response to experience.
• *Reflection* on and *testing* of meaning.
• *Development* of meaning.
• *Response*, leading to new experience.

Articulation
The key vehicle for spirituality is the person's story or narrative. The story brings together experience and all levels of meaning: cognitive, affective, somatic and interpersonal. A good example of this is the spirituality of the psalms in the Old Testament (Brueggemann 1995). The psalmists articulate their story, often one involving hardship or trauma, and how they feel about their situation. A critical part of this

story is previous experience and belief systems as they try to make sense of experience that does not easily fit with views of morality and justice. Invariably, it eventually makes sense in terms of those belief systems, but not always.

Several things happen in this phase. Firstly, it enables the person to gain distance from the self, and so begin to be aware of the effect of experience upon the self and the meaning and feelings which are shaping that experience. Freeman refers to a phase of *distanciation*. This leads to a sense of differentiation: a separation of the self from the self, such that the text of one's experience becomes transformed into an object of interpretation' (Freeman 1993, 45). This is important for the development of empathy for the self.

Secondly, it is a means not simply of expressing but of discovering meaning. Until an idea has been articulated it is not fully understood. Articulation is not simply a bilateral communication. The self can hear what is being said and itself becomes both a learner and an interpreter or commentator, shaping and reshaping the story. Articulation then becomes a three-way conversation, raising the story to a level of publicness, and opening it to examination. This enables the development of self-criticism and, by extension, the capacity to critique others (van der Ven 1998).

Thirdly, once the act of articulation is set in place then the person begins to take responsibility for that spirituality, without which there is no effective integration of meaning and experience. Articulation may occur in different ways. Those who are unable to speak may articulate feelings and ideas directly through the body, as with Margaret's reaching out. However, the more that the story is articulated in the presence of an other the more articulation becomes reflective. With reiteration, rehearsal of the story, the person discovers more about himself and his situation.

Reflection

Once the story is told this provides the basis for a more systematic reflection on the meaning it embodies. This focuses on the different relationships noted above, their significance, and how far they provide faith and hope in the person's life:

1. *The self.* This involves identifying feelings, and clarifying ideas, including beliefs and values or principles. This inevitably leads on to reflection on how the person sees himself, not least as to whether he is someone of value.

2. *Significant others, and their stories.* This examines how the person perceives significant others and how he feels and thinks about them, and what demands they make of him. What meaning do they give to him, and how does that meaning affect his life?
3. *Communities.* Relationships to communities are examined, identifying the core communities which give significant meaning to his life. Do they supply rules for living, a place of comfort, an opportunity for service or success? Such reflection allows feelings and thoughts about such groups to emerge.
4. *The environment.* Is the person aware of the environment? How does he feel about it, and respond to it? What does the environment give to him?
5. *Deity.* Reflection on this may focus on points 3 or 4 above, with many things, ranging from a football team or the environment providing the 'ground of being'. It may centre on one of the religious grounds of faith. In that case reflection should be on the person's image of the divine, and feelings for him.

Each of these reflections are interconnected and involve dialogue between the different parts of the network. Dialogue enables an increased awareness of the values and beliefs of the other. In turn this leads to the clarification of spiritual and moral meaning and greater awareness of the other – hence the development of empathy. With the development of such holistic awareness, the person is then faced by the truth of the other and the inevitable complexities and difficulties.

Firstly, this may involve aspects of the self or the other which have been difficult to face and which thus have been repressed or denied. This may be an emotion, such as anger. It may be an event in the past that has caused shame. In terms of the significant other this may mean looking again at well formed perceptions and exploring alternatives. As Carr notes, many of our perceptions of the other are in fact projections of our own feelings on to the other. Unable to face the anger in our selves we project it on to the other and believe that they are angry with us (Carr 1989, 141 ff.).

Secondly, the dialogue enables the person to test out the meaning of the different parts of her life and begin to relate the moral and spiritual meaning of the wider community to her personal meaning. This is a critical element in the development of spirituality in that it enables the person to own their particular moral and spiritual perspective and also recognise that wider meanings have relevance to her. Hence, there is development of personal agency, the person as subject responsible for her own thoughts and feelings and the development of community. For this to be genuine the person has to be able to critique the thoughts and feelings of the other and allow the other to critique hers. It is here where intertextuality is practised. The different stories that make up the person's network of relationships enter into critical dialogue and thus expand the person's own life meaning (van der Ven 1998).

Thirdly, such reflection inevitably gives rise to an awareness of discontinuities, fissures (Freeman 1993) or dissonances. These contradictions may be at points through the whole range of awareness, for example, between:

- ideas and values, and feelings;
- the attitude of the person to herself and others;
- different values and beliefs held by the person;
- beliefs and values and the practice, the embodiment of meaning;
- the view of the other and 'reality' and
- attitudes and practice in the past and the present.

Some discontinuities point to apparent contradiction but are in reality part of what it means to be human. The self is both bad and good, the same but different, dependent yet in control, free yet constrained. Such discontinuities highlight the tension between human need and limitation and human desires and aspirations. The limitation of our physical nature, ultimately expressed in mortality, means that we cannot survive without support – even at our fittest. Emotional needs demand fulfilment even when the person seems to be at her most independent. Interpersonal limitations mean that it is impossible to relate equally to all who we meet. Such tensions have to be held together. They are a part of what it means to be human.

Other contradictions or inconsistencies are more problematic and may point to the need to change, such as someone who may feel called to answer the needs of other but ignores the needs of the self.

At the heart of these reflections are fundamental questions such as:

- What purpose and function does the person have in his life?
- Who or what is the person's ground of faith?
- What is the person's basis and content of hope?

Such questions can be asked directly, but emerge more naturally as part of the reflection. Many people have built up belief systems without being fully aware of who or what they put their faith in, what is the cognitive as well as affective ground of their faith, or that they may have several grounds of faith.

Developing meaning
The next phase continues the learning process for whoever is involved. Having tested life meaning the person may be unhappy with contradictions or inconsistencies that have emerged. This may lead to a development of life meaning in a different way, perhaps developing the cognitive or affective aspects or focusing on the value of the self as much as the value of others. It may lead to a re-evaluation of faith and hope and to a conscious development of faith in other areas. A good example of this is where the person may move from a conditional faith – one based upon personal achievement of some kind – to a more unconditional one – based upon acceptance of the other. Freeman, using the life of Augustine, notes this as a point of recognition, involving both a recognition of need because of limitations, and recognition of the need to change (Freeman 1993).

The person may already have developed a highly integrated and holistic spirituality, and reflection on experience may simply lead to an affirmation of the spiritual meaning. However, given that all situations are different and challenge life meaning, especially those involving major emotional and/or physical trauma, this still involves learning.

Response
This naturally moves through to an embodying of the spirit in some way. In terms of *shalom* this may mean the acceptance of the other, leading to forgiveness. This views forgiveness not as simply something given to another in response to an action of reparation but rather as process. At its heart is the recognition of common humanity in the other, breaking down the barriers of enmity. Even forgiveness has at its heart a tension, with the unconditional acceptance of the other but also a concern for her response and thus for change. This in turn may lead to action which looks for justice or which leads to some appropriate form of reconciliation (Smedes 1998).

An important part of this response is the negotiation of responsibilities. Finch and Mason argue that such negotiations not only lead to real changes in relationship, they also develop the moral and spiritual identity of the person and the group. In their work with families they noted that the majority did not have a predetermined set of beliefs or values which informed the setting of responsibility for different members of the family (especially for the elderly). Instead, there was a process of negotiation. This was a way of developing 'moral reputation' and literally involved the 'creation and recreation of moral identity' (Finch and Mason 1993). Such negotiations depend on but also enable the acceptance of mutual limitations and awareness of the possibilities in terms of individual and collaborative contributions.

With each aspect of the spiritual process there is both a recognition of the limitations and a move out to the creative possibilities, summed up well in the Alcoholics Anonymous prayer of St Augustine,

> God grant me the serenity to accept the things I cannot change;
> the courage to change the things I can,
> and the wisdom to know the difference. (quoted in Clinebell 1968, 152 ff.)

This is ultimately expressed in action or relationships that embody the spirit, the working through of right relationships, shalom.

Accompanying the journey

If spirituality involves continual reflection and development, both person led and in response to unexpected challenges, it raises the question of how the person maintains continued identity.

Firstly, even where change occurs there is usually some element that remains familiar such as relationships or values. Fowler refers to the 'tent pegs', the coping mechanisms which maintain a sense of identity (Fowler 1996). Secondly, the very act of reflective process provides critical continuity, so that the person can chart a journey and see how they have developed. At the centre of this is the development of integrity with the person taking responsibility for the change. Such responsibility enables her to see both where she has come from, and even if there has been radical change know that it has been caused by her. This sets up the spirituality of sameness and difference, noted above, over time. The person is the same but different from her previous history, but because it is *her* history there is continuity in that change.

Thirdly, there is the need for a 'holding environment', a relationship which keeps faith with the person – enabling faithful change. This might be a community, or it might be simply another person.

The identity of that person may differ from context to context. In systematic religious approaches this is sometimes focused in the idea of spiritual director. Leech offers a less formal and more interesting view of the *soul friend*, literally someone who will keep faith and maintain the person's sense of continuity (Leech 1977). Such support may come from individuals, the environment or divinity. It may come from a formal relationship or one that springs up in a moment of crisis, such as tutor, nurse or doctor. It is something about the focused and attentive presence of the other which enables the person to begin to develop spiritual meaning, or in Lyall's terms to 'hold on to the spirit'. Vanier views this in terms of an accompanier (Vanier 2001, 128).

The image is of someone accompanying the person on her journey or part of it. This is not making the journey for them but being with them and thus helping them to frame a map, however temporary, of where they have been and what that journey means. The accompanier is especially important in moments of crisis, not least where the spiritual map no longer seems to reflect the reality of the journey.

The image can be extended to the world of music, where the accompanist enables the so-called soloist to articulate her melody. It remains her melody, but as the piece progresses it is deepened and enriched in contrast to the underlying harmonies of the accompanist. Sometimes the accompanist will take the melody himself reflecting back what has been heard. Sometimes, that melody will provide the ground for the soloist to develop different harmonic ideas. More often than not the melody will return to the soloist reworked, perhaps even in a different key, having gone through the so-called development. This is a relationship of mutuality that is not strictly symmetrical. Both disclose something of themselves but not in precisely the same way, with the accompanist always seeking to enable the other, and thus to give and share power.

As intimated above this is not a linear process but cyclical. The development of meaning comes around new each time, as new challenges are faced, and old belief systems and awareness challenged. Sometimes, the old beliefs are tested and make sense, sometimes they don't. Sometimes the perceptions which have been relied on for decades breakdown. More fundamentally, this means that the very life meaning and underlying faith is continually being tested by experience and by relationships. Hence, there is no presumption that the spiritual experience will be either easy or comfortable.

Ritual and meaning

Another anchor for continued identity can be ritual. Ritual is often associated purely with the spirituality of organised religions. Moreover, it can be seen in a negative light, as a way of avoiding real reflection and maintaining loyalty. However, as Erikson notes ritual is a key part of each stage of personal development, not least because it enables the development and celebration of shared meaning (Erikson 1977). Rituals can enable shared *attention*, signalling presence there for the other, *intention*, be that long or short-term purpose, aims and objectives, and *affect*, how we feel about each other or certain issues (Stern 1985, 129). Hence, ritual can lock creatively into awareness and appreciation of the other, cognitive, affective and somatic. As such, the ritual can be a key part of the reflective process. It can be both part of the experience which the person or group reflects upon, and as such is open to criticism and change. It can sum up the embodiment of personal or group spirituality, as regular meals together might do for a family. It can also provide part of any continuity over time, acting as a reminder of purpose and hope.

Conclusion

'Definition is a tool of rationality, an instrument which seeks to enclose. The term spiritual however, needs to remain elusive if it is not to betray its very identity' (Bellamy 1998, 185). Bellamy makes an interesting point. Spirituality does have 'soft edges' not least because it focuses on relationships that transcend the self. The danger of her point, however, is that we end up trying to avoid any clear understanding of what spirituality is. Spirituality thus becomes shapeless and ultimately useless for healthcare practice. In this chapter, we have shown that it is possible to define spirituality in such a way that it does not betray its identity.

It involves awareness of the other, the development of the capacity to respond and the development of meaning from that experience. At the heart of this is empathy and unconditional acceptance, which are gradually developed through the spiritual process and in particular through the telling of a story. Story or narrative is able to reveal something about the whole of the person's experience and is thus a critical way of disclosing the person over time. Hence, we can often learn more about spirituality through reading novels than text books.

Spirituality is mediated through physical and psychic presence, and is located in experience. It is not simply knowledge *about* the other but existential awareness of the other. Hence, meaning is learned in that direct experience and from subsequent reflective dialogue with different narratives. To develop that spirituality demands faith in an other and in the self – a faith which both provides the basis of personal identity and also the ground from which the continual discovery and disclosure of the spiritual journey can be achieved. It also requires hope, the capacity to envision a positive future. The development of hope and faith depend upon both a sense of acceptance and a sense of purpose.

At the core of this spirituality is the capacity to appreciate the other in all its ambiguity, not least the central ambiguity of being the same *and* different. Such a spirituality demands both a commitment to the other and also a distance, one which respects the independence of the other. The development of such spirituality demands an accompanist or companion, who can be there on the spiritual journey and who can enable articulation and reflection.

The working definition of spirituality

As a starting point for practice we have offered in this chapter a model of spirituality. It may be asked why should this model be accepted rather than any other. Indeed, it is not clear at first sight what might be the criteria for judging such a model. There are no obvious empirical tests of inclusion, and many different groups lay claim to different perspectives as the truly spiritual ones.

However, there are certain key strengths to this model:

- *Inclusivity*. The model is based in human spirituality whilst also recognising institutional religions as particular expressions of spirituality.
- *Person centred*. Fundamental to this spirituality is the autonomy of the person. Spirituality cannot be imposed upon a person.
- *Other centred*. Balancing autonomy is the recognition of the need for and challenge of others. Hence, it is hard to see spirituality as individualistic or simply created by the individual in a consumer, 'pick and mix' way. A good deal of spirituality is about the givenness and discovery of the other, and what that gives to the person, and how he might respond.
- *Dialogic*. Meaning is essentially developed through narrative and subsequent dialogue. Hence, there is no attempt to develop a normative spirituality. It is possible to speak of a bad spirituality

(one which alienates or blocks off the person from the self or others) and a good spirituality (one which develops awareness of the self and others). However, that cannot be the basis of any attempt to judge another person's spirituality. Any such judgement can only be made by the person themselves, through the development of and reflection on narrative and dialogue.

• *Holistic.* The model takes account of the cognitive, affective and somatic aspects of the person and how these relate. It also shows how all the different views of spirituality fit together, including: spirituality and its relation to energy, transcendence, an inner essence, and life meaning and purpose.

• *Practical.* This view of spirituality focuses on practice and response to experience rather than on theory. As such it offers something which is not a bolt-on extra to the practice of healthcare and which does not require the development of a separate set of skills or knowledge. The basic process of spirituality relates directly to the idea of personal development (Alves 1963) and involves four straightforward phases that relate closely to other therapeutic approaches such as counselling. These areas will be explored in more detail in subsequent chapters.

• *Dynamic.* Spirituality in this model is interactive and dynamic, not a static concept imposed on the other. There is a mutual calling to care for the other.

Spirituality and the scientific perspective

The humanist, existential, narrative model of spirituality that we propose does not, at first sight, seem to fit in well with a scientific approach to spirituality. The scientific approach stresses the presence of observable phenomena that can in some way be measured and thus assessed. Miller and Thoresen, for instance, propose as part of their definition of spirituality that there are three specific dimensions: practice, belief, and experience (Miller and Thoresen 1999, 7). The first of these, spiritual practices, is, they claim, the easiest to measure. The second varies with culture. The third, spiritual experiences, is, for Miller and Thorensen, the most difficult to measure not least because it is not always clear what is being measured, or whether in fact an experience can be measured and assessed.

At this stage we want to make three points that will be developed further in succeeding chapters. Firstly, the scientific approach cannot be used to define spirituality as such. It can only begin to describe and analyse, largely through qualitative means, such as interviews, the phenomena that have already been defined as spiritual. This may have an important function in helping science, and in particular medical science, be clear about the practical outcomes of spirituality, not least in therapy. It can also become a very important part of justifying a focus on spirituality in the therapeutic practice.

Secondly, the scientific approach can co-exist with the person-centred model. Miller and Thoresen's dimensions can easily be located in the four phases of the spiritual process. Spiritual practices are those rituals that sustain and deepen life meaning, be they Lakotan celebrations of the environment, a regular family meal, or memorial services for the deceased. Some may have well developed rituals. Others may have no rituals. Others, may have rituals which are not consciously seen as such, for example rituals involved in 'clubbing' (Lynch 2002).

Belief emerges through the articulation of the narrative and the subsequent reflection and analysis. 'Spiritual experience', something often associated with ecstatic experiences of different kinds is located at points of transcendence, where the person moves beyond himself or is faced by a transcendent other.

Thirdly, there are differences between an exclusively scientific approach and the person centred model:

1. Observable phenomena cannot be assumed. The data of practice, belief and experience can only be gathered through the development of narrative and reflection on experience and life meaning. Moreover, the person-centred approach is one that, by definition, is never fixed but is always evolving in response to experience.

2. The scientist is by definition apart from the observed phenomena, an observer. Of course, there is much material on the effect of the observer in any scientific relationship, be that social or physical, which argues that the scientist will in some way affect the situation (Stannard 1982, 188). However, the key aim is to gather data that is as far as possible not affected by that relationship. The person-centred model of spirituality posits the need of a companion who will enable the person to affirm or develop their spirituality. Such a person then becomes a key part of the spiritual dynamic. Hence, Kohut can write of the empathy itself as critical to the development of meaning and even therapy (Kohut 1982). The main aim here is not to gather data as such, but enable the person to find life meaning in relation to experience. In this the

companion is not a neutral observer, but rather acknowledges her role in helping the person to develop spirituality.

Questions and exercises

1. Reflect on your own spirituality. Is it explicit or implicit? What is important to you? Who or what do you put your faith in? How do you articulate hope? What are the key purposes in your life?
2. As an exercise in empathy work together with a trusted colleague. Each can tell their spiritual story, about their key life meaning, working through the stages outlined in this chapter. The other should reflect back what they have heard about the ideas and feelings that have been expressed.

References

Aldridge, D. (2000) *Spirituality, Healing and Medicine* (London: Jessica Kingsley).

Alves, C. (1963) 'Spirituality and Personal Growth' in *Spirituality for Today* (London: SCM).

Armstrong, J., Dixon, R. and Robinson, S.J. (1999) *The Decision Makers; Ethics for Engineers* (London: Thomas Telford).

Avis, P. (1989) *Eros and the Sacred* (London: SPCK).

Bauman, Z. (1989) *Modernity and the Holocaust* (London: Polity).

Bauman, Z. (1993) *Postmodern Ethics* (Oxford: Blackwell).

Bellamy, J. (1998) 'Spiritual Values in a Secular Age', in M. Cobb and V. Renshaw (eds) *The Spiritual Challenge of Health Care* (London: Churchill Livingstone) 183–97.

Berryman, J. (1985) 'Children's spirituality and religious language' *British Journal of Religious Education*, **7**, 3.

Boyd, J. (1995) 'The soul as seen through evangelical eyes, part 1: Mental health professionals and the "soul" ', *Journal of Psychology and Theology*, **25**, 3, 151–60.

Brueggemann, W. (1995) *The Psalms and the Life of Faith* (Minneapolis: Fortress).

Buber, M. (1937) *I and Thou* (Edinburgh: T. and T. Clark).

Campbell, A. (1984) *Moderated Love* (London: SPCK).

Carr, B.W. (1989) *The Pastor as Theologian* (London; SPCK).

Clinebell, H.J. (1968) *Understanding and Counselling the Alcoholic* (Nashville: Abingdon).

Doyle, D. (1992) 'Have we looked beyond the physical and psychosocial?' *Journal of Pain Symptom Management*, **7**, 5, 301–11.

Edwards, D.L. (1999) *After Death?* (London: Cassell).

Ellison, C. (1983) 'Spiritual well-being: conceptualization and measurement' *Journal of Psychology and Theology*, **11**, 4, 11–21.

Erikson, E. (1977) *Toys and Reasons* (New York: W.W. Norton).

Finch, J. and Mason, J. (1993) *Negotiating Family Responsibilities* (London: Routledge).

Fowler, J. (1996) *Faithful Change* (Nashville: Abingdon).

Fowler, J. (1990) 'Faith/Belief', in R.J. Hunter (ed.) *Dictionary of Pastoral Care and Counseling* (Nashville; Abingdon) 394–7.

Freeman, M. (1993) *Rewriting the Self* (London: Routledge).

Gaita, R. (2000) *A Common Humanity* (London: Routledge).

Gibran, K. (1995) *The Prophet* (London: Penguin).

Goddard, N. (1995) 'Spirituality as integrative energy' *Journal of Advanced Nursing*, **22**, 808–15.

Halmos, P. (1964) *The Faith of the Counsellors* (London: Constable).

Helminiak, D. (1998) 'Sexuality and spirituality: a humanist account' *Pastoral Psychology*, **47**, 2, 119–26.

Hiatt, J. (1986) 'Spirituality, medicine and healing' *Southern Medical Journal*, **79**, 6, 736–43.

Highfield, M. (1992) 'Spiritual health of oncology patients. Nurse and patient perspectives' *Cancer Nursing*, 15, 1, 1–8.

Jacobs, M. (1998) 'Faith as the Space Between', in M. Cobb and V. Renshaw (eds), *The Spiritual Challenge of Health Care* (London: Churchill Livingstone).

Joseph, M. (1998) 'The effect of strong religious beliefs on coping with stress' *Stress Medicine*, **14**, 219–24.

Kelly T. (1990) *A New Imagining: Towards an Australian Spirituality* (Melbourne: Collins Dove).

King, M. and Dein, S. (1998) 'The spiritual variable in psychiatric research' *Psychological Medicine*, **28**, 1259–62.

Kohut, H. (1982) 'Introspection, empathy and the semi-circle of mental health', *International Journal of Psychoanalysis*, **663**, 397).

Kolb, D.A. (1984) (ed.) *Organisational Psychology* (New York: Prentice-Hall).

Lartey, E. (1997) *In Living Colour* (London: Cassell).

Leech, K. (1977) *Soul Friend* (London: Sheldon Press).

Lyall, M. (1997) *A Touching Place: The Pastoral Counselling Relationship* (Edinburgh: Contact).

Lynch, G. (2002) *After Religion: 'Generation X' and the Search for Meaning* (London: DLT).

McFadyen, A. (1990) *Call to Personhood* (Cambridge: Cambridge University Press).

McFague, S. (1997) *Super, Natural Christians* (London: SCM).

Margulies, A. (1989) *The Empathic Imagination* (New York: W.W. Norton).

Mbiti, J. (1990) *African Religions and Philosophy* (London: Heinemann).

Miller, W. and Thoresen, C. (1999) 'Spirituality and Health' in W. Miller (ed.) *Integrating Spirituality into Treatment* (Washington DC: American Psychological Association)

Myers, B. (1997) *Young Children and Spirituality* (London: Routledge).

Otto, R. (1923) *The Idea of the Holy* (London: Oxford University Press).

Outka, G. (1972) *Agape: An Ethical Analysis* (New Haven; University of Yale Press).

Phenix, P. (1964) *Realms of Meaning,* (New York: McGraw Hill).

Reed, P. (1987) 'Spirituality and well-being in terminally ill hospitalised adults.' *Research in Nursing and Health*, **10**, 5, 335–44.

Reed, P. (1998) 'The re-enchantment of health care: a paradigm of spirituality', in M. Cobb and V. Renshaw (eds) *The Spiritual Challenge of Health Care* (London: Churchill Livingstone).

Riceour, P. (1992) *Oneself as Another* (Chicago: Chicago University Press).

Robinson, S.J. (1998) 'Helping the hopeless', *Contact*, **127**, 3–11.

Robinson, S.J. (2001) *Agape, Moral Meaning and Pastoral Counselling* (Cardiff: Aureus).

Rogers, B. (1983) *Freedom to Learn for the 80s* (Columbus: Charles E. Merrill).

Schlauch, R. (Spring 1990) 'Empathy as the essence of pastoral psychotherapy' *Journal of Pastoral Care*, **XLIV**, 1, 3–17.

Selby, P. (1983) *Liberating God* (London: SPCK).

Sims, A. (1994) ' "Psyche"- spirit as well as mind?' *British Journal of Psychiatry*, **165**, 441–6.

Solomon, R. (1992) *Ethics and Excellence* (Oxford: Oxford University Press).

Smedes, L.B. (1998) 'Stations on the Journey from Forgiveness to Hope' in E.L. Worthington Jr. (ed.) *Dimensions of Forgiveness* (Philadelphia: William Templeton Foundation), 341–54.

Stannard, R. (1982) *Science and the Renewal of Belief* (London: SCM).

Stern, D. (1985) *The Interpersonal World of the Infant* (New York: Basic Books).

Swinton, J. (2001) *Spirituality and Mental Health Care* (London: Jessica Kingsley).

van der Ven, J. (1998) *Formation of the Moral Self* (Grand Rapids: Eerdmans).

van Deusen Hunsinger, D. (1995) *Theology and Pastoral Counselling* (Grand Rapids; Eerdmans).

Vanier, J. (2001) *Becoming Human* (London: DLT).

Vanstone, W.H. (1977) *Love's Endeavour, Love's Expense* (London: Darton, Longman and Todd).

3

Health, Illness, Suffering and Spirituality

Patient A

Patient A, ' a woman of 30, was divorced, frustrated and acting out. All she wore over her petite frame was a completely transparent, short nightie. Every morning at 7 a.m., she would make her bed and then curl up on the pillows like a doll, in stark contrast to her three geriatric room mates. The reason for admission was pain in her left groin. "Right here!" she would say, thrusting the offending spot at us. All tests were negative. Nothing. Everyone was polite, but no one took her terribly seriously; she was an irritation. The psychiatrists were summoned. They sifted through her vast piles of broken dreams and traced blind alleys of her life. They paused to note past losses laid to rest in unmarked graves (Unmarked on the surface that is). They nodded wisely, and so did we.

On the day of her discharge she asked her doctors to do a pelvic examination. What?- had no one done a pelvic examination! Embarrassment turned to anxiety and then to guilt when an advanced carcinoma of the cervix was diagnosed. In the days that followed her young doctors smarted from the painful lesson learned: the importance of compulsive attention to detail. They were thankful for relief from the daily reminder of their negligence when she was transferred to the gynaecology ward. Then one day they met her, wheelchair bound for radiation therapy. Above all, it was her face that stood out – radiant, relaxed, at peace, all anguish and distress resolved. Paradox! Her diagnosis had escalated from neurosis to mortal illness, yet her suffering was alleviated.' (Mount 1993, 30)

Patient B

Patient B was a middle-aged woman in hospital for some time first for tests and then an operation. Despite the use of many different pain-killers the post

53

operative pain was not alleviated. Her experience of being in a hospital ward was one of dislocation from the beginning.

'I feel as if I am part of the ward, not me. There is a lot going on around me- and people are doing wonderful things, but it is all so busy that I do not feel in control. I don't really understand what's going on.'

A junior nurse spoke with her one evening when she could not get to sleep and asked her about her family. She started to talk with pride about her role as mother and what her children had done. She soon broke down and spoke about her son, who she had not seen for years. He left home to marry a white Christian girl. B was a strong Muslim who hated the thought or marriage outside the faith. In the short time in hospital after the operation she began very quickly to explore the things which had given her meaning in her life, especially her role as mother, and was eager to speak to the nurse of her guilt, and to begin to review possibilities. She wanted to forgive her son, but also to be forgiven. She was not sure either how her strong Muslim faith could cope with all this. Nothing was resolved, however, and the nurse felt something of a failure when B went home.

Patient C

Patient C was a 19-year old female student, diagnosed with terminal cancer soon after her A level exams. She took up her place at university whilst still being treated. She managed to survive a term there before the cancer took strong hold and she was unable to come back for the second term and died at home.

C. was a natural student who was easily able to cope with a language course. This, however, was almost secondary to her life at university where she was a part of several different networks of relationships: her hall of residence; her department; student volunteer action group; a fundraising group which had been developed at home and which she continued to work with; dance society; her health support network, including community nurses, GPs, radiologists and soon; her family, who came to know the hall well and the health support team. A strong sense of her purpose in terms of serving others bound all these networks together, giving her a high profile in fundraising for cancer. Frequently, towards the end, she commented on how wonderful the previous year had been,

'I have been able to make friends without any of the long hassle of getting to know people – instant friends and the best of friends. There have been so many people supporting me and giving me the chance to really do life to the full. Everything has seemed so much clearer, and I have not been afraid of life, of taking risks. Life has had a meaning.'

Not all had been easy. Apart from the physical pain, she had to cope with many different groups making demands from her. Her courage was an inspiration to others and they, including the press, sometimes placed her on a pedestal. She became increasingly good at making space for herself, though, and good at puncturing attempts to 'elevate' her. Despite her sadness and occasional depression C experienced a real sense of liberation, 'The truth is I never felt so good'.

(Patients B and C both are based in the experience of the authors, and kindly gave their permission for their cases to be used).

The experiences of the three patients show something of the complex nature of illness and health. In this chapter we will draw out that complexity and begin to note how spirituality relates directly to the experience of health and illness, in terms of:

- well-being,
- suffering,
- therapeutic techniques and outcomes.

Patients A and C both had a sense of well-being that was significant despite their experience of major illness. For patient A the key base of well-being was a change in the medical response which began to treat her as a person. It would be possible to interpret her change as simply the gratification of someone with an hysteric personality who now was the centre of attention. However, the change in her character was profound and was more likely in response to two things, a sense of release provided by the truth, and a sense of release which meant that she no longer had to work at conditional acceptance, based upon her physical attractiveness. There was a new meaning to her life, to do with a sense of value, and this enabled her to face and accept the reality of the illness. There was no evidence of cognitive reflection on meaning. Meaning for her was developed at an affective and somatic level and a strong sense of well-being emerged from her suffering.

Patient C developed well-being in a creative and imaginative way. She developed a sense of meaning that was continually being expressed in different ways and in different contexts. For her, possibilities were immense, and she had a clear sense of being of value both for herself and for her contribution to other sufferers. None of this masked the reality of the suffering she experienced. On the contrary she knew that she was facing an ordeal. The important point about her story is that she was open to the ambiguity of the illness experience, the full experience of illness as the other, fearful of what lay ahead, but also learning much from the new avenues the experience opened to her. At the same time this made a great difference as to how she saw and made sense of life. She was far more aware of opportunities as well as limitations, in her situation, her self and in others.

In all this she drew meaning and strength from several different spiritual narratives, religious groups, fundraising groups, the university hall of residence, and friends and family.

Patient B found the experience of making sense of her illness and her relationship much more difficult. Firstly, her experience of illness was one of powerlessness and a loss of identity and control. Secondly, she felt the power which others had over her. She was someone who always relied on a sense of power, over her children, her husband, the house, the food. The result of this was that for a time the vision of her world lost focus and meaning, becoming fragmented, with nothing to hold the different experiences together.

Mount notes two other consequences of illness. Firstly, the world's perception of the sufferer fragments. For the patient this meant that with the loss of her role and power, her family and friends lost a focused perspective of her. Secondly, it fractures relationships (Mount 1993, 31). As mother and carer the patient did not know how to relate to others as dependent and thus became increasingly angry and frustrated.

It is precisely because she reached this level of fragmentation that she began to look again at her relationships and her life meaning. Well-being for her was expressed in a strong religious commitment that gave her a sense of security and straightforward meaning structures. Part of this meaning was the importance of not being ill and not allowing oneself to be dependent, and part was found in rigid cultural patterns of behaviour.

She could only begin to articulate the feelings and explore the meaning in a low-key way, a way where there was no formal receiving of advice or care. It was thus that she began to talk with the junior nurse, when unable to sleep. To share all this with a religious figure or even a senior nurse would for her have been relating to authority and would have made her feel far more guilty. It may also be that she precisely wanted to talk to someone who was nearly her son's age.

For a short while, the search for meaning in the value conflicts which focused on her relationship with her son became more important to her than her physical condition. She was unable whilst in hospital to resolve the issues. This is hardly surprising given that she was also working through meaning that involved issues of gender, sexuality, culture and self image. When she finally left hospital with the therapy a success she had little sense of well-being but did say to the nurse ' I have started to look at myself differently, and I think I have some hope'.

Well-being

These cases offer a complex view that defies any simple definition of health and disease such as the so-called 'medical model'. This model sees disease as essentially the absence of health. It is an objective and biologically-determined phenomenon which is recognisable and treatable through the application of medical science. This model tends to isolate disease from wider social factors and does not take account of the holistic nature of the person (Pattison 1989). There is, in any case, too much evidence of the social nature of disease for this model to be seen as exclusive (White 2002, 18).

The cases above clearly point to a sense of well-being as central to any view of health, something summed up in the World Health Organisation definition: 'Health is a state of complete physical, mental and social well-being, and not merely the absence of infirmity or disease' (Callahan 1998).

This attractive definition takes seriously the holistic, interpersonal and social nature of health (Senior 1998) and with that the importance of social policy in reducing exclusions from health (White 2002, 166). The problem with the definition is precisely its completeness. Few, if any, persons ever experience health in those terms. Indeed, it is reasonable to ask if this is possible, however successful social policy might be. The definition does not take account of the limitations of what it is to be human and therefore to what degree an acceptance of those limitations might be part of any sense of well-being (Moltmann 1985, 273 ff.). In fact this so-called definition of health is more of an ideal aim motivated by a concern for social justice and equality of healthcare. It is more realistic to argue for a complex view of health and disease which see a place for both holism and effective treatment (Nordenfelt 1987).

Miller and Thoresen refer to health as a latent construct, like personality, character or happiness that is, 'a complex multidimensional construct underlying a broad array of observable phenomena'

(Miller and Thoresen 1999, 4). They suggest that health be viewed under three broad domains: *suffering, function* and *coherence*.

Suffering

This takes a variety of forms, from physical pain, anxiety, affective disorders, and distress. Health under this head is categorised as an absence of suffering, and suffering is a common ground for seeking medical help. However, suffering has a subjective element and awareness, and understanding of suffering can be affected by many different things. Hence, 'many healthy people have lived with chronic pain' (Albom 1997). Miller and Thoresen note the possibility of seeing the suffering 'continuum' as involving not merely absence of suffering but also presence of certain qualities, such as energy or enthusiasm.

Function

Health in this domain involves functional ability rather than impairment. Miller and Thorensen note physiological functions such as 'immune competence, neurodendocrine function, blood pressure, muscle strength, physical flexibility, and blood cell count, judging an individual's functioning relative to norms of previous performance' (Miller and Thoresen 1999, 5). Other functions include cognitive, emotional, sexual, and psychomotor. Clearly the effect of the loss of different functions will be felt differently. Cognitive impairment, for instance, would greatly affect a teacher. Once again it is possible to view a person with great impairment as in other respects healthy. In this sense the impairment becomes an acceptable impairment. What makes impairment, or for that matter suffering, acceptable is a function of meaning. This meaning can be generated in different ways:

- socially, with illnesses which are socially acceptable or not;
- interpersonally, with the illness involving guilt or moral stigma, such as HIV.
- personally, through internal perceptions of identity.

Coherence

Miller and Thoresen offer several definitions of this term, from an 'inner peace', to 'a global sense of predictability of one's internal and external environment', to 'resilience', or 'learned optimism' (Miller andThoresen 1999, 5).This focuses very much on the category of the person and thus upon the spirituality which we have been exploring in the previous chapters. Strong coherence could clearly affect how the person deals with suffering or loss of function. A lack of this inner peace could itself be a cause of suffering.

This view includes several views of health which have often been seen as discrete, including health as a virtue (Illich 1977), health as a function, health as social relationship and health as psychosocial well-being (Blaxter 1990). Hence, it can view health both as the responsibility of the self and of others, including the government.

All three domains interact in any particular context, leading to a much broader view of health and health care. Moltmann develops this to a view of health as 'the strength to be human'. This means the maintenance or development of humanity whatever the experiencing of suffering or impairment of function. He contrasts this view with one which sees health, be it a general state of well-being or absence of illness, as the supreme value in life. This, he argues,

> implies a morbid attitude to health. Being human is equated with being healthy.This leads to the suppression of illness in the individual life, and means that the sick are pushed out of the life of society and kept out of the public eye. To turn the idea of health into an idol in this way is to rob the human being of the true strength of his humanity. Every serious illness which he has to suffer plunges him into a catastrophe, robs him of his confidence in life and destroys his sense of his own value.
>
> But if we understand health as the strength to be human, then we make being human more important than the state of being healthy. Health is not the meaning of human life. On the contrary, a person has to prove the meaning he has found in his own life in conditions of health and sickness. Only what can stand up to both health and sickness, and ultimately to living and dying, can count as a valid definition of what it means to be human.'
> (Moltmann 1985, 273)

In a similar vein, Campbell argues that health can be seen as liberation.The liberation is from different aspects of illness, from impairment to lack of coherence or domination by a meaning structure that oppresses or denies humanity (Campbell 1995).Well-being in both these views is linked to empowerment.

Whilst such a view of well-being cannot be simply equated with the spirituality outlined in the last chapter, the links of spirituality and its potential importance to well-being are clear. Awareness and appreciation of the other and the development of life meaning based on those relationships affirms and develops faith and hope and a sense of purpose and function. This process also develops the capacity to live with limitations as much as to appreciate the positive qualities and gifts of the self and the other and the capacity to be at peace with the self and with others. It is precisely in the development of the qualities, virtues (*virtus* originally meaning strength) and skills of humanity that this strength develops and thus enables liberation. Moreover, it is the reflective and person centred process of spirituality which can enable the person to make sense of their particular experience of illness and health and so remain focused on their humanity and value. This view receives its greatest test when it comes to the issue of suffering in healthcare.

Suffering

> *How long, O Lord? Wilt Thou forget me forever?*
> *How long wilt thou hide thy face from me?*
> *How long must I bear pain in my soul*
> *and sorrow in my heart all the day?*
> (Psalm 13 vv.1–2).

The psalmist tries desperately to make sense of the situation he is in. As it happens he ends up praising God. But such endings always seem a little false, as if the party line of God rescuing those in trouble has been tacked on, or presumed. Other psalms, such as 86, do not have such a happy ending, presumed or not. Their search for meaning cannot get beyond the basic experience of suffering. Their expression remains one of lament.

For the different psalmists this suffering was either negative, and was not understandable, or was something which led ultimately to the glory of God – God who would ultimately overcome and might even pay back those who put the psalmist in that spot. These are a good example of humanity's attempts to make sense of suffering, something at the very centre of spirituality, and of direct relevance to any realistic view of health.

In an article in the *Hastings Report,* van Hooft traces attempts from the ancient world to the twentieth century to find meaning in suffering (van Hooft 1998). The most primitive approach was to connect suffering with justice. Suffering was punishment for something done by the person or one of their forebears. This approach to suffering assumes that it cannot and should not happen, it is not just a part of life, and therefore when it does appear there must be a good reason for it. The reason for the suffering may be evident. If it was not, then for such thinkers it was reasonable to assume that the wider picture, which they couldn't see, but the divine could, would contain the answer. Arguments such as these formed the basis of theodicies, attempts to reconcile a good God with the reality of evil and suffering.

This was expanded in later philosophy to the idea that suffering was part of an overall plan which was ultimately for the good of all. In this light everything, even suffering, was for the best in the 'best of all possible worlds' (Lovejoy 1964). With this view suffering moves into a more functional approach. It did not just happen because of certain things, it happened in order that some good might come. Again such good might be evident, or it might be part of an overall plan not seen.

Such a functional view of suffering, however, can also be connected to a negative view of the world. van Hooft notes the example of Plato's Socrates, who, on the eve of his death, welcomes the end because this will take him away from a world of change and suffering into a changeless world where all will be perceived clearly through the Forms of Beauty, Truth and Goodness. Suffering then is ultimately not part of the real world, and can be borne with the aim of moving beyond this world to the more real world. A similar dynamic can be seen in the spirituality of Hinduism and Buddhism, where suffering is seen as inevitably part of life. It can, however, be transcended in and through religious faith.

van Hooft notes that Christian spirituality has tended to dominate the issue of suffering in the West. This has been strongly connected to the example of Jesus, who suffered on the cross to rebuild humanity's relationship with God. The relationship was one of alienation caused by sin, and Christ's sacrifice enabled the relationship to be rebuilt. Suffering then, primarily of Christ, but also of the Christian, is directly connected to salvation, and is interpreted in terms of sacrifice. This does not make suffering *per se* meaningful or good. The experience of suffering is negative and is very real. However, in the light of the larger picture and in particular how the action contributes to a larger positive picture, the pain of suffering can be transformed.

Hauerwas, develops this view building upon the work of Ivan Illich and focusing on the experience of the disabled (Illich 1977, Hauerwas 1986). He attempts to address the assumption that suffering is always bad and that a major aim of modern medicine is to eliminate it. The core of his argument is that the capacity to suffer is a critical part of what it is to be human. He argues that, 'to see the value of suffering we only have to ask what we would think of anyone who did not have the capacity to suffer. Such a person could not bear grief or misfortune and thus would in effect give up the capacity to be human. For it is the capacity to feel grief and to identify with the misfortunes of others which is the basis of our ability to recognise our fellow humanity' (Hauerwas 1986, 25).

Here Hauerwas is connecting the experience of suffering to a basic understanding of what it is to be human and to the development, in effect, of empathy. This involves two parts. Firstly, suffering is part of the human condition. Secondly, suffering is only understood through the development of empathy. If we do not attend to suffering than we can begin to lose this capacity to be aware of humans, including ourselves, and thus the capacity to *be* human. This takes Hauwerwas a stage further, to the suggestion that suffering cannot be understood in terms of general ideas being applied to the situation, nor simply through conceptual analysis. It can only be understood through reflection on particular stories and experiences. It is through such reflection that the positive meaning of suffering may emerge. Hauerwas wants to argue that it is important to discover some positive meaning. Without that, such suffering would be hard to cope with. On the other hand, this must not be at the expense of the reality of suffering.

It is precisely this reality which the psalms of lamentation focus on. They affirm that disorientation is at the heart of our life experience. The world, and in particular the individual's world, is not in good order. The writers also affirm that it is alright to admit this, before the community and before their god, without loss of face or faith. Hence, Brueggemann can write that this is an act of faith,

> It is an act of bold faith on the one hand, because it insists that the world must be experienced as it really is. On the other hand, it is bold because it insists that all such experiences of disorder are a proper subject for discourse with God. (Brueggemann 1984, 52)

The psalms of lament in this context are not simply an expression of despair; they actually form the experience. They enable the person to focus on their emotions and connect the experience to their significant relationships and significant life meaning. This can only be done in this way. Meaning cannot be applied *to* the situation or imposed upon it. It means a dialogue between the affective, cognitive and physical, enabling a testing of and focusing on the feelings and an affirmation and validation of them.

For patient C her moments of anger and frustration had to be shared. In doing so she accepted that this was part of her, and she was able to own those feelings, and validate them, in the sense of not denying them, or trying to suppress them. She was able to feel that *and* remain faithful to her sense of purpose and the people who gave meaning to her life. Such meaning can only be worked through in the light of faithful relationships. In patient C's case several different groups remained faithful to her, through all the physical, emotional and cognitive difficulties.

Such expressions of spirituality thus, as Brueggemann notes,

> lead us away from the comfortable religious claims of 'modernity' in which everything is managed or controlled. In our modern experience, but probably also in any affluent culture, it is believed that enough power and knowledge can tame the terror and eliminate the darkness. But our honest experience, both personal and public, attests to the resilience of the darkness, in spite of us. The remarkable thing about Israel is that it did not banish or deny the darkness from its religious enterprise. It embraces the darkness as the very stuff of new life. Indeed, Israel seems to know that the new life comes from nowhere else. (Brueggemann 1984, 53)

Buddhism is similar to this Jewish spirituality here, at least in the sense that it is less concerned with trying to justify suffering and evil in general and more with practical responses to the experience. Response is focused on the spiritual techniques that will enable detachment from suffering and a movement into enlightenment. Hence, there is the development of a different kind of transcendence (Bemporad 1987, 99).

The Islamic perspective is more directly akin to the Jewish perspective. It has several different views about the reason for suffering in the world, not least punishment for sin and as a test or trial of the faithful. Again there is more stress on response, both active and passive. The active response is to endure one's own suffering and attempt to alleviate others. The passive response is to accept suffering, in the belief that God will not test one beyond one's capacity (Bemporad 1987, 104).

In all this, suffering is both individual, uniquely experienced by the person, but takes place within a wider social context, something which affects the meaning in many different ways. This assumes that meaning will be found in suffering. Hauerwas argues that this goes squarely against the assumption of much healthcare practice, which tends to undermine the possibility of such meaning in suffering, 'In other words medicine tends to break the link between our suffering and our projects by suggesting that suffering is pointless' (Hauerwas 1986, 33, see also Taylor and Watson 1989 and Cassell 1991).

Viewed from the perspective of the Holocaust, Levinas can see no theological narrative providing justification for suffering on that scale (Levinas 1988). He suggests that it is actually immoral to see the suffering of the other as having a purpose. To look at another's suffering and see it as fulfilling a purpose is to see him as a means not an end, and therefore not to respect him. This is another form of denying the reality of suffering, and the fact that it can have no obvious meaning. Levinas then responds in way not dissimilar to Hauerwas, arguing that the only way in which the person can respond to the suffering of an other is through compassion, through being with them, explanation does not help.

Interestingly, though, Levinas does not remain at the level of pastoral care but looks to a broader understanding of suffering based upon this. Suffering, he suggests, actually gives us the possibility of overcoming the alienation and atomism experienced in western society. The suffering of another enables us to be open to the real presence of the other, and leads to the development of responsibility for the other. The negativity and meaninglessness of the suffering in effect provides the real basis for contact with the other. Suffering grounds the ethical response, is the foundation of being responsible for the other. There are problems with such a view, not least the danger that suffering once more can be seen as functional, this time enabling us to commune with the other. However, Levinas's point is that suffering is an inevitable and profound part of our lives, that it cannot be justified in any cognitive way and that compassion and empathy are the only meaningful response.

Such a view severs the old link of theodicies between suffering and justification. As van Hooft writes,

> The challenge of postmodern authenticity is to sever the link between suffering and justice. It is to accept the blindness of fate and the inevitability of bad luck. It is to refuse the false consolations of theodicies or metaphysical theories which make suffering positive. (van Hooft 1998, 19)

This leads us to an even more important point that the competing views of the postmodern world have underlined. The conceptual understanding of theodicies can never of themselves begin to provide genuinely spiritual meaning for those who are experiencing suffering. Not only are they partial, in the sense that they are one of many different views, they are also generalised and purely cognitive. In order to discover meaning in suffering, it has to be particular and has to engage the affective and somatic understanding as well as cognitive.

Patient C worked out her meaning in relation to her situation and the different relationships in each of her networks. This gave her the support systems that she could rely on and also purpose in terms of her contribution. Such meaning was as much affective as cognitive – she *felt* valued and valuable through her relationships. In turn, this allowed her to accept herself not only as an attractive young woman, but also someone who was dependent and 'different'. Questions of identity, sexuality, purpose, trust, hope, acceptance, different images of the good life were all interacting, at the somatic, affective and cognitive levels.

The spirituality of suffering then is not essentially about finding meaning in suffering but rather finding meaning in the self in the context of the particular experience of suffering. That meaning has to be worked out in the light of the particular circumstances and relationships. Indeed, the relationships bring meaning to the circumstances. In this light, it is the nurturing of humanity and the possibilities of humanity even in the midst of pain which give any meaning to suffering.

Similarly, Campbell views suffering as an ordeal in which the aim is not to deny the pain but rather to transcend the effects of the suffering through holding on to and developing the world of spiritual meaning – partly through repeated articulation of narrative, and partly through rehearsal of rituals based in the patient's community of meaning. Campbell notes the example of Terry Waite who, in the midst of his suffering as hostage, with all the isolation and deprivation, repeated the words of the Anglican Eucharist which he knew by heart, thus holding on to his life meaning, church community, friends, spiritual ritual, and God, and thus his humanity, his human identity (Campbell 1995, 36).

Even with the development of such spiritual meaning the experience of suffering emerges as something very ambiguous (Bakan 1968). At one level suffering may destroy meaning, not least through the disempowering of the patient (Weil 1977). The loss of a particular function, for instance, can destroy meaning or meanings in a life. Some suffering may be such that all awareness is dulled. Nonetheless, where there is any level of awareness there is the possibility of some awareness of the other and therefore of a level of meaning and value which reinforces the person. At the same time, the experience of suffering can actually lead to a development of meaning and to an increased awareness of the self and of the other. Woodward quotes one patient who was incapacitated for several months:

> The thing that strikes me about my disability is that it has produced in me an amazing greater level of awareness. It has given me a clarity about the relationships that I have in all their ambiguity and paradox. But above all, at last, after 45 years there are endless things that I have taken for granted that I can now see in such a different light. The colour in the sky, some of the pictures around the house, the wood in the trees in the garden, the quality of a good cup of tea and the small act of care showed through holding my hand or mopping my brow. (Woodward 1995, 10)

Illness then can take us to the edge of experience and perception, and beyond. It can be both an experience of the frightening 'other' but also an experience of discovery about our humanity. How we deal with suffering in this light is, in Campbell's words, 'a product of our broader conception of how human life ought to be' (Campbell 1995, 29). Such a conception involves cognitive, affective and somatic awareness of the self and the other, including the illness and the suffering itself. At the core of any understanding of health and suffering is how 'the self retains its dignity and worth' in the face of pain, disability, and death, three things that we all experience at some point in our lives (Campbell 1995, 42).

Like so many 'big' concepts, dignity has been given some very different shades of meaning. It broadly refers to honour and worth, the sense of being held in esteem. We would argue that the maintenance of dignity is a function of a relationship that develops mutuality and enables the person to develop awareness of her relational network and her purpose in it. Dignity in other words is not something that is simply given, but rather emerges from a relationship, and is worked out in each situation. At the heart of such dignity is the empathy that enables both the patient and the carer to see that illness does not make one into a stranger or an alien, totally different from the other, something that many people feel or fear. Rather that empathy enables them to see the humanity of the person in the midst of suffering.

Spiritual care that enables this development of meaning in one sense does not need justification. It is self evident that this should be fundamental to the concept of care. However, we must also look at any empirical evidence that there might be which connects spirituality to health, not least how it might affect the outcome of care.

Spirituality and therapy

Attempts to make the connection between spirituality and therapy fall into three categories:

* holistic perspectives on therapy;
* the effect of spirituality and spiritual beliefs on therapeutic outcomes;
* the effects of particular spiritual interventions or techniques on therapy.

Holism

There is an increasing amount of work on the holistic view of the person and how this affects health. Benner, for instance, notes the development of *psychoneuroimmunology* – the study of the effects of stress on the functioning of the immune system. Research in this has found that depression, anxiety and repressed emotions play a part in suppressing the immune system (Benner 1998). Strong correlation has been shown between particular diseases and psychosocial factors (1998, 60), including:

* rheumatoid arthritis (associated with suppressed emotions and perfectionism);
* cardiovascular disease (associated with repressed hostility);
* cancer (associated with non assertiveness and the inability to express emotions, hopelessness, and depression).

The effect of traumatic experience has been shown to have an effect on the immune system (Siegel 1984, 148). Several studies, for instance, have noted the suppression of the immune system after bereavement – an effect seen at two months after the experience but not at two weeks (Benner 1998, 60).

Other studies point to the effect of emotional states, lifestyles and life views on the development of disease as well as the maintenance of health (Thomas 1982). It is difficult to pinpoint precise disease vulnerabilities. However, the research suggests that certain characteristics or experiences make individuals 'immunosuppression' prone. These include: conformity, sensitivity to criticism, restricted emotional expression, denial of dependence, major stress (Benner 1998, 60).

There is sufficient evidence of the holistic nature of the person to confirm that attitudes and states of mind do affect therapeutic outcomes. 'Life-coherence' in turn contributes to the development of such healthy attitudes. This reflects a distinction between holism *per se* and spirituality. Spirituality is holistic and enables holism, but is not holism as such.

It is not possible to make grand generalisations about this, but it is reasonable to conclude that concern for the life view of the person and how this connects to her character can be important. Hence spirituality cannot be ignored, and needs to be examined in each patient.

Spiritual beliefs

Many attempts have been made to measure the importance of spiritual and religious beliefs in therapy. Results are surprisingly consistent and show:

- Religious groups with rigid belief systems and practice were linked to greater health and lower mortality then less religious groups or non believers (Idler and Kasl 1992; Kark *et al.* 1996; Strawbridge *et al.* 1997, Pargament and Brant 1998).
- The greater the religious intensity (measured by church attendance, and attitudes) the better the health, and lower the rate of illness. These findings were very pronounced in hypertension and colorectal cancer (Comstock and Partridge 1972, Medalie *et al.* 1972, Larson *et al.* 1989, Levin and Vanderpool 1989).

Similar findings were discovered in wider views of spirituality, including scoring on spiritual, existential as well as religious well-being (Frankel and Hewitt 1994, Shuler *et al.* 1994). Religious practices were also associated with increased tolerance of pain and a higher quality of life (Landis 1996). Religious involvement may also influence the course and eventual outcome of illness. Research suggests an association of religion with better recovery from illness including survival after heart transplants (Harris *et al.* 1995), reduced mortality after other cardiac surgery (Oxman *et al.* 1995), reduced risk of repeat heart attacks (Thoresen 1990), reduced mortality in breast cancer patients (Spiegel *et al.* 1989) and improvement in depression (Propst 1988).

In reviewing research on mental health Swinton (2001) notes that underlying the positive correlation between spirituality and well-being are three key factors:

* Social support. Being part of a community is likely to give the person more support at times of illness, not least through a sense of belonging and self esteem (Brown, Prudo, Harris 1981, Loewenthal 1995).
* Coping mechanisms, enabling both emotion-focused and problem-focused coping (Shams and Jackson, 1993).
* Cognitive realignment, facilitated by a framework within which life can be explained and understood (Sullivan 1993).

The findings of King, Speck and Thomas, however, differed from such positive results, concluding that patients who expressed strong spiritual belief were *less* likely to do well (Speck 1998, 29). The basis of this work was a belief questionnaire, with a nine-month follow up. Items in this, measured on a five-point scale from strongly disagree to strongly agree, included:

* I need to understand why things happen to me.
* My belief helps me during illness.
* Illness is a result of lack of spiritual belief.
* My belief is weaker than it used to be.

Speck suggests several possible reasons for these findings, from strong belief leading to a reduced fear of death and thus less likelihood of fighting the illness, to patients with a poor prognosis developing stronger belief systems. However, more importantly the measurement of strength of belief is in itself problematic. A *strong* belief may well be a limited or brittle belief, that is one that has not been tested empirically, or an essentially cognitive belief whose congruence with affective awareness has not been tested. Such a professedly strong belief may well be more liable to lead to spiritual meaninglessness faced by the illness experience. Research of this nature might more usefully use the stages of the faith model that distinguishes between different kinds of faith and transition experiences (see Chapter 6).

Despite difficulty with the third area of evidence there is sufficient basis to indicate the potential importance of spirituality to health outcomes, and this leads us to the question of how spirituality can be integrated into healthcare practice.

Spiritual interventions

A great deal of research has gone into spiritual interventions and how they affect therapeutic outcomes, including meditation, and different forms of prayer.

Meditation

Meditation enables the development of 'mindfulness'. This is defined as the 'capacity for the human mind to transcend its preoccupation with negative experiences – with fears, anxiety, anger and obsessions – and to become more comfortable with the experiences of compassion, acceptance and forgiveness' (Marlatt and Kristeller 1999, 68).

It involves focusing on and acceptance of the present experience, including negative feelings. Teasdale notes that this aims not to change the content of thoughts but rather to enable the patient to alter her attitude to or relationship with that thought (Teasdale *et al.* 1995).

There are two main processes. Firstly, it leads to an experience and acceptance of 'impermanence', the way in which perceived reality is constantly changing. Secondly, it facilitates the development of an observing self, with the capacity to monitor the self.

Glasser suggests it can be seen as a positive addiction that is intrinsically rewarding (Glasser 1976). Such an addiction:

- is non competitive,
- can be pursued alone,
- has positive value,
- can be done without self criticism,
- is a simple process.

Other research has shown a wide constellation of physical and emotional effects, including:

- reduced oxygen consumption and carbon dioxide and lactate production;
- reduced adrenocorticotropic hormone (ACTH) excretion, producing the opposite effect of stress;
- reduced heart rate and blood pressure;
- reduced activity in the sympathetic branch of the nervous system;

- changes in electroencephalographic brain wave activity and function, consistent with the slowing down of brain and body activities (Benson 1996).

The use of meditation can range widely, including work with anxiety and depression; some severe psychiatric disturbances, such as obsessive compulsive disorder, and heart conditions (Marlatt and Kristeller 1999, 76). It is important to note that this intervention is only part of any therapeutic response (p. 77).

Prayer

Recent years have seen an increase in research on prayer and its effects. At one level this has been parallel to the meditation research, with the effect on the person praying being tested. Once again effects have been positive (Benson 1996). This is well summed up in a *British Medical Journal* article on the effects of rosary prayer and yoga mantras on autonomic cardiovascular rhythms (Bernardi *et al.* 2001). They discovered that both forms of prayer involved, on average, six breaths per minute and that this led to 'striking, powerful and synchronous increases in existing cardiovascular rhythms' (Bernardi *et al.* 2001, 1) Baroreflex activity also increased significantly.

More controversial have been attempts to assess the effects of intercessionary prayer on therapeutic outcomes (Byrd 1988, McCullough and Larson 1999, Astin *et al.* 2000). Whilst results have been generally positive it is not clear how the effect of such prayer can be empirically tested.

Conclusion

In this chapter we have drawn together the relationship between spirituality and health. Spirituality is an important part of any view of well-being. Well-being in this sense is a complex idea that takes into account awareness of and response to others and the underlying meaning. Spirituality is an essential part of dealing creatively and effectively with suffering, not least because it focuses on the development of consciousness and identity which transcends the experience of suffering itself. This moves beyond the traditional religious approach to suffering, to seek meaning in the experience of illness based upon an awareness of the self and others. Such an approach is by definition person centred and cannot be imposed.

This chapter also concludes that suffering is a central part of human experience and thus inevitably part of illness. Such suffering, Hauerwas and Levinas suggest, is part of what it means to be human and can begin to enable the person to develop empathy, and thus deepen spirituality. Any view of healthcare then must take this to account. Finally, spirituality can be seen to play a significant part in therapeutic outcomes.

It does not follow from this that spirituality must play a part in all therapeutic outcomes, and whatever part it plays will depend upon the patient and upon circumstances. It does follow that any healthcare should find ways of being open to and relating to the spirituality of the patient. The question then is raised as to how this spirituality can practically become part of modern therapeutic care. The next chapter will critically examine some ways of assessing spirituality in the therapeutic process. This will be followed by a more detailed examination of person-centred spirituality in healthcare.

Questions and exercises

1. Critically assess the different views of health and illness, and of suffering in this chapter.
2. Note down how you make sense of the suffering that you see in practice.
3. Focus on one situation where the suffering of a patient caused you concern. How did you feel about this and what could you do about it?

References

Albom, M. (1997) *Tuesdays with Morrie* (New York: Doubleday).
Astin, J.A., Harkness, E. and Ernst, E. (2000) 'The efficacy of "distance healing": a systematic review of randomised trials' *Ann Intern Medicine*, **132**, 903–10.
Bakan, D. (1968) *Disease, Pain and Sacrifice: Towards a Psychology of Suffering* (Chicago: University of Chicago Press).
Bemporad, J. (1987) 'Suffering', in M. Eliade (ed.) *Encyclopaedia of Religion* vol. 8 (London: Macmillan – now Palgave Macmillan), 99–104.
Benner, D. (1998) *Care of Souls* (Grand Rapids: Baker Books).
Benson, H. (1996) *Timeless Healing* (New York: Fireside).
Bernardi, L., Sleight, P., Bandinelli, G., Cencetti, S., Fattorini, L., Wdowczyc-Szulc, J. and Lagi, A. (2001) 'Effect of rosary prayer and yoga mantras on autonomic cardiovascular rhythms: comparative study', in *British Medical Journal*, **323**, 922–9, 1446–9, December).

Blaxter, M. (1990) *Health and Lifestyles* (London: Routledge).

Brueggemann, W. (1984) *The Message of the Psalms* (Minneapolis: Augsburg).

Brown, G., Prudo, R. and Harris, A. (1981) 'Psychiatric Disorder in a Rural and an Urban Population', *Psychological Medicine*, **11**, 581–99.

Byrd, R.C. (1988) 'Positive therapeutic effects of intercessory prayer in a coronary care unit population' *Southern Medical Journal*, **81**, 826–9.

Callahan, D. (1998) 'The WHO Definition of "Health"', in S. Lammers and A. Verhey (eds) *On Moral Medicine* 2nd edn. (Grand Rapids: Eerdmans), 253–61.

Campbell, A. (1995) *Health As Liberation* (Cleveland: The Pilgrim Press).

Cassell, E. (1991) *The Nature of Suffering and the Goals of Medicine* (New York: Oxford University Press).

Comstock, G. W. and Partridge, K.B. (1972) 'Church attendance and health', *Journal of Chronic Diseases*, **25**, 665–72.

Frankels, B.G. and Hewitt, W.E. (1994) 'Religion and well being amongst Canadian university students', *Journal for the Scientific Study of Religions*, **33**, 62–73.

Glasser, W. (1976) *Positive Addictions* (New York: Harper and Row).

Harris, R.C., Dew, M.A. and Lee, A. (1995) 'The association of social relationships and activities with mortality', *American Journal of Epidemiology*, **116**, 123–40.

Hauerwas, S. (1986) *Suffering Presence* (Notre Dame: University of Notre Dame Press).

Idler, E.L. and Kasl, S.V. (1992) 'Religion, disability, depression and the timing of death', *American Journal of Sociology*, **116**, 1052–79.

Illich, I. (1977) Medical Nemesis (New York: Penguin).

Kark, J.D., Shemi, G. and Friedlander, Y. (1996) 'Does religious observance promote health? *American Journal of Public Health*, **86**, 341–6.

Landis, B.J. (1996) 'Uncertainty, spiritual well-being, and psychosocial adjustment to chronic illnesses', *Issues in Mental Health Nursing*, **17**, 217–231.

Larson, D.B, Koenig, H.G., Kaplan, B.H. and Levin, J.S. (1989) 'The impact of religion on men's blood pressure', Journal of Religion and Health, **28**, 165–278.

Levin, J.S. and Vanderpool, H.Y. (1989) 'Is religion therapeutically significant for hypertension?' *Social Science and Medicine*, **29**, 69–78.

Levinas, E. (1988) 'Useless Suffering' in R. Bernasconi and D. Wood (eds.) *The Provocation of Levinas: Rethinking the Other* (London: Routledge).

Loewenthal, K. (1995) *Mental Health and Religion* (London: Chapman and Hall).

Lovejoy, A. (1964) *The Great Chain of Being* (Cambridge Mass.: Harvard University Press) 2nd edn.

McCullough, M. and Larson, D. (1999) 'Prayer' in W. Miller (ed.) *Integrating Spirituality into Treatment* (Washington: American Psychological Association), 85–110.

Marlatt, B. and Kristeller, J. (1999) 'Mindfulness and Meditation', in W. Miller (ed.) *Integrating Spirituality into Treatment* (Washington: American Psychological Association), 67–84.

Medalie, J.H., Kahn, H.A., Neufeld, H.N., Riss, E. and Goldbourt, U. (1973) 'Five year myocardial infarction incidence II', *Journal of Chronic Disease*, **26**, 329–49.

Miller, W. (1999) (ed.) *Integrating Spirituality into Treatment* (Washington: American Psychological Association).

Miller, W. and Thoresen, C.E. (1999) 'Spirituality and Health' in *Integrating Spirituality into Treatment* (Washington: American Psychological Association), 3–18.

Moltmann, J. (1985) *God in Creation* (London: SCM).

Mount, B. (1993) 'Whole person care: beyond psychosocial and physical needs', in *American Journal of Hospice and Palliative Care*, January/February, 28–39.

Nordenfelt, L. (1987) *On the Nature of Health; An Action-Theoretic Approach* (Boston: D. Reidel).

Oxman, T.E., Freeman, D.H. and Manheimer, E.D. (1995) Lack of social participation or religious strength and comfort as risk factors for death after cardiac surgery in the elderly', *Psychosomatic Medicine*, **57**, 5–15.

Pargament, K.I. and Brant, C.R. (1998) 'Religion and coping', in H.G. Koenig (ed.) *Handbook of Religion and Mental Health* (San Diego: Academic Press), 112–28.

Pattison, S. (1989) *Alive and Kicking* (London: SCM).

Propst, L.R. (1988) *Psychotherapy within the Religious Framework: Spirituality in the Emotional Healing Process* (New York: Human Sciences Press).

Senior, M. (1998) *Health and Illness* (London: Macmillan – now Palgrave Macmillan).

Shams, M. and Jackson, P.R. (1993) 'Religiosity as a predictor and moderator of the psychological impact of unemployment,' *British Journal of Medical Psychology*, **66**, 342.

Shuler, P.A., Gelberg, L. and Brown, M. (1994)'The effects of spiritual/religious practices on psychological well-being among inner city homeless women', *Nurse Practitioner Forum*, **5**, 106–13.

Siegel, A. (1986) *Love, Medicine and Miracles* (New York: Harper).

Speck, P. (1998) 'The Meaning of Spirituality in Illness', in M. Cobb and V. Renshaw (eds) *The Spiritual Challenge of Health Care* (London: Churchill Livingstone), 21–34.

Spiegel, D., Bloom, J.R. and Kraemer, H.C. (1989) 'Effects of psychosocial treatment on survival of patients with metastatic breast cancer', *Lancet*, **142**, 888–91.

Strawbridge, W.J., Cohen, R.D., Shema, S.J. and Kaplan, G.A. (1997) 'Frequent attendance at religious services and mortality over 28 years', *American Journal of Public Health*, **87**, 957–61.

Sullivan, J. P. (1993) ' "It helps me to be whole person": the role of spirituality amongst the mentally challenged'. *Psychosocial Rehabilitation Journal*, **16**, 3, 125–34.

Swinton, J. (2001) *Spirituality and Mental Health* (London: Jessica Kingsley).

Taylor, R.L. and Watson, J. (1989) *They Shall not Hurt: Human Suffering and Human Caring* (Boulder: Colorado Associated University Press).

Teasdale, J., Seigal, Z. and Williams, J. (1995) 'How does cognitive therapy prevent depressive relapse and why should attentional control (mindfulness) training help? *Behaviour Research and Therapy*, **33**, 25–39.

Thomas, C.B. (1982) 'Cancer in families of former medical students followed in mid-life,' *Johns Hopkins Medicine*, **151**, 193–202.

Thoresen, C.E. (1990) *Long-term 8-year Follow up of Recurrent Coronary Prevention* (Uppsala: International Society of Behavioural Medicine).

van Hooft, S. (1998) 'The meaning of suffering', *Hastings Center Report*, September–October, 13–19.

Weil, S (1977) 'The Love of God and Affliction' in G.A. Panichas (ed.) *The Simone Weil Reader* (New York: David McKay Company) 444.

White, K. (2002) *An Introduction to the Sociology of Health and Illness* (London: Sage).

Woodward, J. (1995) *Encountering Illness* (London: SCM).

4

Spirituality and Assessment

In this chapter, we focus on the practice of healthcare, and in particular the different approaches to spiritual assessment.

Evidence of attention to spirituality in healthcare practice over the last two decades of the twenty-first century is ambiguous and patchy. Oldnall notes that there has been limited coverage of spirituality within theories which cover nursing as a whole (Oldnall 1996). Of twenty-six theories of nursing reviewed, twelve did not acknowledge the impact of spirituality on health care. The other fourteen did make reference to spirituality, but only briefly and without detailed explanation of many of the terms used. These findings would seem to suggest difficulty for the profession in integrating attention to spirituality with the everyday delivery of healthcare. The major exception is Jean Watson, who integrates concern for spirituality at all points of healthcare (Watson 1979).

Alongside this has been an increasing number of books and articles attempting to find a way to address the spiritual perspective of health care. These focus very clearly on the question of assessment of the spirituality of the patient. Gorsuch and Miller suggest four reasons for the caring professions to assess spirituality (Gorsuch and Miller 1999):

- *Prognosis.* As noted above, spirituality can be one variable in predicting outcome and how the patient will handle the illness experience, either negatively in terms of spirituality contributing to the illness or positively in terms of spirituality leading to an effective long-term change;
- *Context.* Regardless of the relationship of spirituality to the problem, spirituality is an important part of a patient's life view and personal development. At one level that spirituality may be affected by an illness experience, and thus the patient should have the opportunity to work through the challenge to his belief systems. Attending to the spirituality of the patient is also important in

ensuring good communication. This in itself may require the carer to test out the actual meanings of a patient's spirituality. For instance, Gorsuch and Miller note the phrase 'waiting for God's call'. This could refer to many things, from everyday decision-making to waiting for death.

- *Outcome.* Given that spiritual functioning is not static there should be a continual monitoring of the spiritual reflection and the way in which this enables coping. Spiritual variables can be important mediators of change and of coping. (Gorsuch 1994, Pargament and Brant, 1998)
- *Intervention.* The spirituality of the patient may well give indications about intervention. At one level this may be in response to some aspects of spiritual distress or may involve a recognition and use of that in therapy. Propst, for instance, demonstrates how using patients' spirituality in therapy can enhance treatment of depression (Propst 1988).

Gorsuch and Miller note that there is already in psychology a large literature on psychometric instruments which assess religious and spiritual variables and that any comprehensive assessment of spirituality would require special expertise (Gorsuch and Miller 1999). Assessment in all this is distinct from measurement – though may include this. The broad aim of assessment is to gain an understanding of the patient's spirituality. Measurement, on the other hand, seeks to determine the strength of spirituality. Hence, it will tend to use scales. However, such scales can only rate some aspect of spirituality, such as strength of belief, feelings, particular quality of life issues as they currently arise. They cannot measure spirituality as a whole. In the light of all, this it is clear that assessment for nurses should not be complex or unwieldy, and that assessment is more important than detailed measurement.

Attempts at developing assessment have varied enormously, and we will examine them under three headings: spiritual practice and belief; spiritual distress; and spiritual well-being. The last two of these categories were set out by NANDA (North American Nursing Diagnosis Association).

Spiritual practice and belief

Several attempts at assessment of spiritual practice and belief stress the religious dimension of spirituality. The NHS Northern and Yorkshire

Chaplains and Pastoral Care Committee, for instance, sets out the importance of spiritual care, charting good practice, and seeking to meet the spiritual needs of the patients (NHS 1995). This rather slim document, produced by the Institute of Nursing at the University of Leeds, was well received across the UK. At the time, it was one of very few documents to discuss spirituality in relation to patient assessment and also in terms of the role of the chaplain, as a spiritual organiser and care giver. It was suggested that the main method of addressing needs is an interview which elicits information on the patient's requirements concerning:

- worship;
- issues which may lead to conflict between beliefs, values and treatment;
- rituals or customs which may need to be practised before death;
- everyday customs, including hygiene or diet requirements.

The gathering of such information is very useful, not least because the patient has a right to have such needs attended to. A slightly different approach is O'Brien's Spiritual Assessment Scale (SAS) (1998, 68). This has a very strong religious component, and is divided into three sections:

- personal faith,
- religious practice,
- spiritual contentment.

Both approaches either attempt to elicit a *formed* and *formal* spirituality, which includes consciously held belief, ritual and value, or measure spiritual strength in relation to such spirituality. However, firstly, for the most part this is exactly what postmodern society does not have. The evidence of ongoing research into the spirituality of the workplace in Leeds, for instance, shows that the majority of respondents saw the interviews as a unique occasion to *begin* reflecting on spiritual meaning and how it informed their context (Randolph-Horn and Paslawska 2002). Even those with a long experience of religious spirituality found this to be a significant opportunity which tested their world view.

Secondly, the assessment tends to be God centred. The SAS asks the patient to respond on a five-point scale from strongly agree to strongly disagree. The first statement is; 'There is a Supreme Being, or

God, who created mankind and who cares for all creatures.' Such a statement immediately sets tight parameters to do with spiritual meaning, reinforced by 17 out of the following 20 questions being focused on God. Hence, the scale for the most part finds its meaning in relation to a particular view of God, whether one agrees or disagrees with that. The view in question posits a creator God, with an implied Judeo-Christian nature, who can have direct personal relations with humans and the world, and might affect a sense of well-being.

In this context the measurement is only of the strength of a particular view of spirituality, and as such is of little use for any but those with a religious background. It is not clear then how significant this can be, not least for the patient.

A third danger of this approach is that it can radically affect the dynamic of any assessment. Those without a formed or formal spirituality may feel marginalised and respond in one of two ways:

• Attempt an answer which fulfils what they believe is expected, 'Yes, I do believe in God. I don't go to church or anything but I do have a great sense of a Being who looks after me.'
• See the assessment as an intrusion and resent it. The patient then can very easily 'privatise' spirituality and dismiss any attempt to even explore life meaning.

In neither case is the patient actually reflecting on meaning in their lives. Indeed, the dynamic moves into an avoidance of such reflection. If a method of assessment exists to encourage reflection then it must focus on the particular narrative of the patient and how meaning relates to his experience of illness, something which Stoll stresses. He is conscious of the need to be open to very different expressions of spirituality and the right of the patient not to discuss such life meaning. In his assessment, he attempts to collect data on the sources of the patient's hope and strength and on the relationship between beliefs and the experience of illness. However, his other two areas involve the person's concept of God or deity and the personal significance of religious practices and rituals (Stoll 1979).

None of this is to say that religion should not be part of any assessment, rather that the reflection on experience and life meaning should be prior to the specific questions about religion. Clearly, any religious perspectives will emerge from this.

Religion can also be dealt with as a matter of rights. In which case this is simply a matter of ascertaining what the faith of the person might be, and ensuring that an appropriate support is found. Importantly, even when religion is focused in any assessment, concentration on the strength of belief or attitude is not sufficient. As noted above, a strong attitude could be a brittle one. In which case the quality of the belief and how this relates to reality is the more important thing to assess. This will be examined over the following chapters.

Spiritual distress

Spiritual distress is a topic in which nurses appear to have become more interested in recent years. Burnard (1987, 377) states that: 'Spiritual distress is the result of total inability to invest life with meaning. It can be demotivating, painful and cause anguish to the sufferer'. Burnard points to a sense of disturbance and loss. Counter to the notion of spiritual distress is that of spiritual well-being. Hungelmann et al. (1996, 52) describe spiritual well-being as a state of acceptance of self and others and of having a positive disposition towards life, with a sense of harmonious connectedness between self, others, nature and ultimate other; an interconnectedness which exists throughout and beyond time and space, achieved through a dynamic, integrative growth process leading to the realisation of the ultimate purpose and meaning of life.

Positive as Hungelmann et al. may sound, it is unlikely that anyone would find themselves in such a state of spiritual well-being over large periods of time. Therefore, spiritual distress can seen as part and parcel of the ups and downs of life in general. If this is so, when attempting to measure spiritual distress, should we not take into account the individuals' usual pattern of behaviours, and measure it against these, rather than what we may immediately and fleetingly see in front of us?

Hay, in the context of hospice care, argues that spiritual needs can be defined and proposes four categories of 'spiritual diagnosis' (Hay 1989):

1. *Spiritual suffering.* Defining characteristics of this include pain, insomnia, non-compliance with the care plan, diminished or extinct involvement with support systems, anxiety, fear, mistrust, hopelessness, and incapacity to forgive or accept forgiveness. Assessment would include focus on: conscious awareness of factors in personal development; breakdown in the spiritual support

system and its causes; and relationship between the interpersonal support system and belief system. Aims of intervention include, increased awareness of personal development, reduction of symptoms such as guilt and anxiety, and greater consistency between belief system and interpersonal behaviour. The means of intervention would include: attention to support systems; enabling reflection on the 'antecedent factors' of development; and encouraging reflection on interpersonal congruence.

2. *Inner resource deficiency.* This is seen as diminished spiritual capacity and its defining characteristics include, low level of self awareness, low aspirations in personal/community goals, and a diminished will to persevere. Outcomes of intervention include the ability to develop awareness of and enable participation in the community.

3. *Belief system problems.* This involves a lack of awareness of any personal meaning system. It is noted in: expressions of the meaninglessness of life; questioning of the adequacy of belief system; and isolation and alienation from community belief systems. Assessment includes the nature of the belief system and the perspective that this has on diagnosis and prognosis. Intervention includes enabling reflection upon the belief system and its relevance to the illness experience, and facilitating involvement in communities which reflect the belief system. As with the other sections intervention may involve referral to other agencies.

4. *Religious request.* This simply involves expression of religious need, and the response includes referral to appropriate agencies including the chaplain.

Hay's assessment approach is very important. It brings together many of the key elements of spirituality and spiritual development and tries to place them in the framework of manageable assessment procedures which any member of the healthcare team can administer, given some training. However, it does have some problems. Firstly, it tends to medicalise spirituality. The very use of the word diagnosis seems to view spirituality as a condition. Such a 'condition' is by definition negative, with a concentration upon 'deficiency', 'pain', and meaning breakdown. The intervention will aim to deal with each of these. This ignores the positive embodiment of spirituality and spiritual development, and indeed implies that unless there are pathological spiritual signs then the spirituality of the patient does not need attention.

Secondly, the assessment tends to concentrate upon process rather than person, with the danger of a concentration upon outcome, leading to a dehumanising effect. Thirdly, it tends to miss much of the elusive quality of spirituality and spiritual relations. For instance, the outcome 'increased awareness of factors in personal development' involves a quasi scientific language which does not begin to touch on the different kinds and levels of awareness which are central to spirituality. Once more this tends to take away from the centrality of the *relationship* between the nurse and the patient. In the next chapter we will note in some detail the importance of that to any spirituality assessment.

Fourthly, the dynamic of assessment is wrong in that what are often seen as 'interventions', for example, encouraging reflection, are in fact necessary for the assessment in the first place. 'Interventions' are better seen as responses. Fifthly, in all of this, spirituality can easily become identified as a separate domain from the body and the mind, with spiritual needs seen as different from the others, leading once more to polarisation. However, as noted, whilst the spiritual is about a particular perspective, involving meaning at several levels, it is not about a separate dimension, but rather about views of all dimensions, and thus is linked to physical and mental health.

Sixthly, there is a danger of self-conscious and formulaic caring in all of this. It is important to achieve a balance between the too-earnest, or task-oriented carer, and to have a relationship of care which is spiritually informed. Seventhly, the assessment form can be used as a means of control. Eighthly, there is a danger of seeing spiritual pain as in essence problematic and needing to be 'treated'. O'Brien lists several views of this, which she refers to as alterations in spiritual integrity, including:

- Spiritual loss. The loss of relationship with God or loss of meaning.
- Spiritual anxiety. The fear of retribution.
- Spiritual alienation. A sense of remoteness from the ground of faith.
- Spiritual despair. A loss of hope (O'Brien 1998, 70).

For O'Brien, pain is defined largely around problems in relationship to God. However, such spiritual pain need not be seen as negative but may well be a positive sign, of spiritual growth towards a sense of well-being. Moreover, as we shall see in the next chapter there is a strong sense in which it is critical that the person be allowed and enabled to take responsibility for that pain herself.

Spiritual well-being

If the religious and medical approaches tend to focus on distress and pain, this might be balanced with concern for NANDA's other category, spiritual well-being. Important attempts to assess well-being include the McGill Quality of Life Questionnaire, which has been used with cancer patients. This includes questions on the meaningfulness, purposefulness and worthwhileness of life. However, even such attempts show how difficult it is to actually 'assess' spiritual well-being (Cohen *et al.* 1997). The concept of well-being is not only vague but has many competing views which only take on specific meaning in relation to person, context and belief system. The experience and history of different people leads to many different perceptions of well-being, and therefore many different expectations. Some depressive personalities, for instance, have a view of life which is essentially negative and which neither thinks in terms of well-being, nor understands the concept. Some belief systems actively extol the virtues of suffering, and see this as a way to develop and grow. These give well-being a negative definition.

Ultimately, however, well-being is only understood through reflection on experience, and dialogue between personal and community narratives which provide different views of meaning. In other words, well-being emerges as a product of life meaning, and life meaning can only emerge through the reflection and dialogic testing of the particular person.

Conclusion

Reflecting on spiritual assessment Cobb asks three questions: (1998, 114):

- Is the assessment practical for the type of patient being assessed?
- Are the language and concepts used appropriate for all patients?
- Is the healthcare professional carrying out the assessment capable of dealing with the immediate consequences of what the assessment may evoke?

The first question demands that spiritual assessment should not take up too much time and should not demand too much expertise. One of the possible reasons why spirituality has not figured highly in recent nursing models is that it is perceived as a specialist area and as something hard to fit into ordinary nursing practice. Another may well be that nurses themselves as a profession are apprehensive about dealing with a topic which has not been fully articulated. There have been several attempts to sum up how nurses see spirituality, but it is not precisely defined in professional codes, or set down in training. In this respect, Watson's nursing theory is a most important approach to ensuring that spirituality is seen as integral to the practical nursing process. It is also an important example of demystifying the spiritual, in which the nurse does not have to be an expert and the spiritual makes most sense in the light of practical decision-making in therapy. This will be examined more closely in the next chapter.

Beneath Cobb's second question is a dynamic that has to be addressed, and which underlines the limitations of all assessment approaches in spirituality. Authors such as Narayanasamy (2001) have developed assessment forms for use in spiritual care. Box 4.1 is an example of such a format:

Box 4.1 Spiritual assessment needs

Needs	Questions	Assessment notes
Meaning and purpose	What gives you a sense of meaning and purpose? Is there anything especially meaningful for you now? Does the patient/client show any sense of meaning and purpose?	
Sources of strength and hope	Who is the most important person to you? To whom would you turn when you need help? Is there anyone we can contact? In what ways do they help? What is your sense of strength and hope? What helps you most when you feel afraid or need special help?	
Love and relatedness	How does the patient relate to: family and relatives; friends; others; surroundings?	

	Does the patient/client appear peaceful? What gives the patient/client peace?
Self-esteem	Describe the state of client/patient's self-esteem How does client/patient feel about self?
Fear and anxiety	Is patient/client fearful/ anxious about anything?
Anger	Is patient/client angry about anything? How does patient/client cope with anger? How does patient/client cope with this?
Relation between spiritual beliefs and health	What has bothered you most being sick (or what is happening to you?) What do you think is going to happen to you?
Concept of God or deity	Is prayer (or meditation) important to you? How would you describe your god or what you worship?
Spiritual practices	Do you feel your faith (or religion) is helpful to you? If yes, tell me more about it? If no, who would you like us to discuss it with? Are there any religious practices that are important to you? Has being ill made any difference to your practice of praying (or meditation) or to your religious practices? Are there any religious books or symbols important to you? Is there anything we could do to help with your religious practices?

In one way or another, many of the forms of assessment which have been devised follow the nursing process model, incorporating the phases of assessment, planning, implementation and evaluation. A number of the earlier models appear to have been overtaken by the Care Planning Approach, where core plans or critical care pathways have been devised which focus on the majority of physical needs within given patient scenarios. Such critical care plans may not immediately, or overtly, facilitate assessment of the patient's spiritual needs. It could be argued that the fundamental principles behind the development of the nursing process in its earliest formats still apply, if a rounded assessment is to take place. McSherry (2000, 79) cautions against the dangers of making spiritual assessment mechanistic by reducing it to a tick-box exercise. The reason for this is that the person's spirituality has a freedom which cannot be contained. Therefore, it could well be that the patient may not have any discernable spiritual needs one day, yet feel extremely down in spirit the next. The causes of such changes in a person's experience may be manifest, or they may not. It is notable that even after long periods of rehabilitation, people who have suffered a spinal injury, often get flash-back dreams, when they are transported back to a point in time before their injury. In these dreams, they are able to walk and undertake many of the more intimate things of life, such as control of the bladder and bowel movements and have some feeling of sexual arousal. Often the person can feel very 'flat' after such a dream, when the dawning becomes a conscious reality again. People don't find such things easy to talk about, often calling them 'the package; this is how I am'. Especially when faced with them every day, they do not want a constant reminder of how life has changed. For some, this means not wanting to look in a mirror as they don't want to see themselves sat in a wheelchair, even though they know that it is a reality of life. No charting of words can make us, as practitioners, understand what it is that people with such experiences are going through. It is only through talking with and being with the person that we might get anywhere near understanding their experience and helping to find solutions, although as in the example given immediately above, permanent solutions may not be attainable.

It should also be recognised that it is impossible to make an assessment form appropriate for all patients. As noted above a majority of patients will not have spent time on spiritual reflection and thus will not have a set vocabulary. Those who adhere to a religion often do not have a single shared vocabulary even within the religion. The view of spirituality which we have been propounding is one in which the only appropriate language and concepts are those which the patient herself develops and owns. The key question then becomes how the patient is enabled to develop her spiritual awareness and vocabulary. The central way of achieving that is essentially dialogic, enabling the person to articulate her narrative. Any assessment form then should be secondary to and supportive of that relationship, providing, for instance a framework which enables reflection. The very idea of assessment tends to be distanced and not collaborative and runs the risk of making the spiritual narrative of the patient fit into the categories set down.

McSherry (2000, 95) points out that there are a number of intrinsic and extrinsic barriers to the delivery of spiritual care, even once it has been assessed. Intrinsic factors include:

• The patient's inability to communicate through illness or loss of senses.
• Ambiguity of what data is required and how it should be handled.
• The nurses' lack of knowledge in the area of spirituality; as discussed earlier it may be too sensitive an area for the nurse to address; it may be emotionally demanding and fear-provoking.

Extrinsic factors include:

• How the organisation operates, and barriers to undertaking such work.
• Environmental distractions resulting in loss of privacy.
• Economic constraints, such as a lack of staff time.
• Educational issues such as inadequately prepared nurses.
• Reduced length of stay in hospital, which makes the exploration of sensitive issues such as spirituality more difficult to engage with; the topic may not be seen by the staff or indeed the patient to be directly relevant to the area of practice; staff and patients may find themselves party to the prevailing opinions of the society in which they live, in which spirituality is seen as something of either a no-go area or something for 'softies'.
• Finally, as there are no easy solutions, it is always going to be an emotionally demanding area in which to work.

This brings us to Cobb's third question, perhaps the most important of all. The importance of the caring relationship is implicit in this.

Such a caring relationship is about enabling the spirituality of the patient to be owned and thus becomes part of the therapeutic response in the most appropriate way. Clearly the intrinsic and extrinsic factors discussed above, need to be taken into account, but once this has been done in a creative way, the potential for the dialogue to develop between the patient and the nurse is opened up. Once the patient begins to open up to his own life meaning and value there is, by definition, a loss of control on the part of the carer. In some senses, the assessment provides a feeling of professional control, with outcomes which are assessable and which are recorded. As we have seen, this leads on to the danger of making it an instrument of control.

The nature of spirituality is, however, dynamic, dialogic, reflective and as noted in the first chapters, risky. It is not controllable and by definition invites the other to take control, to become responsible for the spiritual response at whatever level of awareness they can. This in turn can lead to reactions from the patient which are difficult to handle. Difficulties may be to do with handling the feelings which the patient begins to express. Oldnall also suggests difficulties caused by a fear of intruding in the 'private life', a delicate area of the patient's past or current life. This fear may partly be a desire to tread softly on ground that is holy, set apart, felt strongly about, and a desire not to offend. It is also a fear of not getting it right, or not having enough expertise. In subsequent chapters we will look at the spirituality of the nurse and the importance of developing spiritual confidence, something which is actually about developing an awareness of the very basic and often intuitive skills and qualities which both enable the nurse to engage the spiritual world of the patient. Once again, what enables the nurse to do this is a patient-centred spirituality which begins with an awareness of the person, allowing them to disclose their spirituality in their time, and in their words.

All of this points to two factors which are central to spiritual care: the *presence* of the nurse, which enables the patient to reflect; and spirituality as a *process* of reflection, which points to a narrative and ongoing approach to assessment; and spirituality as part of the nursing *practice*.

Spirituality and religious faiths

We should not forget that Britain has become a multi-cultural environment. It is impossible for the average healthcare worker to keep up to date with the requirements of all the different faiths. Books such as Sheikh and Gatrad (2000) and Henley and Schott (1999) should be on the shelves of every ward where there are regular admissions of patients from different ethnic and religious backgrounds.

The situation is made more complex by the number of people who visit this country from abroad and require healthcare treatment whilst they are here. One of the authors was in New York recently and was asked by a Roman Catholic colleague if English protestants wear crowns at Christmas. It transpired that the American colleague was referring to the paper hats which many people wear on Christmas day. What is interesting here is that this was one Christian, admittedly from another denomination and another country, talking with another. The point is made here in order to emphasise the problems of miscommunication between people of different cultural backgrounds.

However, the best way of obtaining a nursing assessment of the patient's spirituality is by sitting and talking with the patient. The real emphasis needs to be on the quality of the conversation rather than the chart which has to be completed. It is the authors' contention that the expert nurse will be able to cover this ground without the need for a chart, except perhaps as an aide-memoire, and have the ability to report the patient's requirements comprehensively yet succinctly within the written nursing report. Such an approach may not be popular with those nurses who have been educated in a structuralist regime, with the requirement that issues are written in particular ways, along particular dimensions. To do this in relation to a patient's spirituality is to constrain the potential of the deep relationship which can be developed between the patient and the member of staff. To say that nurses are not there to develop such a relationship, is to deride a positive understanding of what the nursing process is about, and reduces the position of the named nurse, to that of a 'gopher', rather than a specialist who is able to assess the needs of the person in a more rounded, fully human way. If authentic relationships are not developed, then both the nurse and the patient become part of a sterile, structured, systematic process which is devoid of integrity and meaning. If this position is taken, how can the nurse ever get near to the patient as a person?

Finally, finding a language between the nurse and the patient is vitally important. This includes understanding what the meaning is behind words that are unfamiliar. It may well be that some foreign languages do not contain the equivalent of some English words and

sympathetic interpreters may have to be sought who will help trans-
late conversation, intention and meaning between the nurse and the
patient. Where both nurse and patient listen to each others' narrative,
they are able to found a common language, which allows both the
nurse and the patient to find new words, refine their understandings,
and ask new questions.

Questions and exercises

1. Having considered in Chapter 2 your own spirituality, how can
   you integrate such understanding to further inform the assessment
   of other people's spirituality?
2. Reflecting upon your own experiences, how have the various
   models of the nursing process which you have used, impacted
   upon your practice of care, particularly in relation to your assessment of people's spirituality in the clinical setting?
3. How can the practice of assessing spirituality be improved?

References

Burnard, P. 'Spiritual Distress and the Nursing Response: Theoretical
    Considerations and Counselling Skills'. *Journal of Advanced Nursing*, 1987,
    12, 3, 377–82.
Cobb, M. (1998) 'Assessing Spiritual Need: An Examination of Practice' in
    M. Cobb and V. Renshaw (eds) *The Spiritual Challenge of Health Care*
    (London: Churchill Livingstone).
Cohen, S.R., Mount, B.M., Bruera, E., Provost, M., Rowe, J. and Tong,
    K. (1997) 'Validity of the McGill Quality of Life Questionnaire in
    the palliative care setting: a multi-centre Canadian study demonstrat-
    ing the importance of the existential domain'. *Palliative Medicine*, **11**,
    3–20.
Gosuch, R. 'Toward motivational theories of intrinsic religious commit-
    ment'. *Journal for the Scientific Study of Religion*, 1994, **33**, 315–25.
Gorsuch, R.L. and Miller, W.R. (1999) 'Assessing Spirituality', in W. Miller.
Harris, R.C., Dew, M.A. and Lee, A. (1995) 'The association of social rela-
    tionships and activities with mortality', *American Journal of Epidemiology*,
    116, 123–40.
Hay, M.W. (1989) 'Principles in building spiritual assessment tools', *American
    Journal of Hospice Care*, September/October, 25–31.
Henley, A. and Schott, J. (1999) *Culture, Religion and Patient Care in a Multi-
    Ethnic Society* (London: Age Concern).
Hungelmann, J., Kenkel-Rossi, E., Klassen, L. and Stollenwerk, R. 'Focus on
    spiritual well-being'. *Geriatric Nursing*, 1996, **17** (6), 262–6.

McSherry, W. (2000) *Making Sense of Spirituality in Nursing Practice: An Interactive Approach* (London: Churchill Livingstone).

Narayanasamy, A. (2001) *Spiritual Care: A Practical Guide for Nurses and Healthcare Practitioners* (Wiltshire: Quay Books).

NHS Northern and Yorkshire Chaplains and Pastoral Care Committee (1995) *A Framework for Spiritual, Faith and Related Pastoral Care* (The Institute of Nursing, University of Leeds).

O'Brien, M. (1998) *Spirituality in Nursing* (Boston: Jones and Bartlett).

Oldnall, B. (1996) 'A critical analysis of nursing: meeting the spiritual needs of patients, in *Journal of Advanced Nursing*, **23**, 138–44.

Pargament, K. and Brant, C.R. 'Religion and Coping'. In Koenig, H.G. (ed.) *Handbook of Religion and Mental Health* (San Diego: Academic Press, 1998), 112–28.

Propst, L.R. (1988) *Psychotherapy within the Religious Framework: Spirituality in the Emotional Healing Process* (New York: Human Sciences Press).

Randolph-Horn, D. and Paslawska, K. (2002) *Spirituality at Work* (Leeds: Leeds Church Institute).

Sheikh, A. and Gatrad, A.R. (2000) *Caring for Muslim Patients* (Abingdon: Radcliffe Medical Press Ltd.).

Stoll, R. (1979) 'Guidelines for spiritual assessment', *American Journal of Nursing,* September, 1547–77.

Taylor, R.L. and Watson, J. (1989) *They Shall not Hurt: Human Suffering and Human Caring* (Boulder: Colorado Associated University Press).

Watson, J. (1979) *Nursing: The Philosophy and Science of Caring* (Boulder: Colorado Associated University Press).

5

Spirituality in Practice

Sunshine Acres Living Centre

The first thing you see up ahead is Mr.
Polanski, wedged in the
arched doorway, like he means absolutely
to stay there, he who shouldn't be
here in the first place, put in here
by mistake, courtesy of that grandson
who thinks he's a shotshot, and too busy raking in
to take time for an old
man. If he had any place to go, you know he'd be out
instantly, if he had any
money. So he intends

to stay in that doorway, not missing
a thing, and waiting
for trouble. Which of course
will come. And could be
you- you're handy, you look
likely, you have

the authority. And you're
new here, another young
whippersnapper, doesn't know
ankle from elbow, but has been given
the keys. Well he's
ready, Polanski. So you go right
to him. Mr. Polanski, good
morning – you say it in Polish,
which you learned a little of
when you were little, and your grandmother taught you
a little song about lambs, frisking
in a pen, and you
danced a silly little dance with your grandmother
while the two of you
sang. So you sing it

for him, here in the dim, institutional
light of the hallway, light which even you find
insupportable, because at that moment
it reminds you of the light in the hallway
in the rest home where, when your grandmother
died, you weren't
there. So that you're also singing
to console yourself. And at the moment you pay her
this silly little tribute, Mr. Polanski
steps out of the doorway. He who had set himself to
resist you, he who made himself
a first, Mr. Polanski,
  contentious
  often combative
  and always inconsolable

hears that you know
the song. And he steps out
from the fortress of the
doorway, begins to shuffle
and sing along.
(Marilyn Krysl, *Midwife and Other Poems of Caring*)

Few caring relationships will be blessed with the immediate rapport found in this poem of Krysl, a first draft of which is used by Jean Watson (Watson 1990). Nonetheless, it neatly and lightly focuses on the essence of spiritual care. Firstly, it reminds us that patients come to a situation of care with a spirituality – it might be defensive, it might be disorganised, it might be dispirited, or disorientated. Mr. Polanski seems to find his identity and value through standing out against 'authority'. His spirituality is tied to a sense of worthlessness and to a family life which has no significant present connections.

Secondly, the presence of the carer focuses on the patient *per se*, not on any dynamic of challenge. The presence of the nurse enables the patient to remember and perhaps rediscover a meaningful identity that opens out to the self and to others. In the poem the nurse reaches out in a beautifully imaginative and simple way. In response to this Polanski is able to reveal something of himself through movement and singing. Of course, few would be able to relate in quite that way. Nonetheless, it does illustrate the movement of empathy well, with a reaching out to the patient enabling him to make connections with himself and others, with narratives and fragments of narratives that give positive meaning and so begin to improve how he copes with his illness.

Thirdly, such spirituality is there in whatever the nurse is doing, from the simple giving of physical care to relating to the patient in the corridor. Spiritual care may well be given in a private moment of intense attention to the patient, but it is not confined to that.

Fourthly, the 'presence' is mutual. Not only do the patient and nurse open out to each other, but they also perceive the same situation in terms of their own history, including their failures. In and through the recognition of each other they transcend the pains associated with those histories. None of this suggests that the pain magically disappears through transcendence. It does suggest that the pain in this interaction is no longer influencing the perception or attitude of the two people, and so they are able to focus on affective meaning that helps them to rediscover their value.

Fifthly, as they meet each other so they accompany each other down the corridor. The nurse becomes the companion or 'accompanist' central to spirituality.

At the core of this encounter is both *process* and *presence*. In this chapter we will examine in more detail the practice of each of these. As we look at the spiritual process we will reflect on the spirituality of the patient and consider the meaning of spiritual pain and distress in this context. We will then look at the nature of spiritual presence and the underlying qualities that enable this.

The spiritual process

As noted in Chapter 2, spiritual awareness is not a static thing but a continual interactive learning process and thus something of a journey, outlined in relation to health in Box 5.1:

Box 5.1   The spiritual process in healthcare

- Developing the spiritual narrative.
- Reflection on the meaning of that narrative, at cognitive, affective, somatic levels and how it links to the experience of illness. This may be termed 'drawing out the spirit', involving clarification of meaning, not least through dialogue.
- Affirming or developing meaning in relation to the illness and the person's social and spiritual context.
- Embodying the spiritual, in relationships which support the patient, or even lead to life-changing practice.

We will now reflect on the whole process, aware that in practice not all of this may be addressed.

Spiritual narrative

For the majority of patients faced by illness, their spiritual narrative may not be well developed or consciously worked through. In any case, making sense of illness, especially major illness, is not something that can be integrated into life meaning before it happens. Hence, when that illness occurs it causes a major challenge to life meaning. Aldridge writes of unity being lost and the person 'separated from the ground of her being' (2000, 35). Hence faith and hope are seriously questioned and the patient 'becomes a refugee within her own soul' (ibid). The natural response to this sense of estrangement is to deny the reality of the experience. For patients experiencing the initial phases of a heart attack, Johnson (1991) notes that symptoms are normalised as flu or a pulled chest muscle. As symptoms persisted one patient spoke of his fear of being a 'cripple', thus destroying his role as a father and threatening his core life meaning and sense of worth. Another patient reported that he only finally went to Accident and Emergency when he thought about his obligations to his family. Prior to that he believed that he could cope with anything himself, and the accompanying fear of dependency was fundamental to his spirituality. For many, then, the spiritual narrative becomes fragmented and unsure.

Others may face the experience of illness and hospital with a spirituality which is very strong or one not articulated in words but which is set out in the dress or appearance of the person. A 68-year old patient came in for an operation wearing a suit with various 'badges' which referred to his military history. He was clear about his life meaning and what had carried him through the experience of war. Here was a rich and sometimes ambiguous narrative that the staff could engage with swiftly. It was set out in many ways from the way he walked, to the ritual of standing or sitting to attention when a doctor came, to the regular rituals to do with keeping his locker tidy. They expressed respect, care and awareness, reminding all concerned about the importance of these values. The spirituality of others may not be so obvious or practised but rather emerges gradually through dialogue.

Either way, the healthcare worker is in the position to enable the patient to begin to articulate the narrative through empathy. The key elements of the narrative are:

- the experience of illness;
- the cognitive, affective and somatic meaning that this has challenged, and which emerges through the telling of a story.

The articulation of the narrative involves the patient gradually
taking responsibility for his story. This is the story that he chooses to
tell and to own. He may tell it for several reasons; to reassure himself,
to impress others and so on. Hence, often the loudest and most insistent stories may be hiding a great fear. As part of the nursing assessment process then, the nurse allows the patient to tell his story. This
may be easily achieved, by picking up on the external signals of the
story – the military insignia, the photos of grandchildren, the sport-
ing regalia and so on. It may be a very direct story expressed in
somatic terms. One elderly stroke patient who had suffered a stroke
and lost speech would communicate his life meaning through physical touch which involved him pulling the nurses ear, and pulling her
head down towards him whenever she sat next to him. Initially, this
was felt as a threat until she realised that this was simply him trying
to get a sense of another person there for him. At one level he was
testing her out, and testing out his value. At another, somatic, level he
was communicating presence directly, without having to verbalise.
Once the nurse accepted this as a ritual of their meeting it became
important. The ritual was then learned by members of the family, two
of whom had found being with him embarrassing with no verbal
communication. Both spoke of a new level of meaning experienced
for their father, and of being released just to *be* with him.

If there are no obvious external signs then conversation about the
family or other centres of value, or simply about the history of the illness,
and how the patient is feeling about it can enable the narrative to begin.
The meaning of illness only begins to emerge through dialogue with the
other parts of the person's narrative. Only in that context do the effects
of it become clear, such as loss of purpose. Through narrative then the
spirituality of the person and his community can be accessed and given
a base from which to work through the experience of illness.

Reflection

As the patient begins to reflect on his narrative so the spiritual meaning begins to emerge. The nurse can focus on particular aspects of the
story that help to develop or affirm meaning and begin to help the
patient to reflect on these. This may involve reflecting on:

- The images and metaphors which the person uses in the story. These may refer to themselves or to the spiritual framework that they draw upon. This often locks into the imagination of the patient, a faculty critical in the development of empathy. How, for instance, does the old man with medals view and feel about the army? For him the army was 'family', giving him purpose and value, what made him still feel secure. Reflection also allowed him to see the downside of that experience, without losing faith in it.
- The values which are critical to the person. The old man's values were discipline and sacrifice. Not only were these values which he felt sustained him, they were also values which he believed he should share with others.
- The beliefs which emerge from this, including the beliefs about people who are valued, including who or what is the ground of faith and hope.
- The experience of the illness and how this challenges his belief system.

The process of reflection leads on naturally to clarification. For some, this is simply locking into meaning which is well rehearsed. For others, there is a discovery of values and beliefs that they may not have been aware of in quite this way. Such discovery can quickly be focused on through reflecting on the things of importance in someone's life. A good example is gardening, as the following scenario shows.

Mrs. B was an elderly woman who came into hospital quite afraid. The various cards by her bedside clearly showed a big flower theme and the nurse explored this. After conversation about her garden and favourite flowers, later conversations were based on the nature of the garden and the quietness and security felt there – a special place, the ground of her faith. Gardening for her was not just a pastime but a very real spiritual experience and one which gave rise to feelings which she had not really registered until she began to articulate the values and images of the garden, its peace and serenity. This allowed her to make connections between the felt serenity of the garden and her experience of illness. Towards the end of her stay this in turn linked in for her to memories of her late husband, and she began to realise that she had avoided reflection both on the importance of the garden and the loss of her husband. She left hospital with a clear understanding how she would remember her husband in the garden, and thus of how she could relocate him.

Clarification then is not merely the affirmation of what has been previously worked out but may be about making connections and discovering new dimensions of meaning and value (van der Ven 1998). This only begins to emerge with the aid of a reflective presence, and subsequent dialogue. It is important to note that this is precisely dialogue and not some finely honed professional skill. It is a natural interest in the other and allowing of the other to disclose meaning, affirming them in their illness experience. Not everyone, however, can make connections so easily.

Spiritual pain

The process of reflecting on and developing narrative, and thus taking responsibility for the narrative and awareness of the environment on which the patient depends, can, to begin with, intensify an initial sense of dis-ease.

It is precisely at this point that the experience of *spiritual pain* can emerge. This is a very real existential pain felt from an awareness of loss of any significant meaning, or an awareness that what has been valuable and significant for life now no longer is. At its most extreme, this is characterised by St John of the Cross in Christian spirituality as the *dark night of the soul* (Fowler 1996, 74). The classic signs of this experience are:

- a sense of the absence of one's ground of faith or god;
- a fearful sense of losing some other important foundation point in one's life, from significant people, to ideals or values, to self image, to purpose, or even gratification;
- a sense of sadness about the inability to grow spiritually, or the persistent failure to effect a desired change to a way of life.

Often these feelings will be associated with an awareness of death as something to be experienced by the person, and thus involve feelings of anxiety, loss of faith and hopelessness. It is very easy at such points to speak of a variety of 'spiritual' phenomena, such as *spiritual anxiety, spiritual loss, spiritual depression* and so on. The dangers of such categorisation are that it can encourage the practitioner to see these as different from feelings of loss and anxiety in general, and thus to set up some kind of higher-level skill necessary to 'spot the difference'. A simpler categorisation is given by Beland and Passos (1981, 1237–8) under three headings: spiritual concerns, spiritual despair, spiritual distress, summarised in Box 5.2.

Box 5.2 A simple categorisation of 'spiritual' phenomena (Belland and Passos 1981)

Spiritual Concerns

Aetiology:
Challenged belief system
Separation from religio-cultural ties
Anticipated role change
Concerned about relationship with God
Unresolved feelings about the concept of death
Search for more meaning and purpose in existence
Disrupted religious practices

Defining characteristics include:
Mild anxiety
Anticipatory grief
Verbalises inner conflict about belief
Questions meaning of existence
Discouraged
Bewildered
Unable to participate in usual religious rituals

Spiritual Despair

Aetiology:
Lost belief in self
Lost belief in treatment
Lost belief in value system and/or ground of faith
Lack of will to live

Defining characteristics include:
Hopelessness
Sense of meaninglessness
Loss of spiritual beliefs
Sense of exhaustion
Sense of abandonment
Sees no meaning in suffering
Withdrawal
Loss of affect
Refusal or passive acceptance of therapy

Spiritual Distress

Aetiology:
Challenged belief and value system
Sense of meaninglessness or purposelessness
Remoteness from God
Sense of guilt/shame
Anger towards God

> *Defining characteristics include:*
> Varying degrees of grieving
> Profound sense of toxic shame
> Disturbance in ideas of and feelings about God and how these relate to
> the illness

Fowler locates experiences such as these in the *transitions* between stages of faith (Fowler 1996, 71). Based on the work of Bridges he indicates four interrelated elements (Box 5.3) which make a helpful framework for the health carer in identifying such a transition phase, and thus some form of spiritual crisis or pain.

Box 5.3   The experience of transition

Disengagement involves a major breakdown in some context of relationships and shared meaning that has helped to constitute the sense of self. Extreme examples of this might be divorce, severe illness.

Disidentification is the internal element of disengagement. It is experienced as the person tries to rediscover her identity in the old patterns of faith and can no longer identify herself in them.

Disenchantment involves a loss of faith in the old perceptions of reality. This can bring with it feelings of anger and resentment, grief, loss, guilt, shame, lostness, and confusion. As Fowler (1996) notes, 'It can also bring a sense of liberation and empowerment', a sense that there are new and exciting ways of envisioning life and value.

Disorientation is the cumulative effect of the other three stages involving a loss of any sense of direction and a great deal of time and energy spent in trying to grasp what is going on. Bridges refers to this as the neutral zone, a time when persons can feel that they are no longer themselves, indeed that they are 'going out of their minds'.

Such an experience is not necessarily the same as depression, not least because the person can still maintain concentration and motivation in searching for resolution. Nonetheless, it can involve real emotional pain, and lead to a sense of despair and consequently to depression. As noted previously, such spiritual pain is no bad thing *per se*. The disorientation may feel bad but is not necessarily pathological and may lead to growth. This is part of the process that may be termed inversion, as the person looks in towards herself and begins to try to find the resources necessary to face the experience of illness.

Any of the four elements of transition may alert the nurse to the need for spiritual reflection. Where spirituality is not set out in the immediate narrative the experience of transition may emerge through expressions of anxiety, resentment or even anger. Such feelings can be directed at the nurse especially if the patient is searching for a 'magical solution' to her pain. By this we mean the view that someone else will solve the problems for the patient, and that she will not need to take responsibility for making sense of experience which is difficult and sometimes ambiguous or contradictory. Faced by such anger and pain the route for the nurse is the same, to establish empathy and to take the patient back to an articulation of the narrative and so an awareness of the affective and cognitive dimensions driving that narrative. Through this, the patient can begin to understand the feeling and the meaning which she is searching for to find ways of coping, including developing her spirituality.

A great deal of life meaning emerges and is challenged through the patient making connections between the different parts of her life. This often highlights contradictions and ambiguities between feelings and ideas, and each of these and practice, which cause anxiety in the patient. The temptation for any carer is try to sort this anxiety out *for* the patient, providing reassurance and 'good reasons' why she shouldn't be anxious. The dynamic of spirituality, however, is not to sort things out but rather, through reassuring presence, to enable the patient to look at what gives rise to the anxiety and begin to make sense of those contradictions – some of which she will have to hold together, some of which will indicate the need to change.

Cases

We will now look at how some of those contradictions can be handled in the following five cases.

Case 1:

One evening the nurse saw that a 60-year-old man was crying when his wife had left at the end of visiting hours. She assumed that he was crying because of her leaving. 'No', he said, 'I'm crying because today was the last payment for my mortgage'. 'Tears of joy then', said the relieved nurse. 'No. What I have lived for over these past 35 years has gone. I went to work every day with that house in my mind. That was my purpose, that was me. Now I have got no reason for living.' Subsequently, the patient had to relocate hope in another function and in a wider range of people. This positively affected how he coped with later treatment.

This was a narrow individualist spirituality without any real base of hope other than through role, function and attainment. The fact of his age and with an operation to come led to tension and confusion, which might have led to depression without a member of the care team and family helping him to use this as a moment of transition, including effecting closure with his function. For him, this was an important learning experience – about finding other sources of faith and hope.

Case 2:

An elderly single female patient was in hospital for a hip replacement was fearful and anxious for a good while even after the operation. Conversation with the nurse revealed that the significant presence in her life was a dog. She feared the loss of this relationship and thus life meaning which was critical to her. Would she able to take the dog out for walks? Would she able to keep it at all?

As she began to reflect on the meaning of the dog in her life she also refused initially to admit that she should be so dependent upon an animal and was thus actually denying an important part of her spirituality. Encouraged to develop her narrative she began to focus on her emotional dependence and understand the part her dog played in her life. It became clear that the dog would have to be involved in the recovery. Simply recognising the importance of the dog for her developed the patient's own sense of spiritual meaning.

Case 3:

A patient showed an apparently organised Christian spirituality, with a Bible at the side of her bed and various Christian get-well cards. She also showed signs of real anxiety about her treatment and began to talk about this as the nurse encouraged her narrative. In particular, during a discussion about religion the nurse noticed that she was also tightly clasping the bedclothes. The nurse gently reflected back to her the perceived anxiety, and the patient began to talk about this, in terms of her fear about dying in the operation and her fear about what would happen to her grandchildren if she did die.

A critical part of this conversation was the patient's 'owning' the feeling of fear. Her faith was strongly cognitive, based in doctrines. She felt that such a faith should exclude the possibility of feeling fear, and thus excluded any affective element. In the presence of the nurse she felt able to acknowledge this and begin to work through it. A little later she asked the nurse to read to her from the Psalms. The nurse, though not a Christian, agreed to do this. In the end, this was all that she required for the newly accepted feeling to be integrated with the old cognitive faith. It is possible for nurses to be involved in a variety of different religious interventions, including the use of meditation and prayer, provided that the patient initiates this. This can be done with integrity even if the nurse is not a fellow believer. The authenticity of the response is relational, with the nurse acknowledging the value of the reading or action for the patient.

Reflecting later on the experience, the patient said that it was important to have the Psalms, because they focused faith on real problems, and also important that she had them read by someone who did not represent her religion. She felt that a chaplain might have reinforced the original cognitive spirituality and made her feel guilty about the experience of fear, and ashamed to express it. This was a good example of a negotiated response to spiritual need, helping the patient to clarify feeling and concept and hold both together. Subsequently, she was able to relate effectively to the chaplain and begin to develop her religious faith.

The imbalance between the affective and the cognitive can lead to a sense of loss of faith. This may indicate referral, with permission, to the chaplain. In the case of the patient above, she was later able to talk with the chaplain at length after her initial work with the nurse. This led to a significant re-examination and re-evaluation of some of her theological ideas. The chaplain was able to use cognitive techniques, where the patient articulates values and then looks at the underlying belief and examines reasons for holding that view (Martin and Booth 1999; Ellis and Dryden 1999). This helped the patient to re-think and feel meaning and thus to a new view of her religion, with God accepting her vulnerability. The nurse can also achieve this kind of reflection if there is time, not least through enabling the patient to articulate and clarify her values and beliefs.

A much more extreme clash occurs when a cognitive spirituality – a strong set of beliefs – becomes the centre of the person's identity, leading to a denial of feelings. Where such a spirituality is challenged, for instance by the experience of fear, this can lead to intense questioning of the self and the development of what Kaufman refers to as shame about shame – feeling ashamed that guilt or shame could affect the person's faith (Kaufman 1980, 104).

Case 4:

A Muslim mother of four exhibited great dis-ease during a stay in hospital that would radically affect how she could care for her children and husband. Her life purpose revolved around her family, and this was reinforced by a strongly patriarchal Islamic faith. Her immense feelings of shame were compounded by the belief that she should not feel this way. To give into such feelings and the resultant depression was a sign of inadequate faith. This was never satisfactorily worked through until she returned a year later following a diagnosis of terminal illness. Only at this point did she begin to work through, with a religious advisor from the chaplaincy, to a resolution that enabled her to let go of the shame-associated behaviour.

On the whole such dysfunctional spirituality, involving internalised shame, focused on the self rather than upon actions, and leading to low self-esteem, would point to referral to the chaplain, religious advisor or counsellor. Fowler notes three kinds of internalised shame that will affect any spiritual awareness:

- *Toxic shame.* This is the internalised shame which views the self as of no worth.
- *Perfectionist shame.* This involves shame at not achieving certain standards.
- *Ethnic or cultural minority shame.* This involves shame associated with being a member of a particular group, be that ethnic, class or gender (Fowler 1996).

Other indications for referral include situations when:

- the patient requests spiritual direction;
- the staff member feels that she cannot cope with the narrative which is emerging, be that because of its complexity or because it is affecting her own equilibrium and sense of meaning;
- there are clear signs of disorientation moving into depression. There is real possibility of dysfunctional spirituality, where no faith or hope is developing, taking a long time to work through, and radically affecting the person's recovery.

Such referral should always be in consultation with and ultimately initiated by the patient.

Case 5:

A Jehovah's Witness had decided not to have a blood transfusion based, of course, upon his view of the Bible. The therapy team respected his autonomy, but late one evening the nurse had time to be with him and learn more about the basis for his belief system. It emerged that he was genuinely unsure about his decision, citing cases where some JWs seemed to have transfusions. But he, as a local leader, felt he had to set an example. The nurse could not attempt to influence the patient's belief. She was, however, able to encourage his continued reflection, enabling him to examine carefully the contradictions in his belief system and the possible outcomes of any decision. This led to the patient discussing matters in more depth with his family and other leaders and eventually allowing the transfusion.

This was a good example of non-directive challenge. The nurse provided the environment within which the patient could honestly examine his beliefs and their justification. As Gillon notes, this constitutes a respect for autonomy, because it enables further development of autonomy, and better decision-making (Gillon 2000). Spiritualities can be challenged then, but only through self challenge in the context of the person's spiritual story.

Developing meaning

As the narrative reveals the different elements of spirituality so the patient can begin to either affirm that which holds together her experience or develop life meaning that will enable her to live with that experience. This may involve:

- developing from a conditional faith (not accepting dependency) to an unconditional one that accepts dependency on others.
- developing from a child-like faith which sees the self as the victim in some way, exemplified by the question 'Why me?', to a faith where the patient takes responsibility for life meaning in the light of limitations, possible resources and necessary changes.

Based on the experience of those surviving a heart attack Johnson writes in terms of finding new meaning and learning to live (Johnson

1991). This is partly about making new relationships in which faith is regenerated and thus new life meaning is built up. This may involve renegotiating function, purpose and faith, as stressed by Finch and Mason (1993). Healthcare staff can become involved in this directly where the family of a patient frequently visits hospital or where they are present at home visits. With the need for change, for example following cardiovascular treatment, there may also be a need to revisit purpose and values and begin to re-prioritise. As Kaufman notes, in psychotherapy, there may come a point where new spirituality has to be explicitly developed, with values articulated and justified (Kaufman 1980, 136). If the person has been through a period of transition it is important that these should be developed to replace values which held old beliefs and behaviour in position. Such a conscious working through of values needs to be located in the process of care. Few healthcare staff have the time to work slowly through this with every patient. However, this is possible to work through in a therapeutic regime that focuses on the important change needed in practice if the person is to either fully recover or live with the condition.

Embodying the spirit

The growing awareness of others enabled through the narrative and reflection naturally leads to the embodiment of spiritual meaning. In long-term nursing, this may involve enabling the patient to develop in a number of ways by:

- Attempting to share responsibility and collaborate with others. In this others begin to be viewed not as competition but as resources that extend the possibilities for the future of all involved, thus creating hope.
- A change in life practice. This may be associated with life disciplines related to food, stress management, meditation, rest and so on.
- Effecting forgiveness and reconciliation. If there is a felt need for forgiveness then the different possibilities for forgiveness and reconciliation can be worked through. This is the development of right relationships, *shalom*, and developing or redeveloping faith in others.

Focusing on heart attack survivors, Johnson (1991, 54) notes several different elements involved in finding new meaning, including:

- preserving the self,
- balancing needs and supports,
- minimising uncertainty.

The first of these looks to the maintenance and development of personal identity in relation to the illness. The second requires clear identification and acceptance of needs and ways of fulfilling them. Core to this is the acceptance of appropriate dependency and the development of interdependency. The third involves the development of an awareness of the embodied self, of limitations and possibilities. Even at this level there is a strong spiritual dimension. Johnson notes how many survivors had lost faith in their body, even to the extent of fearing to go to sleep in case they died in the night. Part of recovery was learning to trust that which was now limited and in one respect weak and flawed.

The virtues

Behind recovery or acceptance of the illness lies the development of what have been referring to in chapters 2 and 3 as core virtues or qualities, including: faith, faithfulness, hope, prudence, the capacity to accept the self and others (love). These are not taught as such but develop in and through the process and in relation to the skilled companion. The presence of the other allows the practice and development of such virtues and so leads to the empowerment of the patient. The faithful patient, for instance, not only has faith in the healthcare workers. He also develops faith in those around him and in himself and his capacity to develop significant meaning in his illness. This will be examined particularly in the experience of dying.

Integrating spiritual care

For the most part the nurse will not be able to see the patient through to the completion of spiritual reflection, especially not to significant life change. Nonetheless, within the everyday practice of healthcare, major reflection can occur directly as part of the treatment. Pearson *et al.* note the case of an elderly patient, Mr. Smith, who had left hospital and returned for outpatient treatment (Pearson, Vaughan and Fitzgerald 1996, 215). They divide the care response into *assessment, plan, intervention, and evaluation,* popularly known as the nursing process, although it should be noted that this scheme of work can be used by any clinician.

Assessment
Since the last outpatient treatment Mr. Smith had lost 5kg.
Conversation revealed that he was very concerned about cooking his
own food, but that he found difficulty in cutting up food resulting in
his meal being cold before he could finish it. He disliked cold food.
However, he did not like 'outsiders' coming in, and turned down
offers of help when he was eating a meal in the Occupational Therapy
kitchen. He preferred to 'struggle along' by himself. The basis of
assessment was both the objective information, such as weight and the
subjective information that was revealed by the patient's narrative.
This gives the impression of a 'strong spirituality' in the sense of a
determination to retain identity, but a weak one in the sense of being
unaware of his limitations and of an inability to negotiate help.

Plan
The nurse planned to put aside time to talk with Mr Smith about his
nutrition. This would be based in the Occupational Therapy kitchen
where he could show how he coped and where different practical
ways of keeping food warm could be examined, such as using a
microwave halfway through the meal.

Intervention
Progress was discussed. The patient was enthusiastic about the help he
was being given, and began to relax more. As he relaxed he was able
to develop his narrative that included his fears of being dependent and
going into a residential care home.
    'Intervention' in this case meant a shared focus on how he might
handle some very particular needs, and dialogue and reflection on
what this meant to him. Through that, he was learning to rely on an
other who respected his need for independence and who did not
encourage over dependency. This enabled him to articulate fears and
hopes, and brought him more into control of his situation, physically
but also spiritually.

Evaluation
Returning to the next outpatient's session the patient brought a
record of his food intake. He spoke of his progress and of the importance of the work in Occupational Therapy. He was pleased with his
independence. For now, he would not have to rely on his neighbours. Nonetheless, he began to speak about how he would appreciate the odd visit from them. It is at this point that reflection on wider

relationships and what they mean to him could be developed, perhaps leading to some relational developments.

In terms of spiritual awareness, the patient had gone through the first cycle of reflection and was now well into the next. The first cycle had seen him reflecting on his identity and focusing this on his treatment need. A good working relationship was built up which showed him possibilities for retaining his sense of identity and agency. The relationship of care itself was critical to his development of spirituality because it modelled an acceptable dependency and a way of negotiating responsibility. The freedom to negotiate was very important for the patient, not least because of his fear that responsibility for the self might be taken away at some point. The second cycle took him into reflection on his own identity and from there to the chance to reflect about need and about others in his life, past and present. With this was also a clarification and development of values. At first he was concerned to be simply independent and avoid total care. This developed into an awareness of freedom as involving partnership and mutuality.

It is from such a process that any patient can begin to widen networks in the family and community, and thus develop more trust and faith, and, with an increase in human resources, more hope.

Spiritual care as presence

As we suggested in Chapter 2, the cycle of narrative, reflection and embodiment is facilitated by the presence of an accompanist. The nurse may be that accompanist over a long period of time or for a moment, or may be in a position to monitor the development as another enables it.

Osterman and Schwartz-Barcott (1996) distinguishes between four senses of presence:

- *Functional presence,* where the nurse is in the same room but taken up completely with a task.
- *Partial presence,* where the primary focus is on task, but with some attention to the patient.
- *Full presence,* where the nurse is fully focused on the patient, psychologically and physically.
- *Transcendent presence,* where the nurse provides a 'spiritual presence'. This is a centred presence in which the nurse is open to the patient and shares a sense of peacefulness and harmony.

No nurse can be always in the last of these, and different encounters call for different functional presences. Nonetheless, it is the last two, with empathy at their centre which enable the patient to relax enough to begin to articulate and reflect upon her spiritual narrative. This can involve several different aspects.

1. *Embodied presence.* All behaviour is communication and thus anything we do communicates something about the nature of care. Eye contact is a good example. The self-conscious use of eye contact can be intrusive, leaving little personal space. For those who have any sense of shame about their condition or self it can seem threatening or judgmental. Too little eye contact can give the impression of the nurse being uncomfortable, thus again giving the patient a feeling of rejection, albeit polite and professional. Eye movement is more naturally to and fro, sometimes focusing on the person and sometimes not. Such eye contact should also sum up the focusing of the attention given to the other and enable an appropriate response (Stern 1985, ch. 7).

2. *Contracting and defining presence.* One aspect of presence is attention given to the patient apart from regular tasks. In this, the nurse has to clearly establish the focus of caring presence, in a way which accepts limitations, of time and energy, just as the patient needs to be clear about her limitations. This is in effect the forming of an informal mutual contract with the patient. A fearful patient may well feel the need to test out the care of the nurse. It is important for the worker then to both clearly set out the boundaries in terms of availability and also establish the genuineness of his care for the patient. The point of such testing is partly to establish, in the patient's mind, the congruence of the care offered. This initial testing and the establishing of expectations for the relationship sets out a 'benchmark'. This may be developed through the time of the relationship with new expectations being mutually agreed. It may be the basis for contact at a time of stress or crisis (Robinson 2001).

3. *Presence as space and silence.* The physical presence of another can sometimes be oppressive. Concern for the patient and especially concern that the patient's pain or spiritual suffering be 'sorted out' can lead to an intrusiveness which gives no space to be patient, to focus on and sort through feelings and thoughts. What shines through in this is the desire to make things better, and the desire to do this for the

patient. Behind this is the view that working with a patient demands a clear outcome, either resolving problems or 'curing'. However, reflecting on and developing spirituality does not necessarily solve problems or complete tasks. Spiritual awareness and growth and the subsequent development of meaning is a continual process that cannot be neatly packaged. Perhaps, more importantly, it is an exploration that demands the person take responsibility for that awareness. They have to have the freedom and space to work through the different levels of meaning. As Vanstone notes in the context of Christian spirituality, this involves giving power to the other, including responsibility for any outcomes. All that can be done is to wait for the other to respond. Hence, the capacity to wait is important (Vanstone 1977).

Presence then has to be there for the other but not to be intrusive. It has to give space for the other to make her decision and own the meaning that she is working through. This also means not attempting to push the patient to what might be thought to be a more mature faith or sense of hope. By definition, such a faith can only emerge through the patient's decision.

In practice, this may mean allowing the person to be alone with their thoughts and feelings. Careful discrimination and negotiation is required with this, and it does not involve the withdrawal of presence as such. The patient should always be reassured that the nurse is available or will return shortly. Leaving the person to be with herself may be indicated if she is clearly stuck and trying to work through ideas and feelings. The nurse can then ask if she wants to be alone and reassure her that she will be available. It may also involve finding the right space for the patient to be alone, for example, office, chapel, or space on the ward or in the home. All this is in light of the nurse's responsibility to provide care appropriate to the context. The factors indicating against leaving a patient alone would include where they are trying to come to terms with a shock, or where there are symptoms of depression, or self-harm. This requires skill at discerning the right moment within changing care pathways.

This creative space can also be enabled through the physical presence of the nurse, and especially through the sensitive use of silence. The temptation to speak or to make things better can easily take power away from the other. Silence on the other hand offers a vacuum that can simply be unfilled or filled by the patient.

4. *Reflective Presence.* The capacity of the nurse to reflect back to the patient the nature of the caring presence is important in confirming

the presence itself. It can be very hard for the patient to actually know that the other has empathised with her. The simple reflecting back of what has been heard and seen clearly establishes that the person has been heard.

This applies to both the words and the contents and feelings behind the words. It also applies to the condition of the patient, whatever that is; his dependency, his physical presentation and so on, precisely things that the patient might be ashamed of. Reflecting back itself also provides a clear indication of a continued, faithful presence. The reflecting back in an even tone demonstrates that the nurse has seen the patient, or heard his thoughts and feelings and is still there, and has remained faithful. She is not discounting any feeling or thought, and she is not dismissing or judging the person. At the core such presence embodies unconditional positive regard (agape).

Such care does not preclude challenge of the patient. It does mean that challenge should be reflective, simply reflecting back the patient's narrative and underlying meaning, and any emerging feelings or conflicts. It is then for the patient to work with these, supported by the faithful presence of the staff member.

5. *Truthful presence.* Any reflection back to the patient also includes the truth of the illness that he is experiencing. In the past this has often been cast as a rather sterile moral debate – to tell or not to tell. Spirituality starts from a different position. The body, including any illness, is part of who I am. If I am to find genuine meaning in my life, I should be aware of the other and the self, including the body. Such awareness is mediated by empathy. The communication of the truth of a diagnosis and the development of life meaning, the context of that truth, then have to go hand in hand. This demands a patient-centred dialogue in which veracity is balanced by faithfulness, and through which the patient can explore, through narrative and dialogue his own truth and faithfulness to himself and to his world.

6. *Mutual presence.* At the heart of the empathic response to the patient is a mutuality, something not always attended to. As Mayer writes, 'Care is seen as something delivered to the powerless from the powerful. There is little awareness in the literature of the patient's capacity to give and thus create a mutual relationship' (1992, 52).

Empathy enables the patient to reveal something of herself and in turn to develop her own empathy which can be aware of the healthcare worker and what they are giving in care. This is not a symmetrical mutuality, in the sense of both parties sharing problems or issues. As the patient shares something of her spiritual narrative, focused in illness, the nurse reveals something of her narrative, focused in the qualities and concerns of care. This exchange may lead to mutual learning and support.

None of this mutuality can be consciously or systematically sought out. It arises naturally from the focus of empathy (Margulies, 1989). As Griffin writes, 'If we sought any of these things deliberately they might elude us – as in the search for happiness. They are, if you like, gifts coming from the proper and authentic involvement in a particular institutional role' (1983, 293). Campbell notes the mutual grace of this relationship, with 'grace' stressing both gift and ease, and how the response of the patient can enable the care of the staff member:

> The professional, who is aware of how much he or she gains in support, enlightenment and personal development from helping others may well feel a greater indebtedness. It is often more blessed to care than to be cared for; and the ability to care is frequently made possible by the understanding and sensitivity of the needy person. Such reciprocity suffuses the relationship with a spontaneity, with a sense of grace which enriches care and cared-for alike' (1984, 107).

7. *Presence and humour.* Empathy is an attitude that is not self-conscious and doesn't draw attention to itself. This partly involves the nurse not taking himself too seriously, and being open to humour (Campbell 1984). Humour, at its best, is a vehicle of empathy, enabling distance and perspective to see the other as same and different and so accept them in their incongruity. Williams, from the perspective of Christian spirituality argues that laughter is the, 'purest form of God's acceptance of us. For when I laugh at myself I accept myself and when I laugh at other people in genuine mirth I accept them. Self acceptance in laughter is the opposite of self satisfaction or pride' (quoted in Pattison 1988, 186).

Where humour is not practised with empathy it can, of course, have the opposite effect, drawing attention to the carer's lack of awareness.

8. *Presence as touch.* By touch we mean using touch to establish therapeutic contact with the patient. This can be differentiated from touch involved in completing a task or touch as involved in healing rituals such as lying on of hands.

The tendency within the medical profession is to minimise touch or to make this purely functional, not least because of the dangers of an abuse of the professional relationship. However, in any spirituality, touch that communicates the caring presence of the other cannot be ruled out. As Lyall notes, touch is a basic need in all mammals (1997). Moreover, the stimulation of the skin can have very positive effects on the mind and spirit (Montague 1986).

The key point about touch is the need for congruence in the carer so that the touch can clearly indicate a caring presence. Such congruence both demands that the carer is aware of the thoughts and feelings in his own mind, and that he is open to the needs and thoughts of the patient.

Indications of non-erotic touch:

- Ritual touch. A regular form of greeting, such as shaking hands, is sometimes important for patients. It signals the beginning of the phase of a relationship, and confirms the presence and attention of the other (Lewis 2000).
- Crisis situations, such as trauma or loss. This is a simple affirmation of the patient. For those experiencing grief there is often a non-verbal negotiating involving sensitivity to the patient's touch. This is seen most clearly where the patient and carer hold hands, and the patient can easily communicate her continued need for this security.
- Focusing of the patient's attention. Where a patient is finding it hard to focus on something important brief touch can help. Such touch can also emphasise a verbal statement.
- Unlocking feelings. Where the patient is clearly troubled and finding it hard to articulate feelings a brief touch of the hand might begin to enable this.
- Calming fear. Touch is a basic reassurance.

Avoid touch when:

- the patient indicates,
- it is simply gratification,
- there is some manipulation.

On the whole touch arises in the context of the caring relationship and thus is formed in response to the need expressed by the patient and confirmed by the carer.

9. *Holistic presence.* The presence offered by the nurse is holistic. It is present to and so takes seriously the cognitive and affective as well as the somatic aspects of the patient – the logical ideas and concepts, and the feelings which emerge as the patient reaches out to transcend the self. This leads to the nurse being able to clarify and challenge all these aspects, and so help him develop greater awareness.

10. *Presence in task and technology.* Like any aspect of care tasks, assessment and observation can be seen as ends in themselves, with completion as the desired professional outcome. Such focus on the task can also become a means of avoiding personal contact.

It can equally be seen as an extension of the self and thus the attention for the patient. In this, the task, however mundane, can be seen as a sacrament, a sign, of care, and of attention to the spirituality of the person. The task and its outcome may well have relevance to the life meaning of the person. Taking blood pressure, for instance, is something that most patients do not understand either technically or in relation to their condition. The nurse can help the patient make those connections, developing somatic awareness and enabling participation and the development of agency. The way in which the task is carried out also enables the nurse to communicate congruence, so that the task becomes an embodiment of her care (Campbell 1984).

This is seen most powerfully in Intensive Care. Seymour stresses the importance of bodily care in the context of so much technological support as embodying and depending upon integrity and trust (Seymour 2001, 147ff.). This in turn sets up an environment that communicates this to the family.

11. *Positive presence.* It is tempting to see spiritual care as primarily reactive, responding to the pain or dis-ease of the patient. It is equally important to be proactive and interactive, alive to the spiritual narrative of the patient as a matter of course. Many patients may have highly significant narratives that form the basis of real value, but do not appreciate them or feel permission to articulate them. The permission to reflect, narrate and appreciate is often not given in an explicit way. Their need is for the actively expressed interest and concern of the other, enabling their narrative to be articulated and appreciated.

12. *Presence as community and environment.* Presence is wider than the individual carer and may involve colleagues, family, and friends

enabling spiritual reflection. Walter Brueggemann describes the family as 'a communal network of memory and hope' (Brueggemann 1985, 8). This network enables the members to feel that they belong and also to 'locate themselves and discern their identities'. In a real sense good communities are an extension of such networks, which health-care workers can either lock into or in temporary ways create. A ward staff or primary care team represents such a community, the underlying meaning of which is expressed in the physical environment and organisation. There may be many different communities, formal and informal, which the patient becomes part of or generates, and which in turn generate meaning. One patient, for instance, after a long spell in hospital would return informally on a regular basis, for a short while, to be with the nursing staff. Other communities form between different patients and peer groups.

One health centre on the edge of a difficult housing estate developed a state of the art environment for antenatal treatment. Attendance, however, rapidly diminished because the smart environment and services focused solely on function and efficiency. The mothers-to-be felt that the meaning communicated by the environment was exclusive and diminishing. The emphasis on efficient service made many feel like cases rather than persons. The values implicit in the service and in antenatal classes were ones that were seen as middle-class and, more importantly, involved standards and perceptions that were either foreign to the patients or perceived as unattainable. They felt themselves to be alien and did not feel valued or that pregnancy itself was a valued and significant experience.

Thus, even the 'best' environments can discourage the patient from finding meaning in her experience or obscure the meaning of care which the team might wish to embody. The health centre had to alter its approach, and did so initially with great success, by increasing home visits and building up a bridge of trust. This in turn enabled greater narrative articulation and the sharing of both fears and values. In turn, the sessions at the health centre became more patient centred.

Empathic presence

The presence offered by the nurse is focused in empathy. As Kohut notes in the context of psychotherapy, 'the mere presence of empathy' has 'in a broad sense a therapeutic effect' (1982, 397). We can perhaps go further and say that such empathy provides a focus of care that enables the patient to reflect on and develop his spirituality in relation to the illness experienced. The nurses themselves thus become a critical medium for spirituality, possibly, even for a short time becoming the patient's ground of faith. In all this, the carer models the empathy for the patient to develop, an awareness of the self and others, the capacity to respond to the other and from this to develop life meaning.

The virtues

Just as there are virtues embodied in the spirituality of the patient there are virtues which underlie the practice of 'presence' (Campbell 1984, Bauman 1993, May 1994). These are summed up in Box 5.4.

Box 5.4 The virtues of nursing

- Unconditional positive regard (agape)
- Empathy
- Integrity
- Hopefulness
- Faithfulness
- Truthfulness
- Pride
- Humility

The foundation of the nurse's empathic presence is the unconditional regard which we referred to in Chapter 2 as a form of love, agape. This is recognised by religious and non-religious writers (Campbell 1984, Bauman 1993). It is not romantic love, but rather a disciplined form of moderated love. As such, it acts as the basis of a faithful, inclusive attitude towards the patient. This is critical in balancing the tendency of large organisations and bureaucracy to ignore the particularity of the patient. It also provides a sense of distance, which is crucial to a professional perspective, so that the nurse does not become over involved, can maintain judgement and competence, and can most effectively develop awareness of and empower the patient. It is precisely such moderated love which enables the virtues of truthfulness and faithfulness to be held together. Hence, it can be seen as the inclusive foundation of the virtues.

Integrity, summed up in Chapter 2, is itself a mixture of virtues, providing consistency and congruence. Narayanasamy suggests that fostering hope in the patient is central to spiritual care, and that this is attached to qualities such as serenity and 'light-heartedness' (1999). Such light-heartedness is connected to the naturalness of empathy noted in Chapter 2, a sense of being at ease with the self, where the nurse is not striving to care or please. Such striving can become very self-conscious and get in the way of communicating empathy.

Faithfulness and truthfulness are intimately connected, as noted above. Pride and humility are also connected, reflecting a proper pride in professional work together with strengths and creativity and a realistic assessment of limitations and weaknesses (Tangney 2000, 74). They also reflect the point that whilst the nurse may be an expert in terms of professional competence, she may be a novice in terms of the application of that competence. The patient, indeed, may become the key person to tell her how to apply them in a particular situation, to show her what he feels he needs.

In addition to such virtues May (1994) stresses the traditional virtues of:

- *Temperance.* Moderation and balance, not abstinence, which is important for effective judgement.
- *Wisdom.* Practical wisdom (*prudentia*) which involves a genuine openness to the past (*memoria*), present (*docilitas*) and future (*solertia*). Campbell (1984) develops this view of wisdom to include:
  Wisdom as folly, reaching out to the patient in her vulnerability, the opposite of a reliance on technology that simply seeks to reduce risk.
  Wisdom as simplicity, the opposite of complex technology.
  Wisdom as discretion, the capacity to know when to intervene and when to remain silent.
- *Justice.* The capacity to give equal regard and respect to all groups (distributive justice), and the capacity to develop and maintain contracts of care (commutative justice).
- *Courage.* Fortitude and resilience in withstanding pressures.

Several points can be noted about the virtues. Firstly, they are interrelated and interdependent, such as truthfulness and faithfulness, each of which is related to unconditional regard. Hence, Aristotle argues that we cannot develop them singly.

Secondly, virtues are linked to skills and technical knowledge (Narayanasamy 1999). Listening and communication skills, for instance, are tied to empathy. Empathy, in turn lies behind the skills of diagnosis and thus of applying technical knowledge most effectively. Competence and care are thus interrelated.

Thirdly, virtues are instrumental, that is at the service of a particular end. In the case of nursing, this is the good of the patient, both in terms of avoiding harm and of enabling positive good. Hence, the virtues are tied to a moral and spiritual vision of nursing.

Fourthly, virtues are not context or discipline specific. Empathy, for instance, cannot be simply identified as a counselling skill. It is a generic human quality which underlies all relationships.

Fifthly, virtues need to be learned and practised. They do not develop without such discipline (Megone and Robinson 2002). Morcover, the nature of virtues, including awareness of limitation and thus of interdependency, requires that they are learned and practised not in the capacity of the individual but in the community or team. The implications for training will be discussed in Chapter 10.

Conclusion

This chapter has outlined the process of spirituality in the context of healthcare. The key to facilitating that process lies not so much within task-specific skills as within the presence of the nurse, enabling reflection and empowerment of the patient. The role of the carer at this point is not to 'intervene' in the sense of solving a problem but rather to help the patient make sense of his illness experience in the light of his relational network and belief system.

The spirituality process is by nature cyclical and the patient may go through it several times over a period, depending on the nature of the illness and the crisis that he is facing. Equally, in extreme crisis the process may be very brief, with the patient showing immediate trust in the nurse, and focusing on unresolved conflicts of value and meaning. This process gives the nurse a framework to allow the patient to take stock at key moments of therapy. It also enables the patient's narrative to develop and any spiritual pain and distress or experience of transition to be addressed and worked through creatively. As discussed in Chapter 4, any assessment forms should facilitate such a process and not become ends in themselves. Hence, what is recorded can refer to evidence of spiritual problems and evidence of positive spirituality, for example, a strong sense of hope or purpose, and what this is based in. Such key words as hope, faith, purpose and reconciliation can be used by the nurse where appropriate, and are most effective when raised in response to the patient's narrative. The nurse can then help her reflect on the strong faith communities, and the points of hope.

The nurse in all this does not have to become an 'expert' in spirituality, still less in the practice of various religions. Where clear religious care is needed this should, with the agreement of the patient, be coordinated by the hospital chaplaincy. The nurse's focus is rather on the *particular* spiritual story of the patient, how she expresses spiritual meaning, whether religious or not. Such person-centred care helps the patient to own her own spirituality in the midst of the illness experience, and regardless of what she might feel she ought to believe or feel. In this the nurse is both expert and novice – expert in providing presence, and novice in the sense that each spiritual story is very different and involves real learning (Benner 1983). The nurse's role is that of skilled companion, accompanying the patient on her journey, and helping her, however sketchily, to map the spiritual region.

Questions and exercises

1. Sketch out how you might apply the stages of the spiritual process to one of your present patients.
2. From your own experience, recount any examples of patients' spiritual pain or distress; how you responded, and how this relates to the spiritual process.
3. How would you differentiate spiritual distress from clinical depression?
4. Is it possible to speak of love and professionalism together, or of mutuality in *healthcare?*
5. Reflect on and detail the professional virtues which you feel you embody. Test this out by sharing it with a colleague.

References

Aldridge, D. (2000) *Spirituality, Healing and Medicine* (London: Jessica Kingsley Publishers).

Bauman, Z. (1993) *Postmodern Ethics* (Oxford: Blackwells).

Beland, I.L. and Passos, J.Y. (1981) *Clinical Nursing: Pathophysiological and Psychosocial Approaches* (New York: Macmillan).

Benner, P.E. (1983) *From Novice to Expert: Excellence and Power in Clinical Nursing Practice* (Menlo Park, CA: Addison-Wesley Pub Co., Nursing Division).

Brueggemann, W. (1985) 'The family as world maker', *Journal of Preachers*, **7**.

Campbell, A. (1984) *Moderated Love* (London: SPCK).

Ellis, A. and Dryden, W. (1999) *The Practice of Rational Emotive Behaviour Therapy* (London: Free Association Books).

Finch, J. and Mason, J. (1993) *Negotiating Family Responsibilities* (London: Routledge).

Fowler, J. (1996) *Faithful Change* (Nashville: Abingdon).

Gillon, R. (2000) 'Refusal of potentially life saving blood transfusions by Jehovah's Witnesses: should doctors explain that not all JW's think it's religiously required?' *Journal of Medical Ethics*, **26**, 5, 299–301.

Griffin, A. (1983) 'A philosophical analysis of caring in nursing.' *Journal of Advanced Nursing* , **8**, 289–95.

Johnson, J. (1991) 'Learning to Live Again: The Process of Adjustment Following a Heart Attack' in J. Morse and J. Johnson (eds), *The Illness Experience; Dimensions of Suffering* (London: Sage), 13–88.

Kaufman, G. (1980) *Shame: The Power of Caring* (Washington: Schenkman).

Kohut, H. (1982) 'Introspection, empathy, and the semi-circle of mental health', in *International Journal of Psychoanalysis*, **663**, 397.

Lewis, D. (Spring 2000) 'Spiritual dimensions of therapeutic touch', *Sacred Space*, **1**, 3, 38–44.

Lyall, M. (1997) *The Pastoral Counselling Relationship: A Touching Place?* (Edinburgh: Contact Pastoral Monograph).

Margulies, A. (1989) *The Empathic Imagination* (New York: W.W. Norton).

May, W. (1994) 'The Virtues in a Professional Setting' in J. Soskice (ed.) *Medicine and Moral Reasoning* (Cambridge: Cambridge University Press).

Mayer, J. (1992) 'Wholly responsible for a part, or partly responsible for the whole? The concept of spiritual care in nursing.' *Second Opinion*, 26–55.

Megone, C. and Robinson, S. (2002) *Case Histories in Business Ethics* (London: Routledge).

Montague, B. (1986) *Touching: The Human Significance of the Skin*, 3rd edn. (New York: Harper and Row).

Martin, J.E. and Booth, J. (1999) 'Behavioural Approaches to Enhance Spirituality', in W. Miller (ed.), *Integrating Spirituality into Treatment* (Washington: American Psychological Association).

Narayanasamy, A. (1999) 'ASSET: a model for actioning spirituality and spiritual care education and training in nursing', *Nurse Education Today*, **19**, 274–85.

Nouwen, H.J. (1994) *The Wounded Healer* (London: Darton, Longman and Todd).

Osterman, P. and Schwartz-Barcott, D (1996) 'Presence: four ways of being there'. *Nursing Forum*, **31**, 2, 23–30.

Pattison, S. (1998) *A Critique of Pastoral Care* (London: SCM).

Pearson, A., Vaughan, B. and Fitzgerald, M. (1996) *Nursing Models for Practice*, 2nd edn. (Oxford: Butterworth-Heinemann).

Robinson, S. (2001) *Agape, Moral Meaning and Pastoral Counselling* (Cardiff; Aureus).

Seymour, J. (2001) *Critical Moments: Death and Dying in Intensive Care* (Buckingham: Open University Press).

Stern, D. (1985) *The Interpersonal World of the Infant* (New York: Basic Books).

Tangney, J. (Spring 2000) 'Humility: theoretical perspectives, empirical findings and directions for future research', *Journal of Social and Clinical Psychology*, **19**, 1.

Vanstone, W.H. (1977) *Love's Endeavour, Love's Expense* (London: Darton, Longman and Todd).

van der Ven, J. (1998) *Formation of the Moral Self* (Grand Rapids: Eerdmans).

Watson, J. (1979) *Nursing: The Philosophy and Science of Caring* (Colorado: Colorado Associated University Press).

Watson, J. (1990) 'Transpersonal Caring: A Transcendent View of Person, Health, and Healing', in M. Parker (ed.), *Nursing Theories in Practice* (New York: National League for Nursing).

6

From the Cradle . . .

All the world's a stage,
And all the men and women merely players;
They all have their exits and entrances;
And one man in his time plays many parts,
His acts being seven ages. At first the infant
Mewling and puking in the nurse's arms;
Then the whining school-boy with his satchel
And shining face, creeping like snail
Unwillingly to school. And then the lover
Sighing like furnace, with a woeful ballad
Made his mistress' eyebrow. Then a soldier
Full of strange oaths, and bearded like the pard,
Jealous in honour, sudden and quick in quarrel,
Seeking the bubble reputation
Even in the canon's mouth. And then the justice,
In fair round belly with good capon lin'd,
With eyes severe and beard of formal cut,
Full of wise saws and modern instances;
And so he plays his part. The sixth age shifts
Into the lean and slippered pantaloon
With spectacles on nose and pouch on side,
His youthful hose, well saved, a world too wide
For his shrunk shank; and his big manly voice,
Turning toward childish treble, pipes
And whistles in his sound. Last scene of all,
That ends this strange eventful history,
Is second childishness and mere oblivion;
Sans teeth, sans eyes, sans taste, sans everything.
(*As You Like It*, Act 2 scene 7)

Shakespeare's character Jaques presents us with a view of the life cycle that is both entertaining and sad. With each time of life we are faced with expectations and challenges, and the developing person has to constantly deal with the tensions between himself and others, her internal and external worlds – all of which contribute to spiritual meaning. Such meaning emerges as a function of physiological changes, family interaction, social role and expectation. The schoolboy, for instance, emulates the snail under pressure from peers, faced by anxiety about his future and by the boredom of a didactic teaching environment.

There is a danger of seeing these stages, which have often been socially validated, as hoops to get through or disasters to face, not least in the popular view of old age. There is equally a danger of seeing these stages as fixed. The whole point of spirituality, however, is that stages and roles are not simply accepted but that meaning is discovered through reflection on the different aspects of the self and other, enabling roles and relationships to genuinely reflect the person and his physical and social environment. As noted above, Fowler focuses on life stages in terms of developing life meaning and faith, and this provides a useful framework for viewing spirituality over time.

In this chapter, we will focus on three areas of nursing connected to this life cycle, childhood, childbirth (and thus beginnings of family) and old age. Much of the 'adult phase' has been covered in the previous chapter. We will look at the way in which life meaning and faith is developed in these times and how this might give indicators for spiritual care for those going through the experiences. At each stage the role of the family in spiritual development and care will be noted.

Stages of faith

We have already noted Fowler's definition of faith as a generic concept (1996, 54). Fowler proposes seven stages of faith that he locates at different ages (Box 6.1). These are based upon the work of Kohlberg who developed Piaget's work in the development of moral meaning and judgement into three phases each with two stages (Kohlberg 1984).

Box 6.1   Fowler's stages of faith

Undifferentiated or primal faith (infancy). This is a pre-linguistic and pre-conceptual stage in which the infancy begins to form a disposition towards an environment that is gradually being recognised as distinct from the self. This stage forms the cradle of trust or mistrust and of self worth based on unconditional or conditional grounds.

Intuitive-projective faith (ages 2–6). This stage builds upon the development of language and the imagination. With no cognitive operations that could test perceptions and thus reverse beliefs, children grasp experience in and through powerful images. The child is thus attentive to ritual and gesture.

Mythic-literal faith (ages 7–12). This sees a reliance on stories and rules, and the narrative that is implied in the family faith experience. The lived faith of the family through practice, ritual, and belief is valued in a concrete and literal sense. This can also involve some testing of the story's meaning.

Synthetic-conventional faith (ages 12– 21). The child in this stage moves on to search for 'a story of my stories'. This looks to the development of life meaning and the person's particular life meaning. At one level this is a product of the development of new cognitive abilities referred to by Piaget as 'early formal operations'. At the same time the developing life meaning is built up of the original faith system, and is thus compiled of conventional elements.

This faith is often accompanied by a strong sense of the need to keep together the faith group as a priority.

Individuative-reflective faith (ages 21-30). Faith meaning is more personally chosen and believed. There is an awareness that one's view is different from others, and can be expressed in abstract terms. The faith developed at this stage is for the sake of the person and of making sense of her life in family or community. It is not developed primarily for the unity of the family.

Conjunctive faith (ages 31–40). In this stage many of the different ideas and perspectives, and the resulting tensions and paradoxes are worked at. Previously not examined these are now held together in balance, with an openness to the perspectives of others. This sees a deepening of appreciation of the complex nature of faith and life meaning.

Universalising faith (age 40 and beyond). This is not so much a stage of faith as a category of individuals who have developed a coherent faith which is grounded in the 'Other', and which enables them to live unfettered by self concern. Membership of this group is very rare and includes, for instance, Mahatma Ghandi and Luther King.

Criticisms of the stage approach include arguments that its is too cognitive/intellectual, and too individualistic. Others argue that the stages are normative with the later stages seen as superior to the early ones. Others question the adequacy of the research (Parks 1992).

Firstly, however, though Fowler sees the stages like Kohlberg, to be invariant, sequential and hierarchical – in other words they have to be gone through in turn – he does not advocate that they be taken too rigorously. They are a useful tool for noting characteristics of faith development, and can help the practitioner to be aware of needs. Secondly, Fowler does argue for a broader rational view of faith including affective knowledge. The intellectual component of spirituality does not make it a superior form. Thirdly, he argues that the needs expressed in the earlier stages are not left behind. Moreover, as noted in the early chapters, those spiritual needs may be most apparent in times of crisis or transition. The faith of the earlier stage is carried over and reworked into the new faith. Indeed, without this, any sense of affective continuity is gone.

This sense of the growth of spirituality that maintains the different styles of faith is developed further by John H. Westerhoff III. Westerhoff also argues that the different styles of faith are added, not left behind. The earlier style of faith can be activated at any time should there be need for it. It is a genuine revisiting of the basic faith.

Westerhoff characterises faith in terms of four styles:

- *Experienced faith.* This is the active and responding faith of early childhood, experienced in the child's relationship to others. This style would be the equivalent of Fowler's first two stages.
- *Affiliative faith.* This is the belonging faith of later childhood and early adolescence which is dominated by the authority of the community.
- *Searching faith.* Common in late adolescence and early adulthood this involves: the development of critical testing; experimentation with alternative understanding or practices; the need for commitment to persons or causes. This can give the impression of inconsistency and fickleness.
- *Owned faith.* This involves the integration of faith into a perspective which is owned by the person for her sake and which is expressed in ideas and practice (Westerhoff 1976).

Westerhoff's approach can be fruitfully used in any practical application of Fowler's faith stages. Firstly, it is possible to see patients who give evidence of many of the different faith stages, depending on context. Illness, as noted in the last chapter, may cause the person to move to an early simplistic faith, often expressed in religious terms, when a more complex faith is maintained with certain relationships. Secondly, as we shall see in death and dying it is possible to move comparatively quickly from an early stage of faith through to stages six and seven in achieving a positive acceptance. In all this, it is critical for the nurse to accept what might seem to be simply regression.

Childhood

> A child's spirit is like a child,
> you can never catch it by running after it;
>   you must stand still, and,
> for love, it will soon itself come back (Arthur Miller, *The Crucible*).

Primal faith

At the core of this stage is the possibility of abandonment. In a pre-conceptual world the infant needs frequent reassurances about the presence of significant others, and the development of some framework of meaning which will mediate that. Stern notes how this is established through the development of different stages of the self, even in infancy. In particular, he argues for the emergence of the subjective self that is discovered through shared attention and shared affect. Through shared attention, nine-month olds can point to or follow the imaginary line from the pointing finger of the mother or significant others, looking in the direction of the point. Stern notes then 'a triangulation between two people and an object of their mutual interest and reference' (Stern 1985, 129).

Even more important is the sharing of affect. Stern notes research which suggests that by nine months infants are aware of the congruence between the facial expression of another and their own affective state. If the parent's face expresses anxiety about a new or dangerous situation the baby will also express this and turn away from the danger. Because it occurs in novel situations this appears to be more than associational imitation. Stern refers to this as 'affect atunement', a complex, dynamic and ongoing operation which involves the caretaker recognising the affective state of the child and communicating that recognition. Again this involves more than simple imitative repetition. It is a communication through tone and bodily attitude that the parent is 'in resonance, in synchronicity' with the experience of the baby. Atunement of this kind falls short of full empathy in that it does not involve the mediation of cognitive processes. Nonetheless, there is the development of a strong awareness of the other through affective and somatic knowledge. Already at this stage then there is the development of a strong pre-cognitive spirituality, communicating meaning and value through affective and somatic knowledge development.

It is very tempting to view children's spirituality in an idealised or romantic fashion. William Wordsworth, fuelled by a belief in heavenly pre-existence, believed that the child was by definition more spiritual and thus was the best educator of adults. As the child grows, so it is in danger of losing this natural spirituality:

> Heaven lies about us in our infancy!
> Shades of the prison-house begin to close
>   Upon the growing Boy,
> But he beholds the light, and whence it flows,
>   He sees it in his joy. (William Wordsworth, 'Intimations of Immortality from Recollections of Early Childhood')

Burkhardt is less romantic in suggesting that children 'live in their spirit more than adults' being less inhibited and more intuitive about spiritual matters. She goes on to suggest that the child has a greater capacity for searching for meaning in life and a sense of relationship to 'self, other, nature and God or Universal Force' (Burkhardt 1991, 34). Perhaps the key point about this view is that the child in infancy, and to some degree throughout childhood, is precisely more open to the other and to the environment in which she exists, and that this is not some mystical 'spirit' but rather a deep awareness communicated through the affective and somatic sharing noted above. It is this openness which is at the base of the searching and exploration which is associated with childhood. As Berryman notes 'young children live at the limit of their experience most of time' (Berryman 1985, 34). A great deal of experience is new and thus there is a real sense of wonder and awe as they transcend their selves and their situations.

It is in this sense that we can speak of an intuitive spirituality, that is one which is open to the other and which discovers meaning in and through relation to the other, and learns faith and hope through that relationship, based upon the somatic and affective sharing. Such spirituality is just as important as the more conceptual approach to spirituality. That we should be surprised by this is purely a matter of being conditioned into accepting the cognitive domination of the western world. In this respect, the child does have a lot to teach us about the spirit.

This affective and somatic way of knowing is very powerful, and acts as the basis of trust. However, no affect atunement can be perfect.

The less the affect atunement the less the baby is confident of the support of the caretaker and the less able, eventually, to open up to the other.

Spiritual care in this stage is above all mediated by touch and felt presence. The confirmation of presence is something which may have to involve frequent visits, and simply being with the baby in a way which enables synchronicity. At the same time, this level of spiritual care may not be possible, and is best given in any case by the parent. This underlines the importance of involving the family in care.

Intuitive-projective faith

This stage shows the development of magical spirituality and imaginative thinking. The child has a 'naive cognitive egocentricism' which sees the world still to some degree as revolving around him. This can lead to a very literal view of cause and effect, with consequences for the child's view of responsibility. He may feel that his behaviour is in some way responsible for the illness itself. He may feel responsible for his parents and family. The resulting sense of guilt or shame might lead him to naively sacrificial behaviour, for example, not communicating the experience of pain in order not to disturb his parents. Such guilt may be a sign of confusion and fear about the experience of the illness or a sign of a dysfunctional spiritual relationship with parents. This inevitably means that the family needs real involvement in the treatment (see below), given that the child at this stage is strongly influenced by the 'examples, mood, actions and stories of the visible faith of primary related adults' (O'Brien 1998, 58). It is important for the care team and the parents to work closely together so that the child is aware of consistency in valuation, and that the basic spiritual needs are fulfilled.

If the child is in hospital there needs to be experience which gives him a sense of belonging and contribution, visible or symbolic ways in which he can be valued, allowing, if necessary, the emergence of the verbal self. It is important to develop rituals and timetables which keep reminding him of his valued place in the group.

Even at this early stage it is important for spiritual care to allow the child to articulate her situation, through play, drawing pictures and so on. O'Brien suggests that it is critical to enter the world of the child and allow him to begin to make sense of the experience. However, the carer should not expect major conceptual reflection to occur. The stories and the articulation will be simply affirming the child's value.

This has the effect of developing faith and also of ensuring that the child does not see himself as responsible for his condition or related crises. In addition to this it is of importance to have an accepting, bright environment, to which the child might contribute, and thus have the contribution affirmed.

The mythic-literal faith

This involves real growth. Firstly there is a move from the simplistic retribution approach in which good and bad are simply rewarded. This means that the child is beginning to operate with some ambiguities. However, there is still no depth of analysis. She does most of her reporting in terms of narrative and story, which are not primarily reflective. There is a development of 'stories, beliefs and observances that symbolise belonging to his or her own faith community' (Fowler 1996, 60).

There is still therefore the need to develop and maintain a sense of corporate spirituality in the family, or the faith community or in the ward. This may be a time of celebration of the group as at meal times. The sharing of food has a strong sense of basic spiritual communion which has often been picked up by the formal religions. This may involve nurses sharing meals with the children, and children being involved in the distribution of the meals. A consumerist approach to distribution can stress a more individualist ethos and lead to a missed opportunity to affirm or communicate a sense of otherness.

In all this, communication of truth remains important. Handzo advocates frank and direct communication (Handzo 1990, 17) There is no doubt that given the strong somatic and affective awareness of the child that she will quickly pick up any incongruence of behaviour or deceptions. One experienced paediatric nurse, quoted in O' Brien's book, sums up this capacity of children: 'You have to have a spirituality which projects total acceptance because, if not, the kids can read right through it; anything that's a facade or put on, they know it in a heart beat' (O'Brien 1998, 213).

This insight is confirmed in the work of Bluebond-Langner. She observed terminally ill children faced by the nursing staff and their family who were colluding in not telling the children about their condition. The children quickly noted the deception, even the underlying meaning of management in the ward, such as in the placement of beds (Bluebond-Langner 1978, 136). They did not, however, challenge the staff or the parents but rather continued to maintain the deception and began to take responsibility for the care of the family in various ways. The patient peer group supported each other and discussed the dynamics of the staff and parents' interaction.

This intimate connection between truth as veracity and the truth as fidelity remains critical. Any frankness or directness has to be in the context of that fidelity – which assures the child that the care is still with them. Equally, it is important to see the truth in relation to the social environment of the child – be that ward or school. This may involve a long process of building up trust.

In addition to the communication of value and the ethos of care, Fulton and Moore argue for the development of 'therapeutic play', which enables the child to develop imagination and articulation (Fulton and Moore 1995, 24). This can generate an understanding of the child's perception of spirituality in the context of her illness. They also argue for the developing of shared story telling or keeping diaries to help the child explore the meaning of her life. As Stern (1985) notes, with the development of the verbal self, this stage of articulation involves statement and repeated statement. Creative use of art can also enable reflection on and confirmation of such meaning, with painting focused on family and history, and with time for reflection on the content.

Synthetic-conventional faith

Adolescence involves massive physical, emotional and cognitive changes, making the child more aware of herself (as a being with interiority) and others. The adolescent is capable of using and appreciating abstract concepts, and so beginning to develop meta-cognition, thinking about how we think, and reflecting on meaning. This leads to the emergence of 'mutual interpersonal perspective taking' (Fowler 1996, 61), an awareness of how others see the self and how the self sees others. In turn this lead to a preoccupation with personality, both as style and substance, and with what others think of and how they value the person.

The search for identity then becomes a matter of trying to hold together the new ideas, feelings, ideals, loyalties, and commitments which emerge from the more self-conscious awareness. In search of this sense of selfhood the adolescent tries on different roles, mostly those which are worn by adults who have proven trustworthy and who trust the adolescent. Hence, as Erikson writes, she 'looks most fervently for men and women and ideas to have faith in, which also means men and women and ideas in whose service it would seem worthwhile to prove oneself trustworthy' (Erikson 1968, 128).

The major limitation to this stage is the lack of what Fowler refers to as 'third-person perspective taking'. This means that 'in its dependence upon others for confirmation and clarity about its identity and meaning to them, the self does not yet have a transcendental perspective from which it can see and evaluate self – other relations' (Fowler 1996, 62).

All of this can lead to the taking of interests and causes, many of which are not thought through and many of which involve contradictions. This may well also lead to different beliefs, frequently and powerfully held. There is real tension between new ideas and the need to conform. Equally, because of this searching element, there is underlying uncertainty about different beliefs and on occasions rebellion against these beliefs, and the expression of anger.

The spiritual care response includes, firstly, to check out the beliefs, allowing articulation. Secondly, unusual signs such as withdrawal from social activities or nightmares should be looked out for. Thirdly, it's important to stay with the person in her contradictions, and also to keep a consistent response. Fourthly, care should be taken to give the adolescent space in which to think through feelings and ideas. Bluebond-Langner observed that where there were no spaces on hospital wards children were apt to create their own spaces and use these for peer group discussion (Bluebond-Langner 1978, 10; Wong 1997, 472). Finally, views of the illness itself should be explored, looking especially for beliefs about the patient being responsible for the illness.

Handzo argues that the spiritual needs of the child are much the same as the adult (Handzo 1990, 17). The key difference is in the way in which they are fulfilled, and in particular in the way that encourages articulation, and involvement, without the kind of cognitive reflection that might be expected from an adult. As noted above, any part of the faith stages may be revisited by the child. In addition, any adult may well revisit them either as a result of trauma or of a search for meaning which is secure and which avoids handling the possible ambiguities in the experience of illness.

Spiritual assessment of the child will thus be much the same as that of an adult. Such assessment should note in particular:

- Underlying problems which may give rise to questions about meaning, such as loneliness related to isolation from the peer group and interruption of school activities. This in turn for older children may lead to anxieties about keeping up with classes and even about the question of the future beyond school.

- The importance of spending time with the family as key givers of spiritual care and as possibly in need of spiritual care themselves. Thus, it is important to assess the relationship of the child to the family – how they generate meaning. In particular, difficulties in communication in the family should be noted. The support of other groups, not least peer groups, should also be assessed. Wong suggests a family assessment interview, including reference to personal religious beliefs and practices, the formal religious orientation of the family, and how their religion influences their view of illness (Wong 1997, 90). Whilst religious questions tend to dominate, it does provide a framework which could refer to a wider spirituality.

- Van Heukelem-Still also includes questions about how the child feels about her illness; how she behaves when frightened; who provides support in times of trouble (Van Heukelem-Still 1984, 5).

Religion

This can be an important aspect of the care of children, not least because children can ask direct questions about God. Firstly, it is important to remember that children also have religious rights, and that they should be given opportunity to exercise them. Secondly, a strong sense of positive and creative spirituality can emerge from the religious experience of the child, and the religious and family community to which the child belongs. Thirdly, care must be taken not to manipulate a child towards a particular religious faith. This does not mean that the child cannot explore religious faith by speaking to a nurse about her personal faith. However, to avoid the possibility of even the kindest pressure it would be important to take the child's questions seriously and include the family and possibly a chaplain in the dialogue.

Hay argues that the spirituality of the child involves a deep-rooted and natural awareness of the other. Over against this are historically-created social pressures which develop what might be called spiritual shame – shame associated with owning or articulating awareness of others and the development of that meaning (Hay 1998). At the root of this is affect and need shame – fear of expressing feeling or admitting need, and thus dependency.

Hay suggests four things that teachers can do to nurture spirituality, each of which can be of use to the nurse or hospital teacher, however long they have with the patient (Hay, 1998, 163 ff.):

1. *Helping children keep an open mind.* At the very least this can mean gently challenging closed thinking or stereotyping which automatically cuts the self off from others.
2. *Exploring ways of seeing.* This might mean use of art work, or modelling different perspectives, or encouraging the child to identify with the figures who he least likes in a story.
3. *Encouraging immediate personal awareness.* This may involve the encouragement of the child's own narrative. It may involve exercises that help the child to focus on even the most insignificant task, such as eating an apple (p. 170). In both cases the child is revisiting something about herself, with reflection which enables everyday life to be 'known for the first time'.
4. *Encouraging awareness of the social and political dimensions of spirituality.* This does not mean classes in politics. It involves making connections between the self and its social institutional environment, noting how they affect each other.

Such strategies give the patient permission to develop and express spirituality in relation to their immediate illness and beyond.

Spiritual needs and the dying child

Such spirituality is critical to nurture in children who are dying. The needs of parents, fears of staff and social attitudes towards death can precisely build barriers that disable the child from addressing his situation. Once again it is important not to generalise. Any child's awareness of death and the meaning that she can take from that will depend upon the context of her family, her illness and so on. Nonetheless, there is good evidence that young children can hold a meaningful dialogue on death, involving quite sophisticated concepts (Sherr 1995, 253). As Sherr puts it, 'Very often the limiting factors for children relate not to their ability to understand but to the willingness of adults to explain' (Sherr, 252). This must not be seen as a criticism of the adult, after all, death cannot be 'explained'. In any case the adult, is trying to deal with his own feelings at the same time. Hence, the health carer has to take into account both the child and the family and response to both involves a more focused approach to spiritual care.

The child

Kate Faulkner suggests the following guidelines for being with children (Faulkner 1997):

- Be 'explicit and literal' in responding to children's questions about dying and death. Euphemisms should be avoided. As noted, children are sensitive to adult attempts to deceive either the child or themselves, and when the truth is not shared can interpret this in many different ways. They may see the reluctance to speak about death as a sign of fear on the nurse's part or a sign of disapproval or rejection. The carer is not just uncomfortable with death but with this person who is dying. It may even indicate to them that they are somehow responsible for the illness.
- Be flexible in approach. At the base of such a flexibility has to be the establishment of presence which will enable the child to see that she is accepted as herself even in the midst of the turmoil of feelings about dying. Bluebond-Langner writes of how she spent long hours simply being with children before they accepted her. In one case this involved sitting through a television programme with the child, without speaking. At the end of the programme the child turned to her and began to ask questions (Bluebond-Langner 1978, 247).
- Be sensitive to non-verbal communication. This involves the development of empathy which demonstrates that the carer recognises underlying feelings and is still prepared to remain for the patient. Just as the child feels pressure not to speak about death, still less her death, so she may feel acute pressure not to express the related feelings. Distress expressed by children of course can have a profound effect upon the carer, not least because the natural reaction is to try to solve the problem which causes the distress. Inability to do so can lead to feelings of inadequacy or failure. All the more important then that the carer should allow the expression of feeling and simply remain with the child. Concern for 'solutions' will only get in the way of the child's addressing the experience of dying, and beginning to find meaning in it. That meaning will be a function of questions about the dying process, such as 'will it be painful?', 'will I die by myself?', about past relationships, not least about feelings of guilt, about present role, and about what happens after death both to the person and to the family. Once a rapport has been established with the child, then she is given permission to ask the awkward questions and express the awkward, disturbing feelings.

Equally, the nurse must feel free to declare her own ignorance or limitations. The nurse, for instance, even from personal faith cannot answer the question 'why me?'. This approach will enable the care to be child centred, so that she is responsible for working out the meaning of her death in her context and experience.

O'Brien (1998) notes the importance of entering the faith world of the child – hence being sensitive to age-related developmental stages. At the same time the nurse should avoid trying to tie behaviour down to 'what is expected' in any stage. Even young children might want to know quite detailed medical knowledge. Equally, though in the younger stages of faith a great deal revolves around the self this does not preclude real concern for others. Bluebond-Langner reports concern from children for their parents which aimed to reduce their anxiety. It is precisely such concern that can give the child immediate purpose.

- Respect the child's right for privacy. The impulse of the carer to do everything for the patient is intensified with a dying child. This can lead to 'over-care' and the result that there is not 'sacred space' for the child to be by herself, apart from the demands of adults.

The family

Stiles notes five ways in which the nurse can provide support to the family (Stiles 1990):

- *Being.* Simply sitting with the family and listening.
- *Doing.* This involves explaining, reassuring and comforting.
- *Knowing.* Sharing an awareness of the dying process and enabling them to understand.
- *Receiving and giving.* Developing a mutuality. This recognises the difficulty of the nursing task and the nurse's own need for support.
- *Welcoming a stranger'.* Inviting the family to take steps to prepare for the death. This can range from reflection on feelings through to practical issues such as finance.

The nurse acts as the 'shining stranger', someone who is both warm but not actually one of the family, who the family look forward to seeing and who radically alters their behaviour when there. The very presence of a stranger in this context helps the family to develop or maintain skills of communication, enabling them to listen more carefully to each other. This context also allows the family members to express their feelings. The underlying pain and anger will often result in family members becoming angry at even small problems of care. Once again, it is important to enable the expression of such feelings. Stiles notes the importance of taking advantage of all opportunities in establishing this care for the family.

Once the family is able to work through the meaning this has for them, including the feelings of each member, from pain to inadequacy and guilt, then they can begin to focus on the family spirituality, something which perhaps they had not been consciously aware of for some time and begin to embody that in the care of the child. One father whose 19-year old student son was on a ventilator and who was close to death spoke of how the family had begun to rediscover each other,

> We have been so busy in the last few years that we became out of touch with each other. Of course I valued my children and my wife! But I wasn't really aware of them. In this past week its been like getting to know each of them from scratch, a new wife and two new daughters. It's been painful but now we are ready for my son.

A well-functioning family provides a strong community for the development and maintenance of spirituality, fulfilling basic faith provisions:

* *sustenance and security*, developing faith stages one and two;
* *communion and belonging*, enabling faith stages three and four;
* *a supportive framework for autonomous behaviour*, facilitating faith stage five;
* *the assurance of life meaning and value*, not least through participation in family rituals, such as meals and gatherings, which ensure meaning and orientation (Nugent 1991, Levy Schiff 1994, Fowler 1996).

In any long term work with a family, the nurse can assess how far it is providing this framework and help them in a small ways to develop some of these functions in relation to the patient. For instance, regular meetings over coffee, however brief, to update the family on the patient's condition can enable the development of shared meaning.

Childbirth

Childbirth is a critical boundary experience. It opens up whole new areas of spirituality for the parents and relatives. The spirituality of the mother is at the heart of this care, and her story may be shaped by many different factors. We will focus on the growing existential awareness of the foetus, the development of meaning that may be mediated by different meta-narratives or myths, the existential meaning found in childbirth, the relearning of relationships at the heart of the transition in pregnancy and childbirth, and finally the response of the midwife and the learning of faith and hope.

The foetus

Hall argues for the importance of this growing awareness of the foetus as other. Whilst some mothers choose to close off the relationship with the foetus, especially where there may be some risk to pregnancy (McGeary, 1994), many have a sense of an other that is part of them but which also has a distinct, particular spirit (Salter 1987). It may not be awareness of that which is discrete other, but for that very reason the relationship has some degree of 'mystery' (Bergum 1989). Technology, such as ultrasound, reinforces some sense of the other (Rothman 1994).

Because of the extraordinary nature of the relationship, it is hard to find empirical evidence that can confirm the precise nature of this relationship or the effects the mother has upon the foetus (Hall 2001, 51). Nonetheless, there is good evidence of the emotional connection made by both parents through researched response to pre and perinatal death. For most who experience this, where the child is wanted, there is strong experience of bereavement, leading to a felt need to have ritual to mark, and find meaning in, the loss of the foetus, such as baptism and funeral (Pye 2001). The following case exemplifies this.

One couple who had been trying for a child for some time found on their second hospital visit that the foetus had died in the womb. The staff knew of their great desire for a child and were initially unsure about how to respond. The couple decided not to have the foetus evacuated at that point but to come back the next day. 'It was important that we say goodbye to him' they said. To do this they had to 'hold him', and to 'feel him' there before them. It was a recognition of the specialness of that being and the narrative and the hopes they had already shared. It was in a real sense recognition of the 'sacredness' of the other. To effect this they went to what was for them a sacred place, an extraordinary collection of rocks and boulders on the moors where they were acutely aware of an accepting presence. 'It was there that we "held" him and the rocks held us'. When they returned to out-patients they were able to share with the staff a sense of meaning which helped the staff to care for them. It did not get rid of the pain but brought meaning and dignity to them and to the foetus. This was a good example of awareness of different others coming together in an experience of suffering and enabling the patient and family to find meaning together. It was also a good example of the sensitivity of the nursing staff, in allowing the narrative and ritual to be developed.

Meta-narratives and myths

Many different factors may cause a relationship to be developed with the foetus, not least the myths or meta-narrative which may give or even impose a sense of meaning on the experience of pregnancy and childbirth. The meta-narratives, or overarching stories, of religious spirituality provide role models such as the Virgin Mary. Some writers suggest that Mary provides both a strong sense of meaning and coping mechanisms in child birth (Magana and Clark, 1995; Hall 2001, 29). Among the suggested reasons for the success of belief systems of this kind is that such faith gives the women a strong sense of self esteem and an extended network of other women with similar values. They also provide a framework of meaning for the pain endured in labour. Such meta-narratives cannot be perfect and run the danger, as we shall see, of being abused. Nonetheless, they can provide a framework of meaning which will give a mother a real sense of continuity and comfort as she experiences the transition of childbirth.

The term myth is one which has come to mean a commonly held belief which is untrue or without foundation. In fact, myths are powerful social and cultural beliefs that offer life meaning and purpose, often mediated by tradition or family rather than by any formal institutions such as religions. For the man, there is the myth of the machismo male, whose purpose is to win bread and sustain the family. This myth can often be sustained by the man's family who might offer negative feedback if he is more involved in the baby's care, or by a lack of role models (Cowan and Cowan 1992). For the woman, there is the more complex myth which presents her as the primary care giver and homemaker. At one level this is sustained by a biological 'imperative' with changes in hormone levels which 'create powerful propensities in the new mother *to be recruited* into the child's nurture' (Fowler 1992, 321) At another level there is the socio-cultural picture of the perfect mum who instinctively knows what to do and who is multi-skilled, able to nurture her baby, keep her man and run the home. The strength of such myths can be very powerful in the mother's search for meaning and value, and sometimes so powerful that she is not aware of the extent of their influence.

Such myths tend, by their nature, to be conditional, affirming the value of the mother if she lives up to them. As such, they can reinforce *perfectionist shame*, shame at not living up to the expectations of significant others, or *affect shame*, shame at expressing feelings such as fear, pain, or uncertainty (Robinson 1998). All of this can reinforce the feeling that myths should not be challenged.

Existential awareness

Alongside such meta-narrative and myth are the more natural, immediate and existential ways of finding meaning. Hall notes a number of cross-cultural studies which point to a broad, humanistic sense of the sacred or transcendence in the experience (Hall 2001, 30). There are strong somatic, affective, cognitive and cultural elements. The body experiences both vulnerability, exacerbated by pain, and great potency. The potency involves the connection between birth and sexuality, and also the action of pro-creation. The idea and experience of such creation cannot be summed up in biological or psychological terms alone. It is not surprising that some religions use the image of birth to express the mysteries and power of creation *per se* (Hall 2001, 33). All this can lead to an experience of transcendence which puts the mother in touch with her creative self or even 'wild self' (Estes 1992). For some, this leads to a strong sense of connection to the earth and nature (Kahn 1995, King 1993). Others seek the spiritual expression of New Age, and alternative medicine.

Relearning relationships

In the midst of all this experience the mother has many different relationships, all of which vie with each other to specify what the ultimate meaning of childbirth is. These include the growing foetus, the baby, the partner, the extended family, with many, sometimes conflicting views of childbirth and the protagonists' roles in relation to that. Such relationships explore and test out meaning and purpose, including major themes about the nature and practice of care, dependence and interdependence. How will the mother relate to an utterly dependent being? How will the new triadic relationship develop? How will care be shared? Developing life meaning in relation to the experience of pregnancy may involve renegotiating relationships with several different people or groups, and with this finding new grounds for faith. The danger lies in the mother developing faith solely in herself and feeling that sharing responsibility with others is a failure.

The support of the midwife

The task of the midwife is to provide competent and supportive presence and, to accompany the woman on her spiritual journey. The midwife may get closer to her in that journey than many of her family, and enable this to be a time of real hope and faith, as summed up in Box 6.2.

Box 6.2   Spiritual support in pregnancy and childbirth

- *Enables the patient to articulate her narrative.* An important aspect of this is to allow her to reflect on and develop her existential awareness of others, not least of the foetus.
- *Enables the patient to reflect on underlying meaning, value and feeling.* This will allow the mother to affirm awareness of the meta-narratives or myths that provide positive support or to examine the value and meaning conflicts that may emerge. This may give the mother the space to deconstruct negative myths (Oakley 1980). This is more than a cognitive exercise. Studies confirm that many mothers have a fixed view of the successful family which they feel that they ought to conform to and that this is often not addressed until they are aware that others share their sense of doubt, or other feelings (Oakley 1979, Painter 1995). Hence the importance of enabling groups that can explore meaning, including disappointments and difficulties, or feelings of failure, such as after a caesarean section. Such groups might be formed for men or women, or in some cases for both (Hall 2001, 43). Page notes the importance of working with men to develop empathy (2000). This in turn enables spiritual meaning to be further explored.
- *Enables connections, both between the different people involved in the process, and between emotions, the body, ideas and culture.* It may be that negative or conditional myths, for instance, discourage the mother from developing a full awareness of the somatic experience of pregnancy and childbirth. This support may be provided through empathic touch. Kitzinger (1997) suggests the importance of touch during childbirth, from *supportive* to *comfort* touch. She also suggests, where appropriate, that is, where requested, the possibility of *blessing* touch, where the birth attendant may use physical contact accompanied by prayers or other spiritual rituals, or forms of massage to help the birth process.

- *Provides secure containment in the process of transition*, especially where this may be confusing. This provides continuity, enabling the woman to develop meaning in her own time.
- *Enables the patient to develop positive views of purpose, faith and hope.* This is often connected to the relearning of relationships. It may involve letting go of an old role, such as dependent daughter, and learning to develop faith in her mother more as friend, or letting go of a conditional faith in her family, and finding more unconditional faith, based in a range of people, including siblings. Part of this might involve suggesting the development in families of rituals that affirm values and meaning from simple family gatherings to baptism celebrations. The more that the parents and significant others are involved in these and their planning, the more meaning is developed through the process. Hope in pregnancy and childbirth is located in several areas, from the hope for a live and well baby to hope of being a good parent (Hall 2001, 35). However, some see hope in the much broader and even ultimate context of leaving a lasting mark on humanity, close to the Hebrew view that immortality is gained through children (*ibid.*). The midwife can help the mother focus on and develop such hopes, giving the experience lasting significance.

Gender and spirituality

Clearly gender issues are very much part of spirituality and it is not surprising that feminism has developed a strong sense of spirituality – as a human and religious dimension. Ursula King describes how the feminist movement has turned away from the traditional dualistic views of the spirit and body as separate. 'Instead they understand spirituality as the search for wholeness and integration, for transformation and celebration' (King 1999, 151). This provides the basis for critique of the old patriarchal attitude to gender, work, family life, the environment and so on.

Such a spirituality can celebrate the experience of childbirth and parenthood as biological, sexual and personal fulfilment and hold these together with the social view of birth which sees the parents and the extended family and friends as sharing in the experience and the tasks. It can hold together both the joy and the pain.

Feminism reminds us not to treat stages of spirituality as targets or standards. King refers to spirituality as both a 'way of seeing' and a 'dance' (King 1999, 153). The way of seeing is precisely empathy, looking beyond stereotypes and second-hand myths to the reality. The metaphor of dance picks up beautifully the dynamic of spirituality as awareness and responsiveness.

Feminism enabled the development of spirituality that moves away for themselves (Pryce 1990).

'oman to find her own voice
? same can be true of men, if
:t and challenge stereotyping

Ageing and the elderly

With ageing comes the many losses which are part of life. It can also involve the specific problem of dementia. We will now focus on both these areas.

The spirituality of ageing

Ageing is an ambiguous process. It is seen both as decline and loss, and also a striking time of growth and development. While each person ages in different ways, shared characteristics include impaired vision and hearing; physical changes in hair, skin and teeth; decreased appetite; skeletal changes due to arthritis and osteoporosis and a lowering in energy levels. These are often accompanied by social changes including the loss of work or community networks and loss of friends or of the immediate family. The world of the elderly is often a monochrome one, with mainly people of their own age in their community. Financial concerns, including the loss of work income, and the loss of social roles in work or play and the capacity to contribute and make a difference, all cause the world of the elderly to shrink further. This can lead to depression and anxiety.

Ageing, however, need not be viewed as decline. Sensory and psychomotor losses may be balanced by increased verbal capacities through the 50s and 60s. Whilst hearing problems are debilitating, they only occur in 26 per cent of over 75s. Along with the increase in reaction time is an increase in creative endeavours through the 60s and 70s. Cognitive losses are largely the cause of illnesses, not of ageing *per se* (Benson 1990, 16).

Jewell notes six areas of concern in the ageing process and in the spirituality of ageing (Jewell, 1999):

1. *Isolation.* A basic human need is to belong, to be a part of a meaningful community. The elderly person's place in established communities becomes under threat, and alternative communities, such as nursing homes, are often monochrome and away from mainstream communities.

2. *Affirmation*. Roles in various networks affirm the worth of the person, the need to nurture and to be needed. A sense of dignity and worth is tied to some sense of being able to contribute. At one level, the role of grandparent becomes critical as the provision of nurture for others.

3. *Celebration*. Jewell argues that this a 'natural instinct for people irrespective of age'. Celebrations root significant events and contributions into the narrative of the group or community. They form part of that narrative and are also a way sharing reflections on the worth of those who are involved in the celebrations, whether as a group or as individuals, or on the ideas and purposes which are being celebrated. Celebrations in old age can easily be lost or be simply individualised, as in birthdays.

4. *Confirmation*. Old age can be a time of profound doubts. There is a need to have the sense of self confirmed, something than can only be achieved through expressing a narrative which is clearly listened to and valued.

5. *Reconciliation*. Even though death may not be imminent, later life brings to mind the unfinished business, the relationships which have been lost or which need mending.

6. *Integration*. Societal views of old age tend to deny the possibility of integration and wholeness. Not only is the old person marginalised, her physical capacities are also denied, from the need for sexual expression and intimate touch to the capacity for energetic sport. The elderly are also often assumed to be less cognitively able. With all these aspects of the person 'denied', the opportunities for the elderly to draw together the different aspects of somatic, affective and cognitive knowledge can be limited.

In addition to Jewell's points we may add *autonomy*. Films, such as *Cocoon* (Howard, 1985), portray a real concern to retain some sense of independence, albeit alongside an awareness of limitations. For many elderly there is a need to define and negotiate this independence and retain autonomy.

Of course, these are spiritual needs common to all ages, but with particular perspective and application in the older patient. O'Brien highlights the particular need for reminiscence, forgiveness, hope and trust, all of which give attention to the patient as subject, and form the basis for a nursing response (O'Brien 1998, 247).

1. *Reminiscence.* The very word tends to be devalued as something of an idle pursuit. In fact, it is a critical part of the articulation of narrative. It allows the person to look back and reassess, enabling an awareness of change and the development of the capacity to accept what cannot be changed and engage what can.

For some more elderly patients this may not involve reminiscence that leads to change but rather a simple repetition of memories. This too fulfils an important function. The repetition of the same stories is a reminder and reinforcement of identity and value. As such the repetitions take on an almost ritual character. In this context, the role of the nurse – despite having heard the story many times – is to become part of that ritual, the ritual listener. By listening attentively she provides the reinforcement of value and identity, enabling the person to be reminded of, and confirmed in, her life meaning. Where possible the carer can take the person through a guided autobiography. This is a particularly important technique for affirmation or development of spirituality. It enables the biographer to see and feel continuity of the self over time, to link life meaning into different relationships and into the social context of the times, and to assess more clearly what there is still to do. The simple reaffirming of the patient's story may help him feel secure in the middle stages of faith, finding life meaning in the groups that he was a member of.

For others, the active listening of the nurse may well lead to the patient's acceptance of dependency, expressed often through the acceptance of role change and development – with the parent for instance no longer caring for the child and increasingly accepting help from the child. Enabling this in the elderly involves listening and reflection which firstly allows the patient to reflect on limitations – with nurse and patient arriving at an agreement about what they are. This might involve an agreed list of functions that the patient cannot fulfil. Secondly, the listening can focus on the needs of the person in the light of the limitations. Thirdly, the patient can be enabled to think through the different ways of handling those needs, in the light of constraints and resources, including the patient's personal ones.

Two important results of this are firstly that dependency becomes seen in terms of objective need. It is not something to be ashamed of, and begins to lose its stigma. Secondly, this process provides the basis of future planning and thus the retention of significant control. Once more the basic life meaning of mutual dependency and freedom are worked through. Reminiscing may also help the person identify past coping skills and strategies, enabling her to deal with present stress.

2. *Forgiveness.* This involves seeking release from the past and from relationships that are not at peace. Once again this involves both a process of active listening and planning which can effect closure or resolution. This may involve forgiving or accepting forgiveness, through confrontation with others (the term confrontation meaning a face-to-face resolution, not aggressive action), possibly through carer-led mediation or some form of ritual. The use of ritual can be effective in enabling 'healing of memories', and forgiveness of those who are lost or dead. Such ritual can range from the planting of a tree to someone's memory, to the development of a context specific service, involving prayers of forgiveness, to the use of the religious rite confession. Clearly such work is best carried out in a team including the chaplain – though she need not be involved in all the rituals.

3. *Hope.* The generating of hope for the elderly may seem strange. However, hope is important in combating fear of the future, increasingly felt by the elderly. As noted above, hope is very much a function of an environment of acceptance and the assurance of faithful presence. Hope for the older patient can also involve focus on a future that goes beyond her life – a grandchild, a bequest, a football team and so on. Finally, hope can centre on the opportunities for learning and for practising skills. As we noted in the case study of out-patient assessment (see Chapter 5), coping skills can enable confidence, the exercise of which gives immediate ground for hope, including the possibility of positive collaboration with family or neighbours, and attainable targets.

In the same context it is important not to focus on skills alone but also capacities and qualities, and roles and purposes that these might fit the person for. The traditional view of the elderly has been that they have wisdom to offer. However, there is little evidence that the elderly *per se* have more wisdom than any other age. Nonetheless, they do have a wide experience and through dialogue and reflection may identify for themselves key qualities and for others key strategies for facing problems.

4. *Trust.* All of the above depend upon the development of trust, which can be a very hard thing for the aged. With the cutting back of the person's life and the increased dependency upon others comes the fear of the loss of control. The simple loss of eyesight, for instance, may make it very difficult to see what is happening or how people are reacting and so more difficult to trust others.

The need is for a trusting community, part of which is the health-care professional, which constitutes something of an extended family, precisely the 'communal network of memory and hope in which individuals may locate themselves and discern their identities' (Brueggemann 1985, 8).

Fowler's final two stages of faith give some indication of the spirituality which can develop if all these aspects are attended to and enabled.

Conjunctive faith

This occurs in mid-life and beyond. In this stage there is a recognition that truth about the self, others and all else must be approached from a number of different directions of vision. It involves an increased awareness of the other and of the different viewpoints and meaning system of the other. The previous stage was confident in its own authority and often in the assertion of the person's own community narrative as the 'best'. Now there is a realisation that any narrative has many different bases, and third party perspectives are important and can be learned from. This leads to an epistemological humility, an openness to learning and to an acceptance of the possibility of and need to maintain many different views.

The development of this stage demands what Marney refers to as an 'ego leak' (see Fowler 1996, 66). This involves the capacity to let go and to accept the limitations of the self and any groups. It demands an environment of acceptance which can clearly signal that acceptance of limitations does not signal rejection of the person. Empirical work on the stages of faith has noted that those who have reached the later stages of faith have been more aware of changes in their life and are more able to accept them. Conversely those who were less mature in faith had 'little or no subjective sense of changing as they grew older (Shulik 1992, 312).

Universalising faith

If the previous stage is not that common, then this is positively rare. This is the final stage of the de-centralisation of the self. The stages of growth have involved a concern for the self and a gradual expanding of the circle of those who are of value and accepted. At this stage concern is focused more on others than the self and there is an acceptance of the life as it is. This stage is associated with serenity, and it is likely that the patient will have a great deal to offer the carer.

In all this, spirituality enables ageing to be a process, one which can negotiate the different stages of life and make connections between them and their related networks. The balance is always between the acceptance of the limitations at each stage and the discovery of new meaning and hope. For active elderly patients with chronic illness one survey notes that the most prized values were hope, comfort, acceptance and peace (O'Brien 1998, 251). In general, they were not content to play 'the role' of the elderly, preferring to reflect on their own particular identity and role. For the homebound elderly this was reflected in another survey where over half the interviewees expressed the ' "desire to be able to discuss their spiritual beliefs and feelings with others, especially in times of crisis" ' (O'Brien 1998, 254). The key phrase here is 'with others', highlighting a need expressed for the elderly, in whatever context, to be part of a community which can enable this kind of sharing. How that community is developed is once more a matter of negotiation. For the homebound, this may mean beginning from a recognition of independence such that the visitors who make up the community should not be seen as 'charitable'. The function of that community and its different members can then be negotiated with, for instance, some regular visitors concentrating upon listening to autobiography and others looking to particular needs. However it is worked out, the community should embody faithful presence in all visits.

MacKinlay (2001) sums up some of the themes and the tasks of the elderly that form the basis of the nurse response in Box 6.3.

Box 6.3   Spiritual themes and tasks of ageing

Themes identified	*Tasks of the individual*
Ultimate meaning in life	To identify source of ultimate meaning
Response to ultimate meaning	To find appropriate way to respond
Self sufficiency/vulnerability	To transcend disabilities, loss
Wisdom/final meanings	To search for final meanings
Relationship/isolation	To find intimacy with God and/or others
Hope/fear	To find hope

Ultimate meaning in this context involves that which gives the person faith, hope and purpose. It does not have to be focused in a deity, though for many in the later stages of ageing such meaning is at least reflected on. For the most part, it is experiential meaning, not simply conceptual. Final meaning begins to look beyond life.

Dementia

Shakespeare sees this as return to infancy – 'sans teeth, sans everything'. It is such a loss of control that is most people's nightmare of old age. Dementia is on the increase and involves a range of organic disorders from Alzheimer's disease (50 per cent of dementias) to Multi-infarct Dementia (20 per cent), to a mix of the two (20 per cent) and finally dementias associated with trauma, drug abuse and degenerative genetic disorders. Though it is associated with old age, dementia is by no means exclusive to old age.

Dementia involves progressive deterioration of cognitive abilities, especially memory; rational, intellectual and organisational skills; the capacity to maintain old or develop new skills; and the ability to process complex concepts. In addition, motor skills are affected, especially spatial coordination. The dementia sufferer may lose a sense of the self and of social continuity, nonetheless there is evidence that somatic and affective awareness can remain intact. However, with a lack of social control the emotions may well be expressed in inappropriate ways which may cause alarm to family and friends or beyond.

The onset of dementia may initially be only slight. However, as the illness progresses, the patient typically experiences anxiety and depression and gradually begins to withdraw from social interaction and lose sense of life meaning.

The effects on the care givers
The effects on family and friends and thus upon the meaning structure of the family are often devastating:

- The onset of dementia can lead to fear and confusion in the family, including attempts to hide the problem and protect the sufferer.
- For many there is the major problem of having to completely reverse roles. At times the patient is entirely dependent, even for the most intimate functions.
- Not only is the child or spouse the 'parent' figure but the person before them gives the impression of having lost all hope. He is no longer a person or even a potential person. When caring for a child

there is at least response to stimuli and the presumption of growth
and development.

• Many families see the patient as in effect dead. When death comes
  it has the effect of being a second death. One widow commented
  at the funeral, 'This is his second funeral.'
• These very different feelings lead to anger, guilt and a sense of
  powerlessness.
• There is a danger of fatigue and a level of stress on the caregivers
  which puts them at high risk (Gaynor 1990).

For the family of dementia patients to be supported they need
imaginative and faithful care. The imagination is in ways of enabling
resolution to guilt and stress – from enabling the family members to
resolve their feeling about the patient (which may well have been
negative before the onset of the disease) to enabling them to let go of
care and share it with others.

The faithfulness is about the family having support which is always
'there' to call on. The care of dementia patients is very much a
marathon and requires a sense of support all along the way. This need
may well tie in with the research of Kaye and Robinson, who noted
that those involved in care showed an increase in formal spiritual or
religious practice and that this was seen as a primary method of
coping with stress. They found that the spiritual perspective both
enabled a sense of meaning which gave value to their care, and also
that it enabled them to transcend the immediacy of the caregiving
situation (Kaye and Robinson 1994). In turn, this confirmed the
importance of the family in the delivery of care for dementia sufferers.

Everett (1999) notes the importance of taking the family's grief
reaction seriously. In the next chapter we examine bereavement as
essentially about finding meaning in loss. The family of a patient with
dementia has to be enabled to work through such grief, both to
accept the limitations of the situation and to find new possibilities
there. Post and Whitehouse (1999) note the critical change in relationship that focuses upon finding meaning in the immediate experience, and upon non-cognitive spirituality mediated by factors such as
the environment and music.

Spiritual care of dementia patients
Care for those with dementia is a particularly important example of
the faithfulness of the caregiver. This is partly about the covenant of

care which remains with the other regardless of the response or non response. It is also about the openness to the patient at all levels – being aware of the somatic and affective person as much as the absence of the cognitive aspects of her life. Given that dementia will not enable guided autobiographies, several ways of the nurse approaching this spiritual care can be identified:

1. Dementias vary greatly in their severity and progression and thus in their impact upon the patient. This may mean that there is some capacity to tell the story albeit the same one in occasional lucid moments. Austin writes of providing care which can respond to the joy of the moment, times when the patient articulates something (Austin 1999). These moments should be of value for themselves and in the context of the life which the person has lead. It may be important for the carer to learn something about the narratives of the patient from another source.

2. Even where there is profound cognitive impairment there is also affective and somatic knowledge which is able to communicate some sense of acceptance, belonging and *shalom*. The nursing staff can communicate this through development of rituals, such as meal times which reinforce the sense of togetherness. It can also be communicated through touch, both regular and ritual, and music (Post and Whitehouse 1999). These reaffirm mutuality and the presence of the other.

3. For those with prior religious associations there are those religious rituals which can give a sense of rootedness. The eucharistic service in particular, but also familiar prayers such as the traditional version of the Lord's Prayer can be powerful. Such rituals can operate at all levels of faith. The Lord's Prayer for instance may root the person in the security of childhood, where it was said on a daily basis at school. Equally, holy communion might relocate the patient to a supportive community of faith. It is a rite too which can stimulate in its own right with tactile elements (eating and drinking), colour in the liturgical dress, and confirmation of the presence of others through the sharing of the peace. Sorajjakool also notes strong evidence of greater concern for religious symbols with ageing (Sorajjakool 1998).

4. Other significant symbols or rituals might include use of old family pictures, of old community film, of paintings, singing, and art

therapy. Treetops advocates the use of a 'memory box' in addition to group reminiscing. This is simply a box for each patient which contains things unique to her narrative, from music to letters, books and photos. It is also possible to develop group memory boxes. The advantage of such boxes is that all the carers can quickly access the particular narrative and memories of the patient (Treetops 1999).

5. Spirituality can also be developed through accessing the non-human environment, in particular through animals and through trips to areas of significance. Once more the trips can be personalised or be relevant to the whole group.

In all of these approaches the primary attitude of the carer is that of openness and acceptance, attending to the patient as subject, even when there is no obvious response at whatever level to confirm that subjectivity.

Conclusion

Spiritual needs remain the same whatever the age. Nonetheless, at different stages in life those needs are set in the context of challenges, capacities and relationships which demand a particular response if the patient or her family are to develop spiritual awareness and subsequent life meaning. At these points, the patient's particular life meaning and stage of faith come together with the experience of illness. It is not the nurse's task to guide the patient on to the next stage in faith. On the contrary, faith cannot be directed. It is the nurse's task to allow the patient to explore her faith and life meaning and move to a different life meaning if they wish, something which might involve a new stage of faith or the affirmation of the present one. For many, especially those suffering from dementia, such life meaning is found in direct encounter. The presence of the nurse enables them to be reminded of this, and of their value, at each moment through picture, touch and however the nurse can communicate her accepting presence. For all, the development of life meaning is centred in some form of community, which in the experience of illness includes the nurse and her colleagues. The family is the key community for the development of life meaning, though faced by the challenges of illness cannot always continue to enable this from its own resources. They too need an enabling community. Importantly, the nurse can play a significant part in enabling the family and significant others to act as a community of value and meaning in and through the shared experience of illness. This results in an affirmation, or exploration and development of faith.

In all this, awareness of the needs and capacities of patients at each stage of their lives, and of the stage of faith which they are able to articulate, affirm and explore or develop becomes important for enabling the appropriate response from the nurse.

Questions and exercises

1. Reflect on your experience of childhood illness and with ill children. How did they make sense of this illness experience? How can the spiritual narrative of the child be enabled?
2. Reflect on your experience of childbirth- as patient, family or nurse. What did it mean to you? How can meaning be enabled in this experience, including faith, hope, purpose and right relationships?
3. How can you sustain any sense of meaningful relationship with a patient suffering from dementia?

References

Austin, C.M. (1999) 'Joy in the Moment: Immediacy and Ultimacy in Dementia' in A. Jewell (ed.) *Spirituality and Ageing* (London: Jessica Kingsley).

Belsky, J. and Kelly, J. (1994) *The Transition to Parenthood: How a First Child Changes a Marriage* (New York, Delacorte Press).

Benson, C.Z. (1990) 'Aging', R.D. Hunter (ed.) *Dictionary of Pastoral Care and Counseling* (Nashville: Abingdon).

Bergum, V. (1989) *Woman to Mother: A Transformation* (London: Bergin and Garvey).

Berryman, J. (Summer 1985) 'Children's spirituality and religious language', *British Journal of Religious Education*, **7**, 3.

Bluebond-Langner, M. (1978) *The Private Worlds of Dying Children* (Princeton: Princeton University Press).

Brueggemann, W. (1985) 'The family as world maker', *Journal of Preachers*, **7**.

Burkhardt, M.A. (1991) 'Spirituality and children; nursing considerations'. *Journal of Holistic Nursing*, **9**, 2, 31–41.

Cowan, C. and Cowan, P. (1992) *When partners become parents: the big life change for couples* (New York: Basic Books).

Erikson, E. (1968) Identity, *Youth and Crisis* (New York: W.W. Norton and Co.).

Erikson, E. (1977) *Toys and Reasons* (New York: W.W. Norton).

Estes, C.P. (1992) *Women Who Run with Wolves* (New York: Rider Books).

Everett, D. (1999) 'Forget Me Not: The Spiritual Care of People with Alzheimer's Disease', *Journal of Health Care Chaplaincy*, **8**, 1/2, 77–88.

Faulkner, K.W. (1997) 'Talking about death with a dying child, *American Journal of Nursing*, **97**, 6, 64–97.

Finch, J. and Mason, J. (1993) *Negotiating Family Responsibilities* (London: Routledge).

Fowler, J. (1996) *Faithful Change* (Nashville: Abingdon).

Fowler, J. (1992) 'Perspectives on the Family from the Standpoint of Faith Development Theory', J. Astley and Leslie Francis (eds), *Christian Perspectives on Faith Development* (Leominster: Gracewing), 320–44.

Fulton, R.A. and Moore, C.M. 'Spiritual care of a school age child with a chronic condition'. *Journal of Pediatric Nursing*, **10**, 4, 224–31.

Gaynor, S.E. (1990) 'The long haul: the effects of home care on the care giver', *Image: Journal of Nursing Scholarship*, **22**, 4, 208.

Hall, J. (2001) *Midwifery, Mind and Spirit* (Oxford: Books for Midwives).

Handzo, G. (1990) 'Talking about faith with children'. *Journal of Christian Nursing*, **7**, 4, 17–20.

Hay, D. (1998) *The Spirit of the Child* (London: Harper Collins).

Jewell, A. (1999) (ed.) *Spirituality and Ageing* (London: Jessica Kingsley).

Kahn, R.P. (1995) *Bearing Meanings: The Language of Birth* (Chicago: University of Illinois Press).

Kaye, J. and Robinson, K.M. 'Spirituality among caregivers', *Image: Journal of Nursing Scholarship*, **26**, 3, 218–21.

Kimes Myers, B. (1997) *Young Children and Spirituality*, (London: Routledge).

King, U. (1999) 'Spirituality, Ageing and Gender' in A. Jewell (ed.), *Spirituality and Ageing* (London: Jessica Kingsley).

Kitzinger, S. (1997) Authoritative Touch in childbirth – A Cross Cultural Approach', in *Childbirth and Authoritative Knowledge: Cross-cultural Perspectives* (London: Berkley).

Kohlberg, L. (1984) *Essays on Moral Development. Vol. 2: The Psychology of Moral Development* (San Francisco: Harper Row).

LevySchiff, R. (1994) 'Individual and contextual correlates of marital change across the transition to parenthood', *Developmental Psychology*, **30**, 4, 591–601.

McGeary, K. (1994) 'The influence of guarding on the developing mother-unborn child relationship', in P.A. Field and P.B Marck (eds), *Uncertain Motherhood: Negotiating the Risks of the Childbearing Years* (London: Sage).

MacKinlay, E. (2001) *The Spiritual Dimension of Ageing* (London: Jessica Kingsley).

Magana, A. and Clark, N.M. (1995) 'Examining a paradox: does religiosity contribute to positive birth outcomes in Mexican American populations?' *Health Education Quarterly*, **22**, 1, 96–109.

Nugent, J.K. (1991) 'Cultural and psychological influences on the father's role in infant development', *Journal of Marriage and the Family*, **53**, 475–85.

Oakley, A. (1979) *From here to maternity: Becoming a Mother* (London: Penguin).

Oakley, A. (1980) *Women Confined: Towards a Sociology of Childbirth* (Oxford: Martin Robertson).

O'Brien, M.E. (1998) *Spirituality in Nursing: Standing on Holy Ground* (Boston: Jones and Bartlett).

Page, L.A. (2000) *The New Midwifery* (London: Churchill Livingstone).

Painter, A. (1994) 'Health visitor identification of post-natal depression', *Health Visitor*, **68**, 4, 138–40.

Parks, S.D. (1992) 'Fowler Evaluated' in Jeff Astley and Leslie Francis (eds), *Christian Perspectives on Faith Development* (Leominster:Gracewing), 92–106.

Post, S. and Whitehouse, P. (1999) 'Spirituality, Religion and Alzheimer's Disease', *Journal of Health Care Chaplaincy*, **8**, 1/2, 45–58.

Pryce, M. (1996) *Finding a Voice* (London: SCM).

Pye, J (2001) *A Winter's Tale: A Pastoral and Theological Exploration of the Responses of Families and their Carers to Pre-natal, Peri-natal and Post-natal Deaths* (Unpublished PhD Thesis, University of Leeds).

Robinson, S. (July, 1998) 'Christian ethics and pastoral counselling revisited', *Modern Believing*, 30–44.

Rothman, B.K. (1994) *The Tentative Pregnancy – Amniocentesis and the Sexual Politics of Motherhood* (London: Pandora Press).

Salter, J. *The Incarnating Child* (London: Hawthorn Press, 1987).

Sherr, L. (1995) *The Psychology of Pregnancy and Childbirth* (Oxford: Blackwell).

Shulik, R.N. (1992) 'Faith development in older adults', in Astley, J. and Francis, L. (eds) *Christian Perspectives on Faith Development* (Grand Rapids: Gracewing).

Sorajjakool, S. (Summer 1998) 'Gerontology, spirituality, and religion', *The Journal of Pastoral Care*, **52**, 2, 147–56.

Stern, D. (1985) *The Interpersonal World of the Infant* (New York: Basic Books).

Stiles, M.K. (1990) 'The shining stranger: nurse-family spiritual relationships'. *Cancer Nursing*, **13**, 4, 235–45.

Treetops, J. (1999) 'The Memory Box', in Jewell, 86–92.

Van Heukelem-Still, J. (1984) 'How to assess the spiritual needs of children and their families'. *Journal of Christian Nursing*, **I**, 1, 4–6.

Westerhoff III, J.H. (1976) *Will our Children have Faith?*, New York: Seabury.

Wong, D.L. (1997) *Whaley and Wong's Essentials in Pediatric Nursing*, 5th edn. (St Louis: C.V. Mosby).

7

. . . to the Grave

Perhaps more than any other area of healthcare, dying, loss and bereavement focus on spirituality. Humankind's relationship with death has always been one of fascination and fear. Unlike other animals we can and, at times, do contemplate our own death. However, despite all the clever ways in which we try to make sense of death or dying there is the simple existential fear of the loss of the self. As Larkin (1993) puts it in his poem 'Aubade',

> This is a special way of being afraid
> No tricks dispel. Religion used to try
> That vast moth eaten musical brocade
> Created to pretend we never die

There may be rational arguments suggesting that in death you will not be aware of that loss. What we might properly fear is the act of dying itself. But we also fear the loss of the self and, with that, the ultimate loss of meaning,

> . . . no sight, no sound,
> No touch or taste or smell, nothing to think with
> Nothing to love or link with.'

Value, the sense of connection and belonging, the consciousness of the other, the affirmation of the self in purposive work, all of these are lost. It is precisely because of this fear that ultimate questions are always just below the surface and that traditional spiritualities and theologies have aimed to give meaning to death.

In this chapter we will briefly look at some traditional religious and cultural ways of making sense of death. These are still important for many, and health workers should at least be aware of them. The chapter will look first at dying and then loss and bereavement. In the first of these, we will consider what a good death might involve, and develop this in terms of spiritual meaning and how the nurse might enable that to develop. In the second, we will examine the process of grieving and the practice of mourning and note how healthcare workers can work together to enable the development of spirituality as part of this.

Death and dying

Tradition

Traditionally, religions have sought meaning in dying and death round the theme of survival after death. Some stress the idea of the immortality of the soul, defined as the discarnate centre of the person's consciousness. This view originates from the Ancient Greeks who saw the after-life as more real than this world. The present world was more a shadowy imitation of the world of 'forms'. This approach was taken up into the Christian faith, which in one tradition sees the soul as leaving the body and going to heaven or hell (Edwards 1999). Other traditions pick up on the more Jewish idea of the survival after death, of the person as whole – mind, body and spirit. Survival involved a resurrection of the whole person in embodied form. Other traditions in the Jewish faith have no sense of survival beyond the grave and thus stress the continuation of human identity and narrative through the family (Neuberger 1994).

Buddhism in contrast does not see survival after death in terms of the separate and distinct entity but sees the person taken up into ultimate peace – Nirvana. For the Hindu there is an eternal soul (atman) that leaves the body and is eventually reincarnated in another living form. This reflects a view of birth, life and death as a never-ending cyclical process. It also helps to explain present suffering seen as the result of transgressions in the previous life (Vatuk 1996). For Christians too there was a linking of justice with the after-life. There will be a day of judgement, where all sins would be taken into account, either individually as the soul leaves the body or at the end of time, when all would be judged together.

All these different views provided a meta-narrative, an overarching story, giving meaning in death, and hope, both for the deceased and for survivors – always assuming that all did actually want to meet in the after-life.

Along with these views of death there were religious and cultural rituals which helped to make sense of the experience of death and bereavement. These were part of communities that faced death as a regular occurrence, and expressed the need of the community. Clark's seminal study of the Yorkshire village of Staithes at the turn of the twentieth century shows how death was never very far away, and that the varieties of ritual which surrounded it centred in the home, involving many different people from the village (Clark 1982, 7). Death had a clear social meaning and the church was able to prescribe what was a good death, including the presence of the family, the rite of confession and absolution and so on. Moreover, in this context it was straightforward to see life as a preparation for death (Cobb 2001, 48).

In a postmodern world things are less clear. Firstly, the grand narratives of religion that offered meaning are no longer understood or accepted by the community as a whole. In turn, funeral ritual has moved away from the churches to the more functional site of the crematorium. Individuals are increasingly encouraged to think through funerals based on their own values and those of the deceased (Gill and Fox 1996).

Secondly, attempts to find meaning through religion have for the most part not been replaced. Aries suggests that this has led to a community 'denial' of the reality of death, something reinforced by increased longevity and modern medicine. This has lead to the perception of death as a failure of care (Aries 1974, 107, see also Smith 2000).

Thirdly, there have been various attempts to see the spirituality of death simply in terms of accepting the inevitable. Building on this theme, Nuland (1993) suggests that we should view death in terms of a much larger picture:

> We die so that the world may continue. We have been given the miracle of life because trillions upon trillions of living things have prepared the way for us and then have died – in a sense, for us. We die in turn so that others may live. The tragedy of a single individual becomes, in the balance of natural things, the triumph of ongoing life. (1993, 267)

Fourthly, there has been a diverse response to death and dying from the healthcare world. Kübler-Ross (1970) tried to discern how we approach a good death. The hospice movement stands out against the medicalisation of death, with a concern for holistic care of the patient in community. However, despite such creative approaches to finding meaning, both for the health carer and the

dying, the majority of people still die 'a
mostly in hospital (Nuland 1993, 255).
to find meaning we examine the narra'
bereaved.

Looking death in the face

Rebecca's story

I am a student teacher and I am dying. I am writing ms .
that by telling my story they may, some day, be better able to help mos.
share my experience.

*I am in hospital - - I can't really remember how long because nobody talks
about such things. I fact, nobody talks about very much at all. The 'everything
is alright' routine is so frustrating and makes me angry. I am left in a lonely,
silent void. Through the 'OK, fine' I can see the staff's own vulnerability and
fear. The dying patient is a symbol of what every human being fears and what
we each know: that one day we will die. I wonder what these carers do with
their own feelings?*

*But what about my fear today and now? Endless people slip in and out of
my room and give me tablets and check my blood pressure. Their fears enhance
mine. Why are they afraid? I am the one who is dying.*

*I guess that what I am saying is that it really is a question of attitude. I
know we all feel insecure. I know we are all on a journey – on a search for
meaning, purpose or truth. I wish these people would stop running away – all
I want to know is that there will be someone to hold my hand when I need
it. I am afraid. Death may get to be routine to them, but its pretty new to me.
I want to talk, to be listened to, I want to have the space to be honest about
fears in a land where I know there are no answers, only questions and anxieties* (recorded in Woodward 1995: 100).

The testimony of Rebecca does two things. First it helps us to look
at the experience of dying. Secondly, it focuses on the often confused
response of the healthcarers. We will look at each of these.

Rebecca was looking for a way through the experience of dying
that would help her to make sense, and there was little meaning or
control in what she was facing up to at that point. Both of these
elements are stressed in the principles of a good death which Age
Concern (1999) sets out in the Millennium Paper, *The Future of
Health and Care of Older People* (Box 7.1).

Principles of a good death

know when death is coming, and to understand what can be
expected.
To be able to retain control of what happens.
- To be afforded dignity and privacy.
- To have control over pain relief and other symptom control.
- To have a choice of control over where death occurs (at home or else-where).
- To have access to information and expertise of whatever kind is necessary.
- To have access to any spiritual or emotional support desired.
- To have access to hospice care in any location, not only in hospital.
- To have control over who else is present and shares the end.
- To be able to issue advance directives that ensure wishes are respected.
- To have time to say goodbye, and control over other aspects of timing.
- To able to leave when it is time to go, and not to have life prolonged pointlessly. (Age Concern 1999, 42.)

These principles stress a person-centred approach to dying and are in effect a list of rights. What the list does not do is to look behind the rights to the experience, and to how meaning, as well as control, is established. A 'good death' is not simply about fulfilment of rights, nor is it simply about the ethics of dying, so often associated with the idea (Badham 1998). Beneath and connecting both of these is the experience of dying and the development of spiritual meaning.

The experience of dying is classically seen in terms of stages, as set by Kübler-Ross (1970):

1. *Denial.* On being told of a terminal diagnosis the patient will not truly believe the doctor. Perhaps the wrong diagnosis has been given, or papers have been mislaid. When the diagnosis is confirmed the patient may retreat into self-imposed isolation.
2. *Anger.* The patient might vent anger on a number of different people, from God to members of the healthcare team. This involves looking for a scapegoat who can be blamed.

3. *Bargaining.* The patient may make promises, sometimes with God, in exchange of an extension of life. The promises are not often kept.
4. *Depression.* The reality of the diagnosis is confirmed and the beginning of anticipatory grief emerges, an awareness of the imminent loss of the important people and things in the patient's life.
5. *Acceptance.* The patient accepts the reality of death and aims to set his affairs in order.

This view of the dying experience is valuable and indicates important aspects that tend to emerge. However, like the principles of a good death it does not capture the underlying spiritual dynamic, something that Rebecca's testimony underlines.

Firstly, Rebecca shows that dying is essentially a social activity. The views and attitudes of others actually affect how the person dies. Moreover, the attitudes of others will strongly affect how the person begins to create meaning for herself. Rebecca experienced this in a negative way, faced by the distance of the healthcare workers and their underlying fear of engaging her. This led to confusion and above all meant that she could not begin to make sense of her experience. This underlines the need for an accompanist who will offer empathy, and the importance of that empathy and unconditional care in enabling positive and holistic spiritual meaning to be shaped.

In research ranging from Menzies (1970) to Kendrick (1998), the difficulty for nurses in general of offering this kind of support to the dying has been set out. All report fear of relating to the dying patients' families and a sense of powerlessness, fear arising from the nurses' own anxieties about death, and uncertainty about coping with patients' questions about death (Littlewood 1993, McNammara, Waddell and Colvin 1995). All this can lead to inadequate care of the dying patient (Hill 1988, Morris 1988, Burnard and Kendrick 1998, Davidhizar and Newman Giger 1998). Also the stage and rights approaches are in danger of seeing the experience of dying in non-relational terms, and this in turn can give permission to healthcare workers to simply complete tasks and not relate to the person or allow spiritual reflection.

Secondly, dying can acutely raise the patient's awareness of the other. At the simple level of awareness of the environment, for instance, the dying playwright Dennis Potter spoke movingly of his awareness of the apple blossom outside his window:

Last week looking at it through the window when I am writing, I *see* that it is the whitest, frothiest, blossomest blossom there ever could be, and I can see it. Things are more trivial than they ever were and more important than they ever were, and the difference between the trivial and the important doesn't seem to matter. But the nowness of everything is absolutely wondrous, and if people could *see* that you know' (Potter 1994, 5).

The very stuff of spiritual meaning then is not simply just beneath the surface, it is right there on the sensitive skin, eyes and ears of the patient. For Rebecca, a central part of her confusion and difficulty was the fact that other things were getting in the way of handling that kind of awareness. Indeed, the attitude of the healthcare workers discouraged either the celebration that someone like Potter felt or the pain that others might feel as they become acutely aware of their present and past relationships and their complex feelings about these and about themselves. Making sense of that increased awareness of the other demands that the patient be allowed to share it as part of their day-to-day discourse. This awareness is now a critical part of who they are. Not to be allowed to share it is to deny something about themselves and to discourage the often faltering steps towards appreciating this awareness, and gaining meaning from it.

Thirdly, all this points to the inadequacy of the idea of stages of dying, and of the particular definition of each of these stages, even if the idea of oscillation between those stages is accepted (Leming and Dickinson 1998). For Rebecca, many different feelings came to the surface at the same time related not just to death *per se* but to relationships and context. As Tarvis notes, in any case an emotion such as anger rarely comes by itself (1982). Moreover, anger is generated not spontaneously but in response to how we see and interpret the world. For Rebecca, there was depression and fear about the thought of death, resentment about her relationship with the care staff, confusion, regret, as well as anger that was doubtless felt about many people. Part of her important work in dying was to sort out those different feelings and sort out what and who they were connected to. Again, this is not simply a matter of being given space to ventilate anger about the thought of dying. On the contrary, it involves enabling the person to articulate her narrative and from that all the related meaning.

Similarly the concept of acceptance does not really plumb the depths of a more proactive process. With increased awareness of relationships and the reflection that allows the person to articulate the value of those relationships, this may lead to celebration or forgiveness and reconciliation. This is not about passive acceptance of death so much as working through and responding to meaning in life. Moreover, in this process there is not first an acceptance, followed by the person then getting affairs into order. It may be that only through working out life meaning, including attempts at reconciliation and forgiveness, can the person 'let go'.

Spiritual reflection in all this enables the development of all the different aspects of meaning, including faith and hope:

Faith

Fowler's stages of faith illuminate Kübler-Ross's stages of dying. The earliest of Fowler's stages of faith can be seen in the response of bargaining and anger. This is a very child-like faith, where even those without religious faith may pray to God to solve the problem. God is seen here in very magical terms of the father figure who can 'sort things out'. Faith at this point is also very much conditional, 'If I do this then will you solve my problem'. The anger and disbelief can also indicate transition between faith stages, involving disenchantment with one view of faith, disengagement, loss of a sense of identity, and disorientation (Bridges 1980).

Often a holding faith is needed, such as Fowler's stages three and four. In this, identity and faith are often found in purpose and belief generated by the group that the person belongs to. A good example of this is where the patient might become involved in fundraising for charities.

As the different feelings are worked through then a more mature faith begins to emerge, one that can accept the support of others even where there is conflict or ambiguity – Fowler's stage Five. It is this stage that leads to possibilities of forgiveness and reconciliation.

Important in the development of faith is the role of the nurse. He may well become a critical, if short term ground of faith for the person. In other words, he may become more than some neutral enabler of spiritual reflection and actually a part of the patient's spirituality. In Rebecca's case, there was a sense in which the nurses could not avoid this. Negatively or positively they were critical to her handling spiritual meaning in her life.

The nurse in all this offers unconditional care. The dying patient is faced by social perceptions of death and can all too quickly buy into that which associates the dying person with the strange and repulsive. The dying person is literally decaying before our eyes, losing hair and body definition. This is made even worse if the patient is suffering from a disease that is felt to be socially deviant in some way such as HIV (human immunodeficiency virus) or AIDs (acquired immune deficiency syndrome). Accepting the self in all this calls for unconditional care which avoids any sense of paternalism.

This means not colluding with the early stages of faith which seek a magical solution. The staff member cannot provide that solution. For some this is precisely why they avoid personal contact and focus on task completion. To face, the patient with unconditional care means the carer having to accept his own limitations. Similarly, enabling a faith which is not conditional means the staff communicating a faithfulness to the patient as person.

Faith in all this is based simply on the accepting presence of the other and the knowledge that the other will still be there for them tomorrow and will remain faithful. Moreover, even if there is no time for lengthy reflection it is possible to establish rapidly that sense of worth. Nouwen, in writing about an encounter with a patient the evening before he died, sums it up thus:

> But when a man says to his fellow man, 'I will not let you go. I am going to be here tomorrow and I expect you not to disappoint me,' then tomorrow is no longer an endless dark tunnel. It becomes flesh and blood in the brother who is waiting and for whom he wants to give life one more chance . . . .
> (Nouwen 1994, 67)

Hope

Developing faith in turn establishes a sense of hope. Hope at the end of life seems an odd concept, and yet it is central to the spirituality of dying. Initial hope may be for survival. This may be important to nurture at early stages to give the patient motivation.

At another level is the hope which is focused on the significant others of the patient. This means the patient reflecting on her network of spiritual meaning, all that gives her worth and value. Through addressing these relationships and looking to effect forgiveness and reconciliation the person can bring her 'business' to an end and have hope for the future through what she leaves behind, through the lives of those important to her.

For others, hope in death is centred in religious belief and concepts of survival after death. It is important in allowing the dying person to articulate her narrative to enable such beliefs to be expressed, and affirmed. As in other experiences of spiritual care, however, there may be times when the cognitive belief in life after death cannot bear the weight of the affective experience of dying. The task of the nurse has to be to allow the person to be afraid, and to express those underlying doubts. This provides the basis for the third level of hope. Such hope is based in the presence of the carer and has little future referent (Robinson 1998). This is the hope that was summed up by one patient in the final days of her life in a hospice, 'Most of my life I felt that I was hope less. My parents said I was, even when I was a parent. They said it as a joke, but I knew it wasn't. I knew I was hopeless unless I got things 'right'. In the past few days I have learned that I don't have to get things right, I am not hope less, and I feel good about that.'

Gillian Rose suffered from terminal cancer and discovered that she did not have to get things right, even her attempts at love. She writes, 'If I am to stay alive, I am bound to continue to get love wrong, all the time, but not to cease wooing, for that is my life's affair, *love's work*' (Rose 1997, 99). This release from conditionality is central to any positive idea of Kübler-Ross's stage of acceptance.

The development of hope is aided by the use of imagination and creativity. This enables the person to develop the capacity to envision the future, be that simply tomorrow in some event or in the distant future, and how that future might be affected by the person's legacy. Such creativity can also develop purposes such as working for others in need, which again provides a sense of hope.

Finding hope, faith and purpose in the experience of dying is a wonderful goal which, of course, rarely happens exactly right. Nonetheless, it provides an aim in spiritual care which underlines that the discovery of life meaning in dying is not simply a passive acceptance of death but about finding meaning in the *life* of the dying person.

Completion, forgiveness and reconciliation

Hope is also discovered in dealing with relationships. This may be a matter of leaving financial affairs or other obligations in good order. It may be a matter of addressing relationships themselves. The awareness of a last chance to set things right increases, with desire both to forgive and be forgiven. Again, this cannot emerge until the patient has the chance to articulate her narrative. It may be in the narrative that she seeks reassurance from the nurse that she doesn't need to forgive or be forgiven. It is important not to simply reassure, but to enable the person to be aware of what she feels she needs to do. In exploring that the nurse can help her to consider what forgiveness might mean and how it might be achieved, through a letter, face-to-face contact, and intermediary (Robinson 2001). It inevitably will lead the patient to explore whether the forgiveness they wish to give should be proactive or reactive upon the acceptance of the other's guilt. In patients who are dying the need for resolution often leads to proactive, unconditional forgiveness. As we will note in the next chapter, forgiveness might not lead to reconciliation. Indeed, it might involve closure of a relationship. Once again there should be no attempt to impose an agenda of forgiveness. It should always arise out of the person's narrative and the reflection on life meaning that emerges from that.

The act of forgiveness can also be rehearsed. This practical reflection can also increase a sense of hope, hope that things can be put right.

Lynn and Harrold (1999) usefully sum up four Rs of the spirit. Their advice is directly to the patient. However, it provides an equally valuable prompt for the practitioner, with areas and ideas that can provide the basis for person-centred reflection (Box 7.2).

Box 7.2   Tasks in dying

Remembering. Take time to reflect on your life and its events. What were your accomplishments? What must be left undone? Who influenced you, for better or worse, and whose lives did you influence? Who did you love? Who do you love? What do those relationships mean to you now?

Reassessing. Take time to see your life as a whole. You may ask what your life really added up to, or who you really were. You might share your thoughts with those who know and love you. Even if you accomplished much in a worldly sense, you may feel you really came up short on doing well with your life. And if life was really tough, you may feel unfairly denied your chances. This is the time to be honest and thoughtful. You are likely to find you did pretty well, on the whole, and you will probably find ways to forgive yourself and others. Surprisingly you will even find ways to see and complete important tasks – instructing a grandchild, affirming the goodness of someone who really needs your support, arranging your finances to protect your spouse, or creating something, whether it is needle point, woodwork or fine art.

Reconciling. Try to be at peace with yourself. You may need to reconcile yourself to not having done things you wanted to do. Your may need to forgive yourself for your shortcomings or transgressions, or forgive those who hurt or disappointed you. You may need others to forgive you. Reconciliation with your imperfections – and those of others – can help you find peace.

Reuniting. Try to be at peace with those who you love. Most of us have had various relationships disrupted over our lifetime, from death, anger, relocation and the many forces that pull people apart. As serious illness threatens, it is important to come together with family and friends, when you can, and to have the chance to say farewells. Don't wait too long to try to see that long estranged sister or son or even to sit awhile with a friend from long ago. (Lynn and Harrold 1999, 30.)

Echoing Potter's point about 'nowness' this list stresses immediacy and whilst it can help the patient to look to the completion of certain tasks, it goes beyond that. Offering support to someone who needs it, for instance, transcends any idea of the patient role or patient's tasks and sees her as resource and caregiver. Once again this provides purpose and transcendent meaning.

Enabling this process may be a one-to-one dynamic or it may involve suggesting ideas, themes or activities that the person can begin to take forward for herself. Again Lynn and Harrold provide some useful ideas for 'shaping meaning' (1999, 32):

Meditation. As a help to centre the self and be open to the increased awareness of the self and the other this can be very effective. It can be facilitated by tapes or by the chaplain or social worker guiding the patient through the process. Meditation is best used to aid reflection, not simply to relax.

Gathering. Opportunities can be found to bring together significant persons. Such gatherings can be low key involving people from separate groups or have the feeling of a ritual or celebration, perhaps a farewell party. Such events can crystallise the person's sense of value and meaning and be important stages or conclusions of reconciliation. They may also be tied to particular rituals in the person's spiritual development. One patient suffering from Motor Neurone Disease had begun to explore Christian spirituality, and for her a ritual and celebration of her discoveries was important. The result was the rite of confirmation, with care workers, friends and family present. All of these groups were part of her spiritual meaning and she wanted all to come together to a celebration that showed her commitment to the meaning she was discovering. Once again there was a strong sense of the caring role of the patient in this celebration. Many of those present spoke of what they had experienced and learned in the celebration through her.

Creating. This can be a way of summing up life meaning. Making a tape, photo album or scrapbook, for instance, can both provide a sense of summary for the patient himself but also a more permanent memorial, which could be used in memorial services or funerals. Art and music, composing or performing can also enable the patient to focus creativity. One patient who learned and performed a song spoke of the real sense of power and energy this gave to her. Energy can be a real product of the dying patient developing spirituality. Some patients speak of finding a 'new life' or a new thirst for life. Such a process can also help the anticipatory grief of the family and friends. In a real sense memories can be created and affirmed.

Giving. Many cultures emphasise the importance of gift giving. Some native Americans give things of value to signify the end of life. Once again this a ritual symbolising something of the person's life meaning in relation to others.

Leaving a Legacy. This can range from conventional wills to a 'value legacy'. A letter or tape recording can sum up the life meaning of the person, allowing his hopes, beliefs and values to be shared with those who he cherished. This may involve simply the person telling something of the story of his life.

Other possible projects that can shape meaning include, making an advance directive, preparing for the person's funeral, or developing altruistic projects.

Advance directives. One of Age Concern's principles of a good death, advance directives express the person's wishes about treatment if they are ever not competent to refuse or agree to treatment. Under case law they have some legal force in the UK, requiring the medical staff to take the patient's views into account (Kendrick and Robinson 2002). They give the person a voice in treatment that can then be amplified and developed by family and friends in dialogue with the medical team. This enables autonomy in the context of shared governance (Kendrick and Robinson 2002). An important supplement to the advance directive is the *values history.* To give the medical team a deeper indication of the wishes of the patient this sets out his core values and life meaning. Developing such a history is in effect consciously reflecting on the patient's spirituality. Unlike the USA, advance directives and values history are not raised by medical staff for the patient to consider as a matter of course. However, it is reasonable to raise this idea as part of the dying patient's spiritual reflection.

Funeral and memorial service preparation. This seems on the face of it to be a negative activity. However, it enables the patient to celebrate his life, thinking about how he would like to be remembered and how the service might sum up his values and relationships (Robinson 2002).

Altruistic projects. In Chapter 2, the case of patient C noted how she raised money for cancer research. Such projects give a further sense of purpose and awareness of the other. They are another way of transcending the patient and dying role, to see the experience as one of giving.

Letting go

It would be easy to contrast the dynamic interpersonal development of faith, hope and purpose with the final more passive letting go of life. However, even the development of faith and hope involve letting go, of false hopes, negative emotions and negative views of the self. Faith and hope emerge in relation to the reality of the person's relationships and possibilities within the context of their immanent death.

Equally, letting go at the end is not simply a passive, individual activity. It remains a social event that in some way is shared by the significant survivors. For many this means being present at the moment of death, keeping somatic contact with the patient, holding hands or lying next to them. For some, this whole event and experience is summed up in more overt religious rituals, such as confession and absolution, anointing, communion, the reciting of confessions of faith, and rituals of farewell (Badham 1998, Leming and Dickinson 1998, 150 ff.).

In one sense such rituals are only relevant to those of particular religious traditions and who ask for such provisions. However, such ritual can be offered by chaplains or religious advisors in a much broader sense. Where a baby or child is dying, for instance, the parents or staff often request baptism. Such a ritual operates in very subtle pastoral ways. It allows the family to feel that they have done everything, and also allows them to let go along with the staff who may have cared intensively for the patient. It can focus on the early stages of faith, as a form of last hope, or on very mature faith that simply accepts the end. Above all, it can embody unconditional care regardless of the niceties of theological ideas or religious commitment (Pye 2001).

There can be other rituals developed around the practice of the department. One specialist baby unit, for instance, passes on to the parents a poem composed by the grandmother of one baby who died. There can be simple moments of silence, or placing flowers next to the bed. The criterion of their effectiveness is if they embody care and enable all concerned to focus and reflect on the value of the person who is dying. Carefully worked out rituals such as these can be especially important when a patient is dying in intensive care units, providing a framework of meaning when the person himself is not conscious. Seymour stresses in this the need to maintain the integrity of personhood (Seymour 2001).

The active movement from initial, through proactive spiritual response to positive acceptance, is well charted by Thomas and Retsas (1999). In work with terminal cancer patients they write in terms of transacting self-preservation, preserving and developing the self through various interactions. This in turn is divided into three phases:

- *Taking it all in.* This involves responding to the initial diagnosis and questioning the different levels of meaning of the experience.
- *Getting on with things.* This involves mobilising, through clarifying purpose and setting goals, and connecting up with the person's network of relationships.
- *Putting it all together.* This involves creating meaning through various actions and response. Reflection on all that enables a final act of discovering the self. Effective spiritual response in all this is therefore a real learning process. Letting go in this context is a positive move towards a new meaning of life.

Family and friends

Developing spiritual meaning in dying has been seen to be interactive, not simply reactive. Hence, the family and friends become an important part of that development. In sharing the person's journey they too are becoming involved in spiritual reflection and in effect begin to work through aspects of grief and letting go, normally only faced much later (Attig 1996, 163). The family may be involved in the gatherings noted above and in certain areas of care (McIntyre 2002). They may also be involved in conference with the staff when reflecting on the right treatment if the patient is no longer competent. Such conferences keep the spirituality of the patient and the family very much to the fore and can in themselves been seen as rituals. Every effort then should be made by the staff not simply to 'support' the family but to enable them to share and help accompany the patient's spiritual journey.

Survivorship
Patients with cancer may well develop their spirituality along the lines noted above (Kendrick and Hughes 2002). However, cancer does not have to be terminal. This raises many issues for those who do survive. Like the survivors of the Holocaust there can be a sense of guilt when other cancer patients have not survived. Equally, with life meaning adjusted to an imminent end, moving into a very different view of hope can be difficult. The nurse once more can provide a bedrock for this transition, and reflection on its meaning. Work done on meaning in dying, however, is likely to provide the basis for a very positive survivor spirituality.

Bereavement and grief

Case A (adapted from Attig 1996)

A's husband was diagnosed with a terminal illness. She was able to work closely with him prior to his death. Together they reflected on his life, affirming his value, through narrative, reflecting on records such as photographs and inviting friends to share their feelings about him, often in the form of letters. This process reinforced his own worth and an increased awareness for A of his life and what he meant to her. They were able to explicitly and mutually sum up their relationship, enabling A to work through anticipatory grief.

When her husband died this gave her a sense of continuity and she continued to talk to him and include him in her decision-making. She formed a sacred space, principally at the graveside where she could relax and converse with him. A was also able to foster this new relationship for her children. On a regular basis they practised rituals of memory, including showing pictures or making floral or pictorial tributes. At the anniversary of his death they developed a more sustained ritual. Each year the children reported that they found new meaning in the repeated ritual. At the heart of the new relationship was still significant life meaning, including faith in the deceased. Faith in this case was based in the ideas, attitudes and qualities of the deceased, which were discovered or affirmed. All this enabled an effective transition and relearning of the way in which all the family related to the deceased. The framework of life meaning had been worked out beforehand and has been sustained afterwards.

The continued relationship did not stop even when A remarried. Her new husband did not perceive the deceased as a rival but rather as part of her life meaning.

Case B

B was a single mother whose daughter had committed suicide. She was a student who had been depressed and increasingly without hope. B had in the week before the death attempted to control her daughter, to get her to come back home at the end of her studies and to follow the path that she had suggested from the outset of the course. Bereavement was intensely difficult. She felt responsible for her daughter's death, but also very angry that she should have killed herself. She also felt very distant because the death had occurred at university. She felt she had lost her daughter 'more than just physically'.

Finding her was a long task, involving something of a pilgrimage to all her daughter's friends, to hear their story of her daughter, her successes and failures and what she meant to them. As she did this she became more and more aware of how her view of her daughter had often involved projecting her negative feelings about herself on to her. B then retold this story to others, her family and friends, her priest and her GP. In so doing she increasingly saw the values and meaning of her daughter's life, in all its contradictions, and her own ambivalence about her.

B began to re-learn her relationship with her daughter. She talked with her, and wrote letters, expressing her need for forgiveness, hoping to learn something from her daughter that she would be able to put into her life and how she related to others. From this, B felt the need to work through some form of penance that would help to symbolise forgiveness and reconciliation. For B this involved putting effort and money into the pastoral care of students. Her daughter, despite her problems, had been very involved in the student version of the Samaritans, and had found purpose in this. The more B built her dialogue with her daughter into her life the more she found a sense of mutual forgiveness. The more she gained empathy for her daughter the more she could accept her, even in absence. Through this empathy she learned to see her at a distance and so begin to understand her as an other, not simply an extension of her self. She realised too that she had used her daughter in some way as a ground of faith for her. B's sense of well-being had very much depended on her daughter achieving at university. Hence, her value and that of her daughter had been very much conditional. She began to discover a faith in others that could help her let go. This led her to change her relationships with her other children. In turn this led to a new sense of faith in the daughter she had come to know. The faith was based on her daughter's vision of life and principles, and upon her honest searching.

Her reflection went wider, leading her to a very different appreciation of God. She had a view of God at one point that saw him as angry with suicides and thus felt that he would both reject her daughter and judge her as a failing mother. However, as she began to experience a sense of forgiveness she was able to see a God of unconditional care. Her affective experience directly affected her life meaning in religious terms. B took three years to get to this point. The pain of her daughter's loss remains very real, and she still lives with regrets.

Theories of loss and bereavement once more take us into stages and phases. Apart from the anticipatory grief stages of Kübler Ross, Parkes offers a four-stage model (Parkes 1972):

* Shock or numbness.
* Pining and 'yearning and protest'. This involves a complex of feelings, including bitterness, irritability and self reproach.
* Disorganisation and despair. This involves depression and withdrawal.
* Readjustment. This includes a redefining of the self.

A complementary approach from Worden suggests key tasks that have to be worked through to deal with the grief, to:

* accept the reality of the loss.
* experience the pain of grief.
* adjust to an environment in which the deceased is missing.
* withdraw emotional energy from the loved one and reinvest in another relationship. (Worden 1991)

According to Stroebe and Stroebe (1991), the dominant, psychoanalytic, conceptualization of grief is of a cognitive process. This process involves the mourner confronting the reality of loss, and by repeatedly going over the events surrounding the loss before and at the time of the event, detachment from the deceased will take place. The function of working through the stages is to enable the mourner to 'emotionally disengage' from the deceased and 'move on with their life', as the full impact of the loss becomes clear (Freud 1917, Bowlby 1961, Parkes and Weiss 1983).

As we suggested in relation to dying such stage approaches are often very useful but do not fully sum up the experience of loss and bereavement or how life meaning is developed. Firstly, what is shown in the experience of A and B is not so much disengagement as a development or relearning of the relationship with the deceased. A had already worked through a great deal of this prior to the loss of her husband. B had to do so much work around forgiveness and life meaning that is normally associated with present relationships. The research of Moss and Moss (1996) shows evidence of newly bereaved old people maintaining and developing emotional ties to the deceased rather than severing them.

This is further reflected in the work of Attig (1996). He argues that the grieving experience is not the passive ' living through' stages but rather an active relearning of the network of relationships which give meaning to the person's life. 'Loss challenges us to relearn things and places, relationships with others, including fellow survivors, the self and even God; and most of all ourselves, including our daily life patterns and the meaning of our own life stories' (1996: 108).

Secondly, the stage approach does not fully take account of the influence of social and cultural factors that help to shape the experience of grief (Kastenbaum 1988, Corr 1991, Littlewood 1992, Costello and Kendrick 2000). For A, a good deal of her grief work was in the context of an upper middle-class culture which enabled very positive reflection. For B, there were many different cultural factors which she had to wrestle with in order to find meaning. At one level her grief for a long time was disenfranchised (Doka 1989). Because of her sense of guilt at her daughter's suicide she did not feel able to mourn in a public way or share her grief. Much of her guilt was, she felt, reinforced by the views of the church. Only when she began to reflect on the many other different narratives did she begin to see any sense of hope emerging both for her and for her daughter's memory.

For B this meant looking actively at the different grounds of faith in her life. She was shocked to find that her daughter had been the principle 'other' whom she had put her faith in, conditional upon success at university. Not only had she lost someone who was close to her, she had also lost this particular ground of faith. Part of the anger B felt was centred here.

B had both to relearn her relationship with her daughter, moving to a more unconditional base of faith, and to review the other points of faith in her life. She came to see all of these as involved in something like a web, with each affected when one was lost (cf. Attig 1996). At one level, this was about relearning social role and functions. At another level, it was critically about discovering and developing faith that she could live with. B's letting go of her daughter was not disengagement, rather letting go of the old relationship with her daughter, developing a new one, and with that developing hope.

For A this same network of faith was allowed to develop, and so include another husband. There was no sense of losing her bonding with her first husband even then.

In all this, then, various developments of faith can be experienced in the relearning of the bereaved person's network of relationships:

• her faith in the deceased person may remain centred on him and his values.
• there may be some from of transitional faith that helps the person to begin to relearn. This might be based in any source, from religion to family, to the community nurse or volunteer visitor.
• faith may grow in others, to replace or supplement the faith in the deceased. Hence, B developed a faith in her daughter's friends.
• there may be faith developed in an entirely new source.

Such faith, like the stages of dying, may well move from a simplistic conditional faith through to one that is able to come to terms with the ambiguity and complexity of the loss and the newly formed relationships (Fowler's stage five).

Thirdly, stage and phase-based models of grief have been criticized for being prescriptive and thus setting up normative targets. However, neither A nor B point to any simple idea of resolution that could be used as a target. B needed to work through her guilt. In working through it, she was able to identify areas where she genuinely was responsible for problems that her daughter experienced, not least the attempt to impose on her expectations of success. This led to attempts to seek forgiveness. Her view of these was ambivalent. She felt some relief, and yet still had to live in the knowledge of her role in her daughter's life. This meant she had to revisit these issues on a regular basis.

Equally, despite the early grief work of A, there was no sense of completion about this. Most of what is conventionally seen as grief work was achieved by her before her husband's death. After his death, her focus was on maintaining that bond. The rituals enabled her to maintain a faith that was already very secure. Klass, Silverman and Nickman note that the active grief work of spirituality does not have a 'completion', only change, renewal and modification of bonds (1996, 352). They suggest that this continued bonding is something new and distinctive. However, many religious spiritualities, especially in the East, have worked out formal frameworks of meaning which allow the bereaved to relate naturally to the deceased, not least through the practice of ancestor worship. Here is a framework of meaning that enables the family or person to show love, respect and loyalty to the other. In a postmodern world, where there are few such guidelines, meaning has to be worked through by the person and the wider family. What is new is how this can be achieved in a person centred way that does not see either the unthinking imposition of the community ritual or the imposition of an assumed obligation of task completion.

Fourthly, it is worth underlining that relearning relationships and redeveloping faith may involve taking guilt seriously. There is a tendency in some non-directive counselling approaches to bereavement to view guilt as wholly bad, even a source of pathology (Robinson 2001). However, genuinely addressing relationships, as we will see in the next chapter, may involve distinguishing between genuine guilt, such as the way in which B related to her daughter, and guilt feelings that have no basis, those which often ascribe some responsibility for the death of the deceased. In accepting some degree of guilt, B was able to work through effectively to a sense of forgiveness, albeit incomplete.

In a real sense the experience of bereavement for these persons had involved all these aspects, leading to either a maintenance of the faith in the other or a change in relationship, to greater clarity about meaning, hope and purpose and the effect of this in all aspect of the relational web. This was all achieved through reflective dialogue and often sustained by the public statement of ritual.

Care response

The response of the nurse is once more based upon an accompanying and enabling role. Broadly this covers three elements in the bereaved person's experience:

Shock and disbelief

The meaning structure of the person's world is such that it is not possible to comprehend a world without the other. This may be because the other is the core source of meaning and faith in the person's life. They perhaps have found purpose through caring for them, or have always left them to deal with critical areas of life – focusing faith on them. The level of disbelief is not simply cognitive but attached to affective and somatic loss. Many bereaved people speak of the sheer physicality of the loss of having another next to them in bed, or the loss of the immediate knowledge of the other through sexual union. The whole body and emotions then are fighting against the proposition that this other will no longer be a part of her life. There is no meaning in this experience, only questions such 'Why me? . . .' 'if only I had . . .'.

Here the carer must avoid imposing meaning on the person's experience, even if these are words aimed to comfort. This applies even when the person may be searching for a religious reason, which may seem to the carer flawed or problematic, such as the bereaved grandmother who believed that God took 'only the good and innocent'.

Enabling narrative

As the person begins to reflect more on the deceased and the meaning of the deceased in her life, then the different feelings and spiritual narratives begin to emerge. This involves reflection on the whole relational web and the different contradictory narratives that will surface. Again, it is important to enable articulation of the narrative, and allow the person to face and work through the meaning of this and any contradictions which may emerge. Whilst it is tempting to always reassure the bereaved person that there are no grounds for feeling guilty again it is important to allow him to explore that himself. What he concludes will determine how his grieving progresses. Hence, he might seek forgiveness in some way.

As the reflection progresses it can be useful to invite the person to work out her own 'faith map'. This involves simply reflecting on how important the deceased was to her and how much and what kind of faith she put in him. She could then consider what other grounds of faith there were in her life and what was important about them. This helps to develop reflection on her relational network. Again it is important not to impose any view of faith, or attempt to push the patient through to a different kind of faith. The bereaved may simply want to remain in the faith she has shared with her husband for fifty years, and will find her own faith in relation to her own relational network.

The revision or renewing of the bond

As noted above, this does not involve solely changing role or perspective but reviewing and reassessing all grounds of faith. The dynamic of this may lead to the development of forgiveness and reconciliation throughout any network of relationship. With this comes the development of purpose and of hope – envisioning a future that is positive and still maintaining a bond with the deceased. Again, this may lead to altruistic projects (Klass, Silverman and Nickman 1996, 354). All this points to a relearning of the self and the development of *shalom* which includes the deceased.

All of this is essentially person centred. It is also other centred and therefore depends upon many other interactions apart from those with the nurse.

Pathological grief reactions

Klass, Silverman and Nickman stress the importance of not rushing into new categories of pathology to replace the medicalised views based on not achieving stages of grief (1996, 352). Older, cultural views of pathology also believed that the bereaved person should be able to get over the experience and return to 'normal'. In all this the cultural rituals and prescriptions, such as length of time for mourning, could be misused.

Any idea of pathology then has to be carefully described in the context of the network of relationships that provide life meaning for the grieving person. Pathology is attached not to the process but to the underlying relationships and how these are lived in the light of the person's loss. The pathology can be evidenced in the way in which relationships that have not been worked through affect the broader life of the person. Tessman, for instance, notes how the inability of one patient to affirm a connection with her dead father affected her subsequent relationships with men who she wanted to be close with (Tessman 1996). In the light of such reflection it is possible to trace a spiritual pathology which involves the inability of the person to find any faith or sense of hope in life. Rubin notes one example of a patient who idealised the past and would not allow any sense of comfort in the present. Such a response does not allow the person to develop empathy and thus an understanding of the reality of the narrative of their relationship with the deceased. It also leads to a lack of empathy for the self, and inability to accept any sense of forgiveness from the other (Rubin 1996).

Communities

A critical part of B's developing spirituality was her interaction with the student friends of her daughter. She gained support from them and thus could see them as a ground of her faith. She also found out more about her daughter from them, greatly affecting how she viewed her and how she might relearn her relationship with her.

It is important for the healthcare worker to monitor and, where appropriate, enable interaction with different groups, and to avoid a medicalised view of grief and mourning. A good example of interaction is in the preparation of memorial services.

Memorial services are increasingly used, especially in the death of children or young adults (Robinson 2002). A good illustration of this is services provided for students. The preparation of a memorial service can enable many different groups to come together and begin to find shared life meaning through dialogue. At one level, this is important for the family to find the life meaning of the deceased through dialogue with the fellow students, much as B did. At another level, the sharing of memory and life meaning as the students and family reflect on and prepare for the memorial service provides ways in which death and loss can be talked about openly and creatively. For many students, this is the first opportunity to express feelings and develop vocabulary which looks to find meaning in death. The memorial service itself then provides a public statement of life meaning based around the memories of the person. It is important to note that reflection on the embodied meaning of that person is more than saying goodbye. It enables those at the service to reflect on value and practice and how the life meaning of the deceased affects them now and in the future – data gathering, value clarification, and the articulation of purpose that can be valued and shared.

This is a good example of how postmodern spirituality can be enabled through inter-textual dialogue which allows the different groups and people to articulate and test out life meaning in relation to the deceased. The final event reflects not a simple overarching spirituality but the complex spiritualities of all the communities involved, and how they interrelate through reflection on shared experience (Robinson 2002). Healthcare staff can be involved in such services via the chaplaincy, and in relation to community agencies, including local religious or community centres. By becoming involved they further enrich the meaning.

The same dynamic can be involved in the preparation of funerals and other rituals, such as candle lighting, the planting of trees, wakes and other celebrations of the person's life.

Staff bereavement

Professional distance is always important to ensure a competent use of skills. However, it is often difficult for staff not to become involved with the patient, especially if the patient is using him as a ground of faith, or there has been mutual faith development. In the light of this the staff member may well also feel bereaved. In that case it may be important to include him in the reflections and rituals which may be used, and also ensure support. The chaplain can play an important role here in support of the nursing staff.

Conclusion

Spirituality is at the centre of care for the dying and bereaved. It is partly there in finding meaning in dying and death, and partly in the meaning found in the underlying network of relationships, both past and future. It is partly there in helping the bereaved and dying to find a voice. It is also there in helping the deceased to find a voice in the life of the bereaved. Sometimes this will emerge from one-to-one reflections with the nurse. Sometimes rich meaning will emerge from or be confirmed by gatherings and rituals, all of which can include health workers. Such meaning revolves around the development of faith, hope, value, purpose, and reconciliation in the relearning of relationships.

We have noted that some staff find direct engagement with a dying patient difficult. This is hardly surprising, as there are few guidelines that can help them. Without such guidelines it is easy to slide into medicalised and individualist views of death and dying. The first sees the staff member as healer, not involved with death. The second sees dying and bereavement as essentially personal activities. The first can become task oriented and ignore the person. The second is unaware that dying and bereavement are essentially social and interpersonal experiences, ones that are about trying to make sense of the meaningless. The staff member also brings to this experience his own belief system and fears about death and dying.

However, spiritual care of the patient depends upon the empathy of the staff, enabling the patient to develop meaning and so generate faith and hope. This may lead to reconciliation and forgiveness. It is precisely the development of such meaning that can bring about a sense of new perspective and even new life and which can generate real energy for the dying or bereaved. The staff are not exclusively responsible for enabling this spiritual reflection. On the contrary it will be most effective when all the relational networking of the patient is involved. The staff may enable that or simply help the patient to reflect on that. Of course, there may not be time to do any networking. However, as Nouwen reminded us even the shortest time with a dying patient can establish empathy and care and so establish the building block of spiritual meaning, a sense of being valued:

> Let us not diminish the power of waiting by saying that a life saving relationship cannot develop in an hour. One eye movement or one handshake can replace years of friendship when a man is in agony. Love not only lasts forever, it needs only a second to come about (Nouwen 1994, 67).

The nurse in all this remains the skilled, faithful companion (Campbell 1984, 49). His task is to simply accompany the patient on her journey and by staying with her help her to make sense, even of its final moments. To provide such care a person-centred and flexible team is crucial, to collaborate and refer within and beyond the team, including to community care and local religious centres.

Klass, Silverman and Nickman (1996, 355) suggest that the movement toward a more creative view of dying and bereavement is just the beginning of a break away from the old models. Ultimately, it must involve bringing 'death into the conversation about the living'. It means finding ways, such as through discussion of advance directives, in which death can be acknowledged as a part of life, without affecting the tone and delivery of healthcare (Guroian 1996, Age Concern 1999).

Questions and exercises

1. Reflect on your experience of death and dying. What meaning do you find in death? Where, for instance, can you find hope in the process and experience of dying? How do you react to a dying patient? What feelings does such a relationship raise for you?
2. How can you help develop faith, hope, purpose and right relationships in a dying patient?
3. How can you enable such life meaning to develop in the bereaved person?

References

Age Concern (1999) *The Future of Health and Care of Older People: The Best is Yet to Come* (London: Age Concern England).

Aries, P. (1974) *Western Attitudes towards Death: From the Middle-ages to the Present* (Baltimore: John Hopkins Press).

Attig, T. (1996) *How We Grieve: Relearning the World* (Oxford: Oxford University Press).

Badham, P. (1998) 'Should Christians accept the validity of voluntary euthanasia' in R. Gill (ed.) *Euthanasia and the Churches* (London: Cassell), 41–59.

Bowlby, J. (1961) 'Processes of mourning', *The International Journal of Psychoanalysis*, **XL11**, 317–40.

Bridges, W. (1980) *Transitions: Making Sense of Life's Changes* (Reading, Mass: Addison Wesley).

Burnard, P. and Kendrick, K. (1998) *Ethical Counselling: A Workbook for Nurses* (London: Arnold).

Campbell, A. (1984) *Moderated Love* (London: SPCK).

Carter, S.L. (1989) 'Themes of grief', *Nursing Research*, **38**, 354–7.

Clark, D. (1982) 'Death in Staithes' in D. Dickenson, and M. Johnson, *Death, Dying and Bereavement*, (London: Sage), 4–10.

Cobb, M. (2001) *The Dying Soul: Spiritual Care at the End of Life* (Buckingham: Open University Press).

Corr, C. (1991) 'A task based approach to coping with dying', *Omega*, **24**, 81–94.

Costello, J. and Kendrick, K. (2000) 'Grief and older people: the making or breaking of emotional bonds following partner loss in later life'. *Journal of Advanced Nursing*, **32**, 6, 1374–82.

Davidhizar, R. and Newman Gigor, J. (1998) 'Patients' use of denial: coping with the unacceptable', *Nursing Standard*, **12**, 43, 44–6.

Doka, K. (1989) *Disenfranchised Grief* (Lexington: Lexington Books).

Edwards, D. (1999) *After Death?* (London: Cassell).

Freud, S. (1917) *Mourning and Melancholia* (Hogarth Press: London).

Gill, S. and Fox, J. (1996) *The Dead Good Funeral Book* (Ulverstone: Engineers of the Imagination).

Guroian, V. (1996) *Life's Living Toward Dying* (Grand Rapids: Eerdmans).

Hill, J. (1988) 'Bereavement Care', in J. Wilson-Barnett and J. Raiman (eds) *Nursing Issues and Research in Terminal Care* (Chichester: John Wiley and Sons).

Kastenbaum, R. (1988) 'Safe Death in the Post-modern World' in A. Gilmore, and S. Gilmore, (eds) *A Safer Death* (London: Plenum), 3–15.

Kendrick, K.D. (1998) 'Theories of bereavement', *Professional Nurse*, **14**, 1 ,57–62.

Kendrick, K.D. and Hughes, N. (2002) 'Spirituality', in D. Clarke, J. Flanagan, and K.D. Kendrick (eds) *Advancing Nursing Practice in Cancer and Palliative Care* (London: Palgrave).

Kendrick, K. and Robinson, S. (2002) *Their Rights: Advance Directives and Living Wills Explored* (London: Age Concern).

Klass, D., Silverman, P. and Nickman, L. (1996) *Continuing Bonds* (Philadelphia, Taylor and Francis).

Kübler-Ross, E. (1970) *On Death and Dying* (New York: Macmillan).

Larkin, P. (1993) 'Aubade' in D. Dickenson and M. Johnson, *Death, Dying and Bereavement* (London; Sage), 78–9.

Leming, M. and Dickinson, G. (1998) *Understanding Dying, Death and Bereavement* (Fort Worth: Harcourt Brace) 4th edn.

Littlewood, J. (1992) *Aspects of Grief: Bereavement in Adult Life* (London: Routledge).

Littlewood, J. (1993) 'The Denial of Death and Rites of Passage in Contemporary Societies', in D. Clark (ed.) *The Sociology of Death* (Oxford: Blackwell).

Lynn, J. and Harrold, J. (1999) 'Handbook for Mortals' (Oxford: Oxford University Press).

McIntyre, R. (2002) *Nursing Support for Families of Dying Patients* (Philadelphia: Whurr).

McNamara, B., Waddell, C. and Colvin, M. (1995) 'Threats to the good death: the cultural context of stress and coping among hospice nurses', *Sociology of Health and Illness*, **17**, 224–44.

Menzies, N. (1970) *Communication and Stress: a Nursing Perspective* (London: Macmillan – now Palgrave Macmillan).

Morris, E. (1998) 'Death and Loss: helping patients', *Nursing*, **3**, 2, 5–7.

Moss S.M. and Moss, S.Z. (1996) 'Remarriage of Widowed Persons: A Triadic Relationship', in D. Klass, P.R. Silverman, S.L. Nickman, (eds) *Continuing Bonds: New Understandings of Grief* (Philadelphia: Taylor & Francis) 163–77.

Neuberger, J. (1994) *Caring for the Dying in Different Faiths* (St Louis: Mosby).

Nouwen, H. (1994) *The Wounded Healer* (London: Dartman, Longman and Todd).

Nuland, S. (1993) *How We Die: Reflections on Life's Final Chapter* (New York: Alfred A. Knopf).

Parkes, C.M. (1972) *Bereavement: Studies of Grief in Adult Life* (London: Penguin).

Parkes, C.M. and Weiss, R. (1983) *Recovery from Bereavement* (New York: Basic Books).

Potter, D. (1994) *Seeing the Blossom* (London: Faber and Faber).

Pye, J. (2001) *A Winter's Tale: A Pastoral and Theological Exploration of the Responses of Families and Their Carers to Pre-natal, Peri-natal, and Neo-natal Deaths* (Unpublished PhD thesis, University of Leeds).

Robinson, S. (1998) 'Helping the hopeless', *Contact*, **127**, 3–11.

Robinson, S. (2001) *Agape, Moral Meaning and Pastoral Counselling* (Cardiff: Aureus).

Robinson, S. (2002) ' "Thanks for the Memory . . ." Death of a Student: Memorials, Mourning and Postmodernity' *Contact*, **138**, 16–25.

Rose, G. (1997) *Love's Work* (London: Vintage).

Rubin, S. (1996) 'The Wounded Family: Bereaved Parents and the Impact of Adult Child Loss', in Klass, Silverman and Nickman, 217–34.

Seymour, J. (2001) *Critical Moments – Death and Dying in Intensive Care* (Buckingham: Open University Press).

Smith, R. (2000) 'A good death', *British Medical Journal*, **320**, 129–30.

Stroebe, M.S. and Stroebe, W. (1991) 'Does "grief work" Work?', *Journal of Consulting and Clinical Psychology*, **59**, 479–82.

Tarvis, C. (1982) *Anger: The Misunderstood Emotion* (New York: Simon and Schuster).

Thomas, J. and Retsas, A. (1999) 'Transacting self-preservation: a grounded theory of the spiritual dimensions of people with terminal cancer', *International Journal of Nursing Studies*, **36**, 191–201.

Tessman, L. (1996) 'Dilemmas in Identification for the Post-Nazi Generation: "My Good Father Was a Bad Man?" ', in Klass, Silverman and Nickman, 329–48.

Vatuk, S. (1996) 'The Art of Dying in Hindu India', in H. Spiro, M. McCrea, E. Curnen, L. Palmer, L. Wandel (eds) *Facing Death* (New Haven: Yale University Press), 121–8.

Woodward, J. (1995) *Encountering Illness* (London: SCM Press Ltd.).

Worden, J.W. (1991) *Grief Counselling and Grief Therapy: A Handbook for the Mental Health Practitioner* (London: Routledge), 2nd edn.

8

Spirituality and Mental Health

The Fragile Rock of My Being

I was in a Jewish choir rehearsal and suddenly for an instant
I saw in my mind's eye a rock – stronger than any rock I had ever seen –
Rainbow coloured, living in some of the people in the choir, in the centre of
their being.
That experience led me to ask Jesus into my life two days later with the
encouragement of another believer.
The rock I had seen had an identity and a character and that was Jesus.
I have based my whole life on that rock, combining my Jewishness with my
belief in Jesus.
My creative life – I am a painter and a poet – is based upon the religious
implications of the initial experience.

But my experience of life on a daily basis is that God and life are not a rock,
but are like shifting sands and there is no refuge or comfort in them.
Faith hasn't helped me build my life up, which has been shattered in illness (a
schizo-affective disorder). I've had to do it myself against all the pressures of
life.
I feel I am not acceptable to God in my 'ill-state' despite all my efforts at
acceptability. Although I don't feel the presence of Jesus tangibly, I believe in
what he stands for – 'for binding up the broken hearted' – and I emulate his
personhood in my being.
My paintings and poetry are a creative defiance in the face of a daily struggle
to maintain my consciousness.
What is in my heart is the rock of Jesus, but he doesn't relieve the heavy
weight of the fragile wiring of my being.

Dan Clouts

*Dan Clouts' 'story', is one of a number written by people who have, as the
title of the book says, come together with, The Courage to Bear Our Souls: A
Collection of Pieces Written Out of Mental Distress (Mental Health*

Foundation 1999). Clouts was brought up in the Jewish faith, no doubt an experience during which Jesus would have been looked upon at least sceptically, and possibly with derision. The purpose here is not to look particularly closely at either Judaism or Christianity, for this is not a book about religions, but Clouts' story is interesting because although he is Jewish, he has clearly been affected by what he calls his belief in Jesus. Life has not been easy for Clouts, he has endured a schizo-affective disorder, and for all his Jewishness and belief in Jesus, he has not felt the warm glow of faith that many faith evangelists promote, but has had to face life, in the raw, on his own and yet not on his own, for as he points out he has felt Jesus to be a rock, particularly in what Jesus stands for, in healing and binding up the broken hearted. There is an ambivalent chord in Clouts' story. Although Jesus is seen as a rock, he is not seen as relieving all of Clouts' problems, more it is in the nature of Jesus as a role-model, the emulation of which Clouts attempts, in living out his own life, which has been of help. Such ambivalence within one's own faith and towards or away from other faiths, points up that the faith business is a murky, messy world, through which those who have a faith have to trawl to make sense of, especially during periods when experiencing the dark night of the soul, for example in the stews of depression or chronic mental illness.

The focus of this chapter is on mental health as much as mental illness. The reason for this is that many people experience variability in the state of their mental health, without ever being diagnosed as having a mental illness. This can include staff as well as patients. It is not the work of this chapter to summarise the different levels of mental illness, acute and chronic, but to cover some of the generalities of spirituality as related to mental health. We will examine the search for meaning which lies at the base of mental health, summed up well in symbolic interactionism. We will then turn to the issue of depression, sometimes termed as the common cold of mental health problems, noting the experience of sufferers. Through two case studies we will examine how spirituality lies at the heart of the therapeutic process and relationship. Finally, we will note reviews of spiritual need and assessment in mental health, and briefly detail a number of different alternative therapeutic approaches, often viewed under the heading spiritual'.

Mental health, meaning and spirituality

Frankl argues that the core factor that motivates the person and helps them to develop and maintain mental health is the need for meaning, and with that in particular, the need for purpose and the related sense of hope (Frankl 1962). As we have noted it is precisely this which attention to the spiritual narrative enables.

It is this meaning which is discovered through story. In psycho-analysis, people tell their dreams to uncover hidden truth (Bausch 1995, 5). They tell their stories, as storyteller, to the listener, in this case the psychoanalyst, who is the other, and who becomes an actor within yet another part of the storyteller's story, the storyteller redefining the story, in the light of the other's listening. Story allows the storyteller to revisit an old situation in new ways. The past, the unchangeable that cannot be changed, is just what it is. It cannot be changed by the person's story. Reality is what it is, and yet, the story form can be used to reinterpret the unchangeable creatively. It helps the person to go back and relive the event and to see its outcome in new ways. A story well told is the listener's dream, for we are able to sit back and relax our sense of curiosity, lulled into security by the well-modulated voice and the full nature of that which is to be told. But to tell a story is a symbolic act requiring a symbolic interaction, and Hewitt's theory of symbolic interactionism sums up the underlying dynamic. When analysed, the symbolic interactions performed by an individual take three forms:

- Human beings act towards things on the basis of the meanings that things have for them;
- The meanings of such things are derived from, or arise out of, the social interaction that one has with one's fellows;
- These meanings are handled in, modified through, an interpretative process used by the person in dealing with the things he encounters (Hewitt 1979, 5).

Although these propositions appear simple enough on the surface, they summarize a deceptively complicated set of ideas about the nature of the human world and how people act within it. They are based on a knowledge and understanding of the interaction between a set of variables; objects, meanings, action, social interaction and interpretation. Each of these will be explained below.

Objects
Most people are able to describe an object, for example, a table. When we talk of the purchase of a table to a friend on the telephone, the other will have a picture in their mind of this real object which has

been purchased. In symbolic interactionist terms an object means something other as in, for example, a child who 'sees' shadows on a wall. The child is able to designate the shadows and name them as, say, a ghost and act towards the shadows as though the ghost existed, jumping under the bed-clothes for security. Assuming that a ghost didn't exist, we have here the creation of an object by symbolic designation. The ghost doesn't exist, only the shadows, yet the child acts towards the ghost as if it were as real as the table by her bed.

Meanings

We all look for meaning in social interaction, whether at a party or in the 'awkward question' at an interview. Meanings in turn give purpose to activity, though meanings rely on perception of the spoken word, and the non-verbal cues which are provided for us by the other.

Action

The way an individual acts does not consist merely of what may be observed by others, but also contains an internal process of control in which the individual directs his conduct towards some goal or object. Other people in a room at a party, are as much objects as the table upon which the drinks are served. If we see the people who are present at the party as 'friendly' then we act towards them as though they are 'friendly'. It may be of course that they are not true friends but are putting on a social act. This raises a very interesting question for the health service professional. 'Who are you when you interact with the patient or client?' Do we present ourselves as the 'professional'? Nominally it would be right to do so, because the patient or client comes to us for some service or another. Do we present ourselves as being friendly? Presumably yes, as this will help gain the confidence of the patient or client. The real question to ponder is how far down the road are we prepared to go, to lay out who we are ourselves to the storyteller, in order that an authentic relationship is developed, which in turn creates an environment for an authentic story to be told.

Social interaction

Individuals interacting with one another do so in part by taking one another's perspectives towards themselves, meaning that situations of social interaction become structured in terms of role. Group members name and act towards one another, creating a sense of group structure.

The people in the group, (which may be defined as two or more people) then start to 'play' roles relative to one another. Thus the storyteller is just that, and the listener is the listener. Again, if there is to be an authenticity in the relationship, it has to be understood that each is there for a purpose, though the formation of a story, especially if told for the first time, is no easy thing for the storyteller. Nor is it easy for the listener to grasp the nuances and detail.

Interpretation

Individuals do not learn about themselves or experience themselves directly. We see ourselves as others see us, learning to use the name given to us by others, but more subtly than this, to use the terms of value, respect, hatred, liking, social location and definition which others give to us and we apply to ourselves. These are learned from our families, friends, work colleagues and from the social structures around us which may define who we are, nurse, doctor, priest, audiologist, criminal, patient, or hopeless case.

All of this points to meaning and purpose that is negotiated in various ways as part of life. This contrasts sharply with the historical view of mental illness. The mentally ill were perceived by definition to be unable to negotiate meaning, be that logical or moral (Digby 1985). On the contrary they were entirely different, entirely 'other'. Hence, they were viewed as a threat, not least to order and moral meaning, which had to be controlled (Jones 1972). Others have viewed mental illness as in itself a form of possession by the other, requiring exorcism (Rosen 1980), or in a more positive light as a sign of prophetic or divine ecstasy (Wilkinson 1998). The development of a more scientific view of mental health and illness has often not attended to questions of meaning, looking either to control behaviour through drugs or other techniques (Pattison 1989). However, meaning, and often the loss of it, is at the centre of much mental disturbance, something exemplified in depression.

Depression

In Chapter 5 we noted that the 'dark night of the soul', a crisis of spirituality which involved the general category of sadness, differs from depression (Stone 1998). Sadness is seen as a healthy reaction to life situations involving loss, disappointment or confusion, often closely related to grief. This may be part of a depressive illness but need not lead to clinical depression. Such depression is a complex mood disorder involving the entire psychobiological organism, characterised by

stently negative views of the self, the world and the future. This
lead to a collection of symptoms of which the slowing down of
the whole organism predominates (Fairchild 1990). Gilbert (1992, 1)
notes that these symptoms affect emotional, cognitive, and biological
operation, with a general lack of motivation. Whilst there are a broad
range of causes, including genetic predisposition and/or endocrine or
neurochemical imbalance, there are also causes which focus on life
meaning, critically the patient's attitude to the self. Kohut argues that
depression often springs from a loss of 'external inputs', especially
human relationships, which give and maintain positive feelings about
the self (Kohut 1977). Kohut argues that depression is related to a
painful sense of disappointment, and related shame, and thus argues
that the key to treatment is the articulation of that disappointment
and working through the life meaning which has been learned and
internalised.

Recent qualitative research by Swinton also focused on meaning
in depression. It involved three men and three women being inter-
viewed, using an unstructured interview technique for between 45
minutes and one hour. All of the participants had experienced depression for at least two years. Each interview opened with the question,
'What is it that gives meaning in your life?'

The central themes which emerged from the interviews provided
a rich mixture of useful data:

- *The meaningless abyss of depression*: If there is no meaning in a
  person's life, where is the motivation to carry on? For some of the
  interviewees, there was a feeling of being in an abyss, that black pit
  of meaninglessness into which the person with depression slides.
  This is bad enough, but worse is to come if there is no apparent way
  of finding a foothold out of the abyss, in the form of feelings of
  doubt about self, others, and life in general.
- *Questioning everything*: The movement from a meaningful universe
  to a meaningless one presented in all the participants. Therefore the
  familiar is constantly questioned.
- *Abandonment*: Feelings of abandonment, either by others or by God,
  or both, was a common theme which ran through all the interviews. We are constantly told by people of authority within faith
  institutions that God loves us. If we feel that we are unloved and
  unwanted, it is as though God has abandoned us. Being told that
  God is carrying us when we are at absolute rock bottom and feeling abandoned is not only tactless, but verges on the absurd. Telling

people they are not alone when they clearly think they are is unhelpful. Showing that they are not alone, by being with them, and here we return to the notion of the carer being the accompanist on the journey, is an entirely different matter.

- *Clinging on*: In the midst of meaningless, all the participants clung on to their faith, not necessarily in terms of their religion, but in a personal relationship with God. The person's spirituality helped the individual relocate him or herself within the world, helping them to find identity, worth, purpose and hope. As Swinton puts it, 'In the midst of the hopelessness and helplessness that depression brings into a person's life, spirituality provides a reason to be, a purpose and sense of meaning which reaches beyond their immediate situation . . . enabling a person to cling on in the midst of the darkest storms' (Swinton 2001, 116).

- *The desire to relate and the failure of relationships*: Depression drains the physical and psychological strength out of the person and the strength required to fight is lost. This makes physical and psychological relationships difficult to sustain, because the person simply does not have the strength to do it. Such a lack of strength may well be at odds with the person's deep-seated desire for relationships, the failure of which inevitably makes the depression worse.

- *Being ground down*: The constant battle against depression becomes demoralising, grinding the person down, and in extreme cases, to the point at which they lose the will to live.

- *Being trapped into living*: This is likened to the person feeling ground down. When suicidal thoughts occur, because of an individual's positive spirituality, it becomes double edged, with feelings such as, 'God wouldn't want me to kill myself' emerging, and also guilt, and fear of eternal damnation. This has meant that although suicide has seemed to the individual to be the most logical next step in the depressive cycle, they feel trapped into living because of the consequences once they have succeeded in the act.

- *The crucible of depression*: For some, the journey through depression brings new spiritual insights. One participant in Swinton's research called this the 'crucible'. Everything having been put in the melting pot, the pot is put into the refiner's fire, and impurities that come to the surface are skimmed off. That which remains is pure and wholesome. Such an experience radically changed the participant's view of life. The term 'refiners fire' is drawn from spiritual tradition, and the meaningless and hopelessness of depression is reframed as a necessary part of his spiritual journey, discovering spiritual and personal insights which might not have been discovered if the depression had not been experienced.

- *The healing power of understanding*: All of Swinton's participants stressed the importance of feeling understood by those who offered care, and that this helped them to see their own needs more clearly. Although it varied in degree, all of the participants found that the Christian Churches to which they belonged were wholly unprepared to deal with their mental health problems. The reasons for this varied, including, intellectualisation of the religion, rather than practical dimensions of care, and lack of education within church communities about mental health problems. Unsurprisingly, those who were the most effective at caring were those who had experienced suffering themselves. Unfortunately, the professional healthcare givers fared no better. Whilst tolerant to spirituality, none of the professionals provided any active spiritual support or intervention. To the contrary, it was sometimes thought by the staff that the participants had 'gone religious on us' . . . 'a bit dodgy'. This brings us back to a problem referred to earlier, that it is very difficult for healthcare workers to relate to the spiritual needs of an individual if they have no real understanding of their own spirituality. It is insufficient for a nurse to agree to an in-patient going to a church service, without exploring why this is important to the individual. Such an exploration would give valuable insights into the person's spiritual requirements. If spirituality is seen to be an added extra, to be given by staff who are seen by others to be so inclined themselves, then a vitally important dimension of healthcare is being ignored.

- *Liturgy and worship*: When the intellect seemed to be failing, a primary experience of the participants was that other senses can enable spiritual contact through the symbols, hymns and sacraments of the church; for some people, the non-cognitive elements of ritual and symbol become extremely important. This need is not confined to members of particular faiths.

The phenomenological approach which Swinton has used has much to offer mental health practitioners. His research gives more than a flavour of the richness of feelings and experiences held within an individual patient's frame of reference and those within a selected group. There is nothing within that described which should cause us to be surprised. It is in the acknowledgement of such feelings and experiences, and how they focus on meaning or the lack of meaning, that care staff can start to become supportive accompanists to the individual as he journeys on through, and hopefully beyond illness.

Two case studies will now illustrate some key elements of the development of spirituality in the therapeutic relationship.

Case A

A came to her therapist suffering from what had been diagnosed as bi-polar affective disorder. She exhibited initial uncertainty about the process and kept apologising for wasting the therapist's time. Initially she spoke of problems experienced at work, in the religious community that she was involved in, and with her family. She felt responsible for both her boss and for the leader of her community, both of whom were under pressure caused by major change. She also felt responsible for her younger cousins who she felt were being badly treated by their parents.

After several sessions she began to share how she had been emotionally and sexually abused as a child by both her parents. For several sessions she alternated between a sense of deep depression and one of knowing just what she needed. These needs would be expressed often just before the end of the session. At one of these she said 'I know it sounds odd for a woman of my age, but I think all I really need is a hug . . . but it is the thing I most fear. God I'm strange'.

She spoke further of her depression and of how she felt impelled to self-harm. A recurring image for her was of smashing her wrists through glass.

The spiritual world of the patient

A had come to her therapist with a very clearly defined spiritual world. From her experience of abuse she had built up a sense of self-esteem which was built on conditionality. She could only be worthy if she pleased her parents, which by definition she could not do. From this conditional world she had built up a very explicit value and belief system, such as responsibility for others, self-reliance, and moral taboos on feelings such as anger. This system had arisen out of her *affect shame* (shame about feeling), and *need shame* (shame at declaring need) (Kaufman 1980). Hence, her spiritual perspective had arisen from her experiences, and feelings of low self-esteem.

This system was both evidence of her problem and also was seen by her as a key way of coping. She had to survive by her own efforts and she felt that she had to take responsibility for many different people, especially those she saw as victims. She knew it created problems but did not want let go of it. In turn, this explicit spirituality caused a distortion of data, from her view of the abuse, which she thought to be her fault, to her view of others who she polarised as either entirely for or against her.

Narrative

As the therapist enabled A to articulate her narrative, she was able to gain distance, which led firstly to a clearer view of the data. Her desire to break glass turned out not to be a suicidal desire but rather based in the memory of the abuse. On the first occasion it occurred near a window. She could not find a voice to cry out, but desperately wanted to reach the window to smash it. With a clearer view of the data she also began to have a view of herself as a victim.

In articulating the narrative A was continuously testing the therapist, looking out for conditional responses. Often the revelation would be accompanied by the phrase, 'You must find me revolting'. At about this time A tentatively but seriously raised the question of therapeutic touch. She wanted, but feared mostly of all, to be hugged. This led to a contract, which included holding hands with the therapist, when A initiated it. The touch enabled her to develop her narrative, and it confirmed the building of a bridge of unconditional acceptance which existentially began to erode the basis of her spiritual world. Articulating the need to be hugged in particular, she began to question her need shame. The therapist's response affirmed that this need was good and that human beings shared it.

Clarifying and testing meaning

The narrative had already caused contradictions to surface. One was the view of herself as both responsible for the abuse and also the victim. A second was the emergence of anger and the prohibition of anger. A third was the concern for others and a lack of care for herself. The therapist reflected back these contradictions to A, giving her the responsibility of working through them (Halmos 1961). This non-directive approach allows the client to begin to work at life meaning and begin to question it in the safety of the therapeutic relationship. This naturally led to two levels of spiritual development. Firstly, A was able to focus more on her anger. This meant identifying this feeling, along with many other (Tavris 1982, 94). As she identified the feeling and articulated it in the context of the therapeutic relationship so she was able to existentially experience anger which was not destructive. Secondly, and in parallel, this led to her reflecting on her religious spirituality. This she believed provided moral support of her view that anger was wrong. When asked about the religious justification of this she pointed to the example of Jesus and the general destructive effects of all anger. The therapist's role at this point was not to enter into a religious debate, or push her away from a negative spirituality, but to enable her to explore her own religious views in a critical and creative way. Through her own resources she found examples of positive anger in her religion, and thus began to chip away at the cognitive belief which had helped to hold in place her affect shame. This helped her to begin to move away from a conditional, non-accepting view of faith, through to one which was increasingly able to put faith in people and ideas which were ambiguous (Robinson 1998).

A great deal of the clarifying and testing of meaning comes through the inter-textual dialogue that we referred to earlier (van der Ven 1998). In A's case this involved reflection on the different texts that were part of her story. This included experience in the Christian Church, the family, school, and work. Each of these tended to reinforce the others in her stress on conditional value. However, the more she was encouraged to articulate the different texts and what they meant to her the more differences began to emerge. These differences provided the base for inter-textual dialogue which challenged each of the texts. The strong sense of personal support experienced in school, for instance, enabled A to question the conditional worth felt within the family. This, in turn, enabled A to question the church 'text' which seemed to support the conditionality of the family. Once the church text was more positive it could also critique the conditional view of worth. The task of the therapist was simply to enable the story and the different texts within it.

Finding new meaning

As A began to question her old spirituality she had to begin to finds values and beliefs that could replace the one that she had relied on. Kaufman writes of the need at this point to find new meaning, and of, 'the need for meaning in life, for a sense of purpose to what we do, that quest for belonging to something greater than oneself, the search for significance which springs from the identification need' (Kaufman 1980, 136. Cf. also Foskett 1984).

For A this involved the development of a new moral and spiritual meaning which was focused on the concepts of care and love. This was based in the unconditional therapeutic relationship which both gave her a sense of such love and also enabled her to question her old spirituality safely. This led to a development in her religious faith. Prior to this reflection she had seen God as judgemental and very much in cognitive terms. He was the focus of 'good' ideas. Now she could begin to personalise her faith and even to see God in feminine terms. As she moved into a different view of God she was also able to focus on the church community which she had never felt a part of and see it as supporting her. Hence, she began to develop a much more complex and existential faith. With all this she began to develop critical qualities and virtues, principally empathy for herself and others, a more rounded sense of care , and humility and pride in the sense of being aware of her limitations and strengths.

It is important to note that this development of faith did not necessarily take away from the experience of suffering. It did provide a way of living through and responding to that suffering. Cashman notes that other abuse survivors have found different ways of developing a faith, such as one client who formed a spiritual relationship with nature. She said, 'I got mothering from the landscape then, and I do now, and that's where I feel closest to God' (Cashman 1993, 86).

Embodying the spirit

The new meaning had to be embodied for A to take this forward. At one level this meant A renegotiating her responsibility with others. As she practised this, she was able to let go of the felt need to care for all the vulnerable she knew. Alongside this, she began to address her relationships with her parents. This moved into questions of forgiveness and reconciliation. It meant moving away from any sense of religious obligation to forgive, to focusing on those relationships. At first, this meant accepting that her parents were not monsters. Recognising their common humanity enabled her not to simply seek revenge (Smedes 1998). At the same time, facing the reality of what they did demanded justice. Hence, her search was for *shalom,* a sense of right relationships. In her case this led to communicating her feelings to her parents and stating her forgiveness, and to the conclusion that she could not be reconciled with them. Forgiveness in this sense was proactive, with reconciliation seen as dependent upon the response of the other (Smedes 1998). None of this precluded her expression of anger, indeed the force of the anger was empowering, enabling her to both forgive and close the relationship.

At various times, her embodiment of spirituality could not be simply articulated in words. It needed a sense of ritual to encompass the many feelings that were struggling to be articulated. Hence, for instance, she had a gathering of her friends to celebrate and cement her renegotiating of responsibilities. This had been the first time that she had entertained others in her house. When it came to closure, she had a service which gave up her parents to God, and gave him responsibility for them. She spoke of a great sense of release from this.

All of this enables her to develop hope in a realistic and creative way. At one level, this was about an increase of life options now that she was able to share responsibility. At another level, her previous spirituality had by definition not allowed her to envision the future in any positive or creative way.

This case shows how the simple process of spiritual reflection can be an integral part of the therapeutic process itself. It remains essentially non-directive, but does not preclude the use of techniques such as cognitive-behavioural therapy, in focusing on and testing beliefs and belief systems (Martin and Booth 1999, Robinson 2001). It should also be stressed that this can be used either by the therapist as part of the process, by the nurse when taking the role of therapist, or by the nurse in collaboration with the therapist. In using this approach explicit questions about faith, hope, purpose, forgiveness and reconciliation can be used non-directively, to enable the client to reflect on these areas of her life, such as where she places faith and what is the nature of her hope.

Case B

B is seen by many to be a pillar in the community, a retired professional and regular churchgoer. Whilst in hospital he approaches the chaplain after the Sunday service and asks for the sacrament of reconciliation, involving confession and forgiveness. As he shares his story it become clear that he is anxious and depressed about the fact that he has spent time in his local newsvendors looking at soft porn magazines. He feels that he has sullied his relationship with his wife of forty years by looking for gratification elsewhere.

This case raises issues of guilt and shame. Many therapists view the idea of guilt as by definition pathogenic. Moreover, religion is often seen as attempting to control through guilt (Avis 1989, 61–2,

Cashman 1993, 84). In this light the client should be released from guilt, enabling him to move on. Enabling the client to address his spirituality reveals a more complex picture.

On the face of it B is driven by a form of negative guilt which is causing him anxiety in his therapy. The chaplain initially felt that it was important to help B let go of this. However, as he articulated his spiritual narrative it became clear that this was not one driven by negative religion reinforcing a negative, and thus destructive sense of guilt. B's wife was central to his spirituality. In many respects, she was as great a ground of his faith as the church. His experience of illness had caused a real sense of the loss of his wife – even though she came to visit him regularly. In the light of that he genuinely felt that he had let his wife down, and that he needed to make reparation. In that light the chaplain enable B to reflect on the underlying meaning of this, and just what the guilt was. It emerged that B felt that he had lost the physical side of his relationship to his wife and that part of the reason for this had been his concern, first, with increased voluntary work and also with several other women. Whilst none of this had led to unfaithfulness he did see this cumulatively leading to him not paying attention to his wife, and thus losing awareness of her. The ritual of reconciliation was able to focus on that for him and move him further on to examine ways in which he could begin to renew his relationship with his wife. This included plans for a holiday after the operation.

Critical to this whole process were two things. Firstly, it was important to distinguish between pathogenic guilt, which either has no basis or is the cause of ill health, and healthy guilt, the awareness of the person's own responsibility in any situation or breakdown of relationships (Robinson 2001). It is important to be aware of the possibility of the latter and its potential importance to therapy and developing spiritual meaning. Secondly, distinguishing between the two is critically not the role of the therapist or priest, but of the client himself. Only through articulating his narrative can the client begin to objectify the meaning and thus begin to examine for himself the basis of the feeling of guilt. Once that is done then the pathogenic guilt can be talked through in the light of the unconditional care offered and the healthy guilt can move on to ways of embodying forgiveness, reconciliation and *shalom*.

Both these cases underline two points. Firstly, factors such as shame can be blocks to the development of spirituality. Secondly, some spiritualities can be unhealthy. In other words the person may have developed a belief system which has no awareness of appreciation of the other and thus generates life meaning which has either no faith or hope or builds faith and hope on inappropriate foundations. This may mean, for instance, putting faith in the other to achieve what it cannot, or putting too much faith in the self. In one sense this highlights the point that no spirituality is fully formed. It is, by definition, a learning experience, developing in response to new situations. As such, it is perfectly reasonable to enable the challenge of any spirituality. This is not to impose a new spiritual perspective on the person, but rather to enable the person to challenge and test her life meaning for herself. Where such life meaning is well developed testing will simply affirm it. Where it is inadequate or the cause of an emotional problem then testing in the light of the non-judgmental presence of the nurse, as described above, will enable further development.

Empathic presence

The empathic presence of the therapist or nurse is once more the key to enabling appropriate spiritual reflection. As noted in Chapter 5, Kohut argues that empathy *per se* has a therapeutic effect, both in the clinical setting and in life in general (Kohut 1982, 397). He notes two major elements of empathy in therapy. Firstly, it has a methodological function, enabling observation and reflection, both by the therapist and the client. Secondly, it is a psychological 'bond' and 'nutriment', the very oxygen of the therapeutic relationship. This relates closely to the dynamic noted above, with the client learning through the acceptance of the therapist to accept her self and from this to develop new spiritual meaning which can help to support and maintain recovery.

The very person of the therapist is thus critical to the development of spiritual meaning, enabling this to be a part of the therapeutic process. Swinton can thus speak of spiritual meaning in mental health as enabled by therapeutic understanding (Swinton 2001, 140). Blise (1995) stresses the difference between explanation and understanding in the therapeutic context. Explanation stresses the importance of distancing in order to see a particular condition or problem. As such it is focused in therapeutic outcome and problem solving. Understanding seeks to focus on what gives the person their life meaning and to communicate that the therapist has recognised that life meaning, as the client has articulated it, be it in a cognitive, affective, or somatic way. Blise notes the case of a psychotic patient who suffered from the delusion that he was being chased by the FBI. At one level she took note of the delusion *per se* and continued with the drug regime. At the same time she responded to the patient's story, recognising his fear and communicating how fearful she would be if she felt the FBI were pursuing her (Blise 1995, 18). Hence, whilst the facts of her patient's story might be challenged, the underlying feelings could be affirmed and explored, with the therapist encouraging a development of his story. This same approach then can be developed with those suffering from psychoses, and alongside any drug regime.

Spiritual needs and assessment in mental health

Swinton (2001) sums up the spiritual needs in mental health in Box 8.1.

Box 8.1   Non-religious spiritual needs

Values and structures of meaning
Hope
Faith
Search for meaning/purpose of life
Dealing with guilt and initiating forgiveness

Relationships
Therapeutic presence
The possibility of intimacy

Transcendence
The need to explore dimensions beyond Self
The possibility of reaching God without the use of formal religious structures

Affective feeling
Reassurance
Comfort
Peace
Happiness

Communication
Talking and telling stories
Listening and being listened to

With story at the centre of articulating needs this allows values and affective feelings to emerge and be explored together. Story also enables the person to transcend the self. As noted in Chapter 2 the dynamic of empathy is about transcending the self to identify with the other. It is also about transcending the self to see the self more clearly and identify with it. Such a dynamic of transcendence leads to a reframing of perspective, enabling the person to see the self and others in a different light. This in turn enables the development of faith in the self and other.

In many respects spiritual needs arise directly from human needs. Kaufman, in Box 8.2 (1980) lists six human needs that tie directly into the definition of spirituality in Chapter 2: Life meaning is mediated through the fufilment of such needs.

Box 8.2   Spiritual needs

- The need for relationships – to be in close interpersonal relationships with others who want to be in relationship with you.
- The need for touching and holding, to provide the primary basis for the development of security and trust.
- The need for identification – to know others 'from the inside' and to gain a sense of belonging.
- The need for differentiation to experience oneself as a separate being and capable of mastering developmental tasks.
- The need to nurture – to feel that the love and care one has is good and valued by others.
- The need for affirmation – to feel worthwhile and valued for ones uniqueness. (Kaufman 1980, 40 ff.)

Fitchett (1993) suggests a framework for spiritual assessment, summed up in Box 8.3. This can be used as a means of analysing the spiritual narrative, or helping the client to reflect on hers.

Box 8.3   An assessment framework

- *Belief and Meaning.* 'What are the beliefs that give meaning and purpose to a person's life and what are the important symbols that reflect them?' Do any aspects of the person's narrative and her present situation come into conflict with this life meaning? How far is the world view consciously articulated or simply implied in the narrative?

  Attention to such details will enable the nurse to reflect back what she hears and so enable the explicit meaning of the narrative to be developed.
- *Vocation and obligation.* Questions of importance here include, what sense of calling and obligation does the patient have in her life and how are these expressed in her relationships? How does this relate to her present illness?

- *Experience and emotion.* How does the experience of illness and the associated feeling relate to the patient's life meaning?
- *Courage and growth.* This axis involves questions about how the person has coped with crises in the past and how adaptable is her faith now.
- *Ritual and Practice.* This explores the rituals which support the patient's life meaning and asks how they are being used in the present situation.
- *Community.* This axis asks questions about the faith community of the patient. Who is the core community who give life meaning to her? How does the patient relate to that community- as an active or passive member? How does the faith community relate to this experience of illness?
- *Authority and guidance.* Where does the patient look for guidance about life meaning in moments of stress? Is this fixed or flexible?

Therapeutic techniques

Questions such as these help to assess how far the psychological problem has a spiritual source and how far spiritual support can assist in therapy. As noted in Chapter 3 there is a great deal of research which ties spiritual care to mental health and emotional well-being (Levin 1989, 1994, Koenig and Futterman 1995). Some of the more striking recent research findings have been in terms of forgiveness and forgiveness therapy. Several studies have found that psychotherapies that involve forgiveness lead to improvements in many of the indices of well-being, including reduced blood pressure, fewer negative emotions, less depression and anxiety, and higher levels of self esteem (Freedman and Enright 1996, Coyle and Enright 1997). Forgiveness is also associated with the creation of more supportive networks and the reduction of chronic hostility (McCullough 2000).

Such research has led to the development of techniques associated with spirituality such as meditation. The effects of meditation have been shown to include:

- reduced heart rate and blood pressure
- reduced activity in the sympathetic branch of the nervous system
- changes in electroencephalographic brain wave activity, consistent with the slowing down of brain and body activities (Benson 1996).

The use of meditation has included work with anxiety and depression, and some severe psychiatric disturbances, such as obsessive compulsive disorder (Marlatt and Kristeller 1999, 76).

The aim of meditation as a part of therapy is to develop 'mindfulness', an awareness of the self and one's physical and social environment. Box 8.4 gives an example of preparation and instructions for meditation adapted from Marlatt and Kristeller (1999, 74).

Box 8.4   A meditation technique

Ask the client to take a comfortable sitting position, with back straight and either sitting on a cushion with legs folded or on a chair with both feet on the floor. The aim of this is to promote a 'relaxed wakefulness', rather than relaxation that results in sleep. Eyes should be closed, or might be focused on an object such as a lighted candle.

The following instructions (and variations on them) can then be given. 'First, take a few deep breaths and notice the flow of air as you inhale, then gently exhale, again noticing the physical sensation of your out breath. Throughout this time your job is to pay close attention to your breathing, breath by breath. Breath in through you nose and out through your mouth. Allow your breathing to relax and gradually assume a natural pace and rhythm, as you in hale and exhale deeply. Pay close attention to the physical sensations of each breath. Notice the effect on you nose and mouth. Notice the rising and falling of your chest and abdomen as you take each breath. Be a relaxed but aware observer of your breathing process as it occurs naturally.

When you become distracted by events other than your breathing, such as thoughts which arise in your mind, sounds in the room, or feelings that occur in your body, first become aware of these feelings, and then aware that they are distracting you. Then gently return your full attention to your breath, its rising and falling. Treat all distractions (external sounds or outside events) in the same gentle manner'.

Allow the client to practise this for 10 minutes and if appropriate then remind him of the instructions. At the end of the period of meditation agreed with the client, a small bell or gong can be sounded and the client asked to gently move back into the space of the room and slowly open his eyes.

It is important then to debrief the client, see how he felt and see what this awareness might have led to. This might involve unexpected awareness. Marlatt and Kristeller, for instance, report one client who had meditation to help her stop smoking and became increasingly aware of internal conflicts which were associated with an experience of child sex abuse.

The crucial role of meditation in spirituality is not simply to help the patient relax, or to be aware, but also to reflect on the life meaning contained in the experience. The client, for instance, might have found the experience uncomfortable, and in reflecting on this discover a sense of unease about her body, an inability to develop awareness and appreciation of her physicality.

Once the client has practised this approach and feels safe with it he can be encouraged to use it himself during the week, building up a discipline. A useful reinforcement for the practice is for the client to reward himself after each meditation, relaxing in some way, before moving into other jobs.

An accompanist of another kind

Much can be learnt from other situations and the lesser known professions, who can help us to transfer knowledge from one professional scenario to another for the benefit of the patient. A good example is the work of Nigel Hartley, music therapist at Sir Michael Sobell House in Oxford. Formerly a professional concert pianist, his work is not merely about the provision of palliative care. It is about allowing people to find a way of expressing, for themselves, that which they cannot express in other ways. To listen to excerpts of Hartley's work with patients is to hear the dialogue between the therapist and patient in music. His accounts of his work with people who have Aids or are HIV positive at London Lighthouse and with people at Sir Michael Sobell House – provide remarkable insights, not only about the work undertaken between therapist and patients, but also of the open relationship which is required to allow creativity and newness to shine through (Hartley 2001). This is shown in the following related case:

One patient, an elderly woman called Mary, asked if she could see him. She had been in hospice for a few days and was completely wrapped in blankets, all round her head and was shaking. Hartley talked to her for a few minutes about music and after a few minutes the blankets came off and she said she wanted to write a song. . . 'Why do I worry'. Mary asked Hartley to play a chord, which he did, and off she went, making it up as she went along. Listening to a playback of the tape recording, Mary wanted to change this and that, and within an hour a song had been written. Mary was enormously worried about dying; her death was imminent. What was released in her song, was a way of talking about it, and some sort of affirmation that it didn't matter whether you worried or not, it was going to happen. Although Hartley had thought the song was going to be terribly sad, it was quite happy in the end, with Mary saying, 'I am not worried about dying because my husband loves me and he's going to be there and I'm going to see him again.' Mary's husband had died two years previously.

What is demonstrated here is that Mary needed to say what she did, through the medium of song, in a complete way. Hartley didn't interrupt her, but went on her journey with her. He didn't focus on what she was saying even though it was vitally important, but gave her space for it to be said, held and put together.

In his work, Hartley has recognised that the uniqueness of the therapist–patient relationship in music therapy is that the therapist plays with the patient, the patient is not expected to play alone. This is a strength of the work, and provides just one example of a therapist accompanying, not just in a professional sense, but in an authentic accompanying presence, the patient on their journey. Hartley reflects that whilst he was a professional musician, although he played regularly in all parts of the world, he didn't really relate to the music but felt somehow separated from it. It was when he had to learn to improvise, using music as a therapeutic medium with patients that the music had to come from within himself.

This raises a particular question for all healthcare professionals. Do we play a part, guarded by our professionalism, when we interact with patients? Or do we allow ourselves to be the people we are, in touch with ourselves, in order to bring the best of ourselves, and who we are meant to be into the caring, accompanying relationship?

New developments

A Spirituality and Mental Health Forum, set up in 2001, brought together a number of interested parties who were keen to develop a better understanding of the various groups who were working in this field. It is chaired by a member of the Anglican Archbishop's Council. Running alongside this work is the National Institute for Mental Health in England NIMH(E) which is taking forward work on a number of initiatives including; a mental health consultation focusing on Minority Ethnic Groups and Women in Mental Health. It is likely that there will also be a programme on spirituality and faith communities in the near future.

One of the problems for all professional groups, including those working in mental health, is the development of an understanding of what skills are required to deliver a quality service and how these skills might be developed. As we saw in Swinton's work, there is at least some scepticism within psychiatry about spirituality, as a subject, and as an issue which needs to be attended to beyond that of sending someone off to a church or chapel service on Sunday. Swinton's work points out that, whilst the liturgical elements can be vitally important to people at certain stages of their mental illness, attending to a person's spiritual needs will in most cases require much more than that. One idea is that there needs to be a fusing of clergy and the psychiatric services professions. This may or may not be right, but experience in some mental health chaplaincy services has shown that the chaplain is an important part of the team, in supporting both patients and staff in their various needs, and as being seen as an intelligent observer of and commentator upon that which is occurring in the clinical setting. Attempts at fusing clergy and psychiatry has very real echoes of William Temple's projects, with his work in the development of the National Council for Pastoral and Medical Co-operation, set up nearly seventy years ago, and referred to earlier in this book.

Conclusion

The discovery and development of shared meaning is at the base of mental health, something informed by spirituality with its stress on faith, hope, purpose and forgiveness and reconciliation. Mental health is helped by the negotiation of such meaning, focused on the development of the spiritual narrative. Such narrative then can be at the centre of therapy, with conditional spirituality often being a cause of mental problems and the development of new spirituality a critical part of successful therapy. This has been at its most explicit in addiction therapies with the use of processes such as the twelve-step treatment, centred on spiritual awareness (Clinebell 1990).

For some there is a need to tell and retell stories. Sometimes it is only after hearing the story many times that something new is revealed, or heard in a different light, by either or both the storyteller and the listener. The story might be told through different media; art, song, writing, and speech. All too often psychiatry has encouraged therapy that has been primarily about containment and security, precisely concerned not to listen to the story of the patient. In the late 1970s, two of the authors of this book experienced hospitals where admission interviews of patients involved taking nursing histories of the patient. Looking back it is very clear that the different professional groups were breaking up the patient's story into slots of professional interest. In a real sense the essence of the person could be lost in the gaps between those slots. With no story there was no power, and with no power, no real hope.

Similarly, in research, the patient was often perceived as the object of scientific testing, reinforcing a medical or mechanistic model of health. Swinton's hermeneutical phenomenological approach to research is both action and relationship based. It recognises that the spiritual narrative is essentially a learning experience, and can only take place in the context of an empathic relationship that enables mutual reflection and responsibility. It also recognises that multiple realities exist, and that there is an inevitable involvement of the researcher in the research.

Mental health must also be seen in its wider context, in the community and work. Occupational health, for instance, can introduce meditation, quiet rooms, or spiritual retreats (opportunities to reflect in a more systematic way) to the work place in a proactive way. Randolph-Horn and Paslawska's research (2002) has shown that many workers, in all sectors, would value such opportunities. Such approaches look to developing whole communities as places of hope, and can connect the professional development stress on transferable skills to the positive psychology that focuses on the development of virtues such as hope and serenity (Connors, Toscova and Tonigan 1999, Yahne and Miller 1999).

Questions and exercises

1. How does spirituality relate to mental health and illness?
2. Reflect on your relationship with a mentally ill person and consider how you might enable his or her spiritual story to develop in the context of the treatment.
3. Take time out with a colleague to practise meditation and consider how it might be introduced to a patient.

References

Avis, P. (1989) *Eros and the Sacred* (London: SPCK).

Bausch, W.J. (1995) *Storytelling: Imagination and Faith* (Mystic CT: TwentyThird Publications)

Benson, H. (1996) *Timeless Healing* (New York: Scribner).

Blise, M.L. (1995) 'Everything I learned I learned from patients: radical positive reframing'. Journal of Psychosocial Nursing, **33**, 12, 18–25.

Cashman, H. (1993) *Christianity and Child Sexual Abuse* (London: SPCK).

Clinebell, H. (1990) 'Alcohol Abuse, Addiction, and Therapy'. In Hunter, R. (ed.) *Dictionary of Pastoral Care and Counseling* (Nashville: Abingdon Press), 18–21.

Connors, G., Toscova, R. and Tonigan, J. (1999) 'Serenity', in W. Miller (ed.) *Integrating Spirituality into Treatment* (Washington: American Psychological Association).

Coyle, C.T. and Enright, R.D. (1997) 'Forgiveness intervention with post abortion men, *Journal of Consulting and Clinical Psychology*, **65**, 6, 1042–6.

Department of Health *The National Institute for Mental Health in England; Summary Consultation* (2001) (NIMHE: Manchester).

Digby, A. (1985) *Madness, Morality and Medicine*, (Cambridge: Cambridge University Press).

Fairchild, R.W. (1990) 'Sadness and Depression', in R.J. Hunter (ed.) *Dictionary of Pastoral Care and Counselling* (Nashville: Abingdon), 1103–06.

Fitchett, G. (1993) *Assessing Spiritual Needs: A Guide for Caregivers* (Minnesota: Augsburg).

Foskett, J. (1984) *Meaning in Madness* (London: SPCK).

Frankl, V.E. (1962) *Man's Search for Meaning: From Death Camp to Existentialism* (Boston: Beacon Press).

Freedman, S.R. and Enright, R.D. (1996) ' Forgiveness as an intervention goal with incest survivors', *Journal of Consulting and Clinical Psychology*, 63, 510–17.

Gilbert, P. (1992) *Counselling for Depression* (London: Sage).

Halmos, P. (1961) *The Faith of the Counsellors* (London: Constable).

Hartley, N. (2001) 'On a personal note: a music therapist's reflections on working with those who are living with a terminal illness' in *Journal of Palliative Care*, 17, 3, 135–41.

Hewitt, J.P. (1979) *Self and Society: A Symbolic Interactionist Social Psychology*, 2nd edn (Boston, Massachusetts: Allyn and Bacon).

Jones, K. (1979) *A History of the Mental Health Services* (London: Routledge and Kegan Paul).

Kaufman, G. (1980) *Shame: The Power of Caring* (Washington: Schenkman).

Kiev, A. (1972) *Transcultural Psychiatry* (London: Penguin).

Koenig, H. and Futterman, A. (1995) 'Religion and Health Outcomes'. Paper presented to: *Methodological Approaches to the Study of Religion, Aging and Health*; Washington.

Kohut, H. (1982) 'Introspection, empathy, and the semi-circle of mental health', *International Journal of Psychoanalysis*, 663, 397.

Levin, J.S. (1994) 'Religion and health: is there an association , is it valid and is it causal?' *Social Science and Medicine*, 38, 1475–82.

Levin, J.S. (1989) 'Religious Factors in Aging, Adjustment and Health' in W.M. Clements (ed.), *Religion Aging and Health: A Global Perspective* (New York; Haworth Press) 133–46.

McCullough, M.E. (Spring 2000) 'Forgiveness as human strength: theory, measurement and links to well-being', *Journal of Social and Clinical Psychology*, 19, 1, 43–55.

Marlatt, G.A. and Kristeller, J.L. (1999) 'Mindfulness and Meditation' in W.R. Miller, 67–84.

Martin, J.E. and Booth, J. (1999) Behavioural Approaches to Enhance Spirituality, in W. R. Miller, 161–76.

Miller, W.R. (1999) (ed.) *Integrating Spirituality into Treatment* (Washington: American Psychological Association).

Mental Health Foundation (1999) *The Courage to Bear Our Souls: A Collection of Pieces Written Out of Mental Distress*, London: Mental Health Foundation.

Pattison, S. (1989) *Alive and Kicking* (London: SCM).

Randolph-Horn, D. and Paslawska, K. (2002) *Spirituality at Work* (Leeds: Leeds Church Institute).

Robinson, S. (1998) 'Christian ethics and pastoral counselling revisited', *Modern Believing*, Summer, 31–44.

Robinson, S. (2001) *Agape, Moral Meaning and Pastoral Counselling* (Cardiff: Aureus).

Rosen, G. (1980) *Madness in Society* (Chicago: University of Chicago Press).

Smedes, L.B. (1998) 'Stations on the Journey from Forgiveness to Hope' in E.L. Worthington Jr. (ed.), *Dimensions of Forgiveness* (Philadelphia: William Templeton Foundation), 341–54.

Stone, H. (1998) 'Depression and spiritual desolation', *The Journal of Pastoral Care*, Winter, **52**, 4, 161–72.

Swinton, J. (1999) *Building a Church for Strangers* (Edinburgh: Contact).

Swinton, J. (2001) *Spirituality and Mental Health Care* (London: Jessica Kingsley).

Tavris, B. (1982) *Anger, The Misunderstood Emotion* (New York: Simon and Schuster).

van der Ven, J. (1998) *Formation of the Moral Self* (Grand Rapids: Eerdmans).

Wilkinson, J. (1998) *The Bible and Healing* (Edinburgh: Handsel).

Yahne, C. and Miller, W. (1999) 'Evoking Hope', in W. Miller (ed.).

9

Spirituality and Learning Disability

> People with a profound mental handicap possess a limited ability to reason at the complex level, and are therefore not able to work through any doubts or develop any sort of faith. (Birchenall and Birchenall 1986, 150)

> Such an existence gives no real opportunity for inner spiritual growth, or the nourishment of the human spirit, both of which are important when coming to terms with the meaning of Christianity. It gives no real opportunity to experience the joy of seeking a lifetime relationship with the Almighty, because the concepts involved are complicated and require a level of awareness which the profoundly mentally handicapped do not have. (Parish 1987, 75)

The area of profound learning difficulties is one of the most important tests of spirituality, and the possibility of developing life meaning. In this chapter we will focus first on the definition of learning disability and upon the difficulties this raises for practical consideration of spiritual care. We will then note what learning disability has to give to any concepts of spirituality and finally consider how spirituality might be developed in the care of the learning disabled, through routine tasks, in a personal sense and in and through community expressions of meaning.

Learning disability

Learning disability is a broad concept, including:

- *Mild learning disability.* This involves only basic reading and writing skills. Generally such people are independent and not seen in the healthcare context

- *Moderate learning disability.* This involves limited language skills, requiring some help with general care. Many people with moderate learning disability can do simple jobs.
- *Severe learning disability.* Some words or gestures can be used to communicate basic needs, and activities can be undertaken with supervision.
- *Profound learning disability.* With this a person has no learning or self-care skills (Swinton 1999, 13).

Nonetheless, there is a long history of such persons being seen as all radically different from the norm. The norm for the two quotes above, from nursing and from the church, is to do with the capacity to reflect and in particular the capacity to reflect intellectually. However, the very difference of the learning disabled dramatically challenges views of the person, spirituality and spiritual care.

Firstly, the learning disabled challenge the common concept of person, as an autonomous rational decision-maker. Some philosophers such as Kant even see such rational capacity as the unique aspect of human nature – compared to the animal kingdom – and the reason for respecting persons in the first place (Kant 1949). There are, of course, major moral objections to such a view. It excludes some human beings from the definition of personhood on the basis of difference or limitation. This is always an arbitrary judgement, one that ultimately runs the danger of moving into eugenics. The whole point about the spiritual perspective which we have argued for is that awareness of the other demands openness to difference as well as sameness; it demands the presumption of personhood in all living human beings, all of whom have limitations of some kind or degree. This takes us back to the empathy that recognises the humanity of the other, and reminds us that the person is social, known through how she relates to others in her life.

Secondly, the two quotes above assume that spirituality is not possible to access if there is no capacity for intellectual reflection or dialogue. However, our definition of spirituality refers to awareness of the other and stresses awareness as involving affective and somatic elements as well as cognitive. Indeed, it could be argued that the intellectual side of awareness has been given too great an emphasis in western history (Benner 1998). This has led to an undervaluing of affective and somatic awareness and lack of development of the necessary skills for developing these. We implied above that it is in fact highly developed somatic and affective awareness which act as the basis of intuitive knowledge of the other. This is often seen as a knowledge about the other which does not appear to be based on any straightforward empirical evidence, such that some people view intuition as almost extra sensory. On the contrary, intuition could be perceived as highly sensory, an acute awareness of the other in somatic and affective terms. This can pick up indications of unease, ambivalence or contradictions in the other and in relationships with others. Equally, such knowledge can act as the basis of strong faith, where the person can be aware of the congruence and care of the other, without this having to be confirmed conceptually. Hence, intuitive knowledge is closely connected to empathy.

Thirdly, the learning disabled person challenges any idea of spiritual care and healing and health. This is not 'a condition' that can be cured. For many parents this is precisely what makes their life so difficult. They were responsible for bringing this person into this life. For many this leads to a life of exhaustion and anxiety. For many there is regret that their child will not grow to be as them, or fill them with joy at achievement, such as the gift of grandchildren. Guilt is not far from all this, be it for bringing the person into the world in the first place or for having these negative feelings at all.

Despite the reaction of others the learning disabled most often do not perceive themselves as 'in need'. As Hauerwas writes,

> Even if they do not suffer by being [*learning disabled*], they are certainly people in need. Even worse they do not try to hide their needs. They are not self sufficient, they are not self possessed, they are in need. Even more, they do not evidence the proper shame for being so. They simply assume they are what they are and need no justification for being such. It is almost as of they have been give a natural grace to be free from the regret that most of us feel for our neediness. (Hauerwas 1986, 176. [Our italics and term. Hauerwas uses the anachronistic term 'retarded'.])

All of this rightly challenges the simple medical model of health (Pattison 1989), with its stress on pathology and mechanistic cure. Indeed, it makes it hard to see how the learning disabled can easily fit into any conventional pattern of care.

The care response

Driven by a desire to care for the learning disabled, and therefore from the highest of motives, it is tempting to face these challenges through one of two strategies – to infantilise or idealise. By definition, the first means taking the part of a nurturing parent to provide protection and to 'do' for the other. The danger in this is that the learning disabled person is not respected for who she is and the goal of treatment becomes control. Control should come as no surprise, since this has been the main objective of therapy for the learning disabled down the ages. Bannerman and Lindsay (1993) note the way in which the church down the centuries mixed pharmaceutical treatment with moral exhortation and judgement, underpinned by religious ritual and prayer, all to control people who were perceived as subhuman. This improved with the medicalisation of therapy. Yet still, the learning disabled were seen as mentally ill and placed in asylums, for control (Narayanasamy 1997, Thomson 1998).

The second approach simply does not reflect reality. The learning disabled have been known in parts of Ireland as 'God's children', however they are not angels. They have the same needs as the 'normal' person, not least for sexual expression and security (Birchenall 1997, 87ff.). They can suffer behavioural problems (McCue 1993) and are as much prey to anger or self-deception as any other person.

How then do we relate to these persons in any sense of mutuality? One response of care services might be to stress the process of normalisation. This has been a major movement in the care of the learning disabled. Wolfensberger (1972) has attempted to take this idea from the theory of equality into practice. He defines normalisation as the:

> Utilization of means which are as culturally as normative as possible, in order to establish and or maintain personal behaviours and characteristics which are as culturally normative as possible.

Part of this involves stress on the rights of the learning disabled, such as self-determination, work, and acceptable living standards (Emerson 1992). More importantly, it involves the presentation of the learning disabled in normal contexts which will diminish that sense of difference that ultimately runs the danger of dehumanisation. Hence, Wolfensberger looks to develop learning disabled lifestyle in the community, living in normal houses and going through normal community routines, such as work and shopping.

O'Brien takes this further in practice, detailing the following 'accomplishments' of any service for the client:

- *Community presence*, involving an integrated lifestyle;
- *Making choices* about lifestyle;

- *Enabling competence*, through the development of skills and attributes valued in the community;
- *Enhancing respect*, through improved self presentation;
- *Community participation* and the widening of social networks.

All of these are important elements in the development of identity and social networks. However, as Birchenall *et al.* (1997, 58) note, there is the danger of simply making the learning disabled conformist and 'grey'. In focusing on the spirituality of the learning disabled there are important questions about how their very difference is important and how a real sense of mutuality can be developed in the light of that.

It is possible to see the learning disabled as teaching us to care, drawing from society the qualities of care. This is close to the Hauerwas argument about suffering (1986). However, there is little to commend it, because of the danger of making the person instrumental – seen as only there for the furthering of the moral and spiritual growth of the carer (Pailin 1992, 102). Moreover, it once more runs the danger of stereotyping and idealising the learning disabled.

To relate to the learning disabled as they are means, at one level, recognising the nature of the learning disabled and what they have to offer, including what Dan O'Leary refers to as spiritual qualities. Firstly, like a child the disabled person tends to live for the now. O'Leary writes about one disabled person in this way,

> Joseph is not often consumed by regrets about yesterday or anxieties about tomorrow. This freedom from a condition which is a chief limiting factor in most human spirits enables Joseph to live in 'the now' to a most unusual degree. And here, I would say is the heart of Joseph's spirituality – the immediacy of his being to the world around him. (O'Leary, 1991)

Secondly, the learning disabled person tends to be aware of and appreciate others in a very clear and immediate way. This can include a 'simple reverence' for the other, exemplified in the caring response to babies from many learning disabled. Thirdly, meaning in all this is gained not so much in reflection but in the act itself, in the encounter with the other. What learning theory may refer to as a sign or symbol of the caring relationship becomes for the learning disabled the embodiment of the care itself, as we shall illustrate below.

Fourthly, learning disabled people are often able to enter into play and initiate play in an unselfconscious way. This can open up the 'child' in others giving them permission to enter and enjoy play. Fifthly, learning disabled people often exhibit a capacity to trust and develop faith in a very direct and speedy way. This is a major challenge to a culture often taught to be suspicious of the other. Sixthly, as already noted, learning disabled people exhibit the capacity to accept difference without regret. In real sense they embody difference and challenge others to embrace it.

Such qualities can have a profound effect upon community, enabling the community:

- to expand awareness of and to celebrate difference- to accept the stranger in its midst.
- to accept what it shares with the learning disabled, not least that of the child which never goes away – the need for security, for reassuring touch, for play. Hence, the learning disabled can enable the community to be open to its dependencies and basic needs.
- to be open to the important levels of knowledge which are so often lost in the stress on intellectual development – not least the affective and somatic awareness.
- to recognise that spirituality is not an individualistic matter but one shared and generated by community (Vanier 1999).

In all this the learning disabled are not instrumental in teaching 'the normal' how to care, drawing forth compassion. They are rather teaching 'the normal' how to be human, how to be open to themselves and embrace sameness, difference and limitation in a way that does not imply some form of judgement. This demonstrates the possibility of developing asymmetrical mutuality, such that the learning disabled person can contribute from somatic and affective awareness, and the carers respond with a framework in which to enable 'direct reflection' and the development of meaning. Montgomery notes the way in which nurses who allow themselves to be close to patients can therefore experience the positive effects of caring (Montgomery 1991). Part of this can involve the development of the nurse's own spirituality.

The spiritual framework of care

Spirituality can be expressed in and enhance care of the disabled in three ways:

- personal interaction,
- community interaction,
- a combination of personal and community interaction.

Personal interaction is very much about the personal care of the patient, with the staff member attempting to relate to the particular needs in the context of holistic care. This involves careful attention to emotional feelings, and in particular the need to explore meaning and feel secure. Narayanasamy and Owen (2001) stress this approach compared to the more conventional religious approach to spirituality, and see meaning emerging through a more counselling-centred approach that supports the client in crisis.

Community interaction is a side of care explored in therapeutic communities such as Jean Vanier's L'Arche. It would be wrong to see such an approach as purely religious. As we shall see, it is rather person and community centred and does not attempt to impose religious meaning on the client.

The third approach reinforces the need not to have exclusive ways of providing services. The meaning that is generated by community or in the interaction of the individuals can be applied in both contexts. A useful way of examining this interaction is through Fowler's stages of faith.

Spiritual care and the stages of faith

Dennis Schurter notes that Fowler's first and second stages of faith would seem to be most relevant to the learning disabled (Schurter 1992). He does, however, point to a pre-stage that is also relevant.

Pre-stage and tasks

The pre-stage is the time of 'undifferentiated faith' which usually involves infancy to around two years of age. It is important because during this period 'the seeds of trust, courage, hope and love are fused in an undifferentiated way', underlying all that comes later in faith development (Schurter 1992, 298). Fowler spends little time in this period, not least because his research method demands the capacity to respond to questions on reflection. However, it is important in working with the profoundly learning disabled, those who require the most care in feeding, bathing and so on. As Schurter notes, the needs of such persons include love and trust 'which can be demonstrated through consistent care, mutuality of eye and voice contact with others, aid in controlling and using an adult body with an infant mind – all of which help combat a person's fear of insecurity and abandonment' (Schurter 1992, 298).

Such tasks can be shared with other key persons not least members of the family. It is precisely in and through fulfilling such mundane and often difficult tasks that faith can be nurtured between the patient and carer. Schurter notes the non-verbal communications from the patient, smiles, eye contact, affirming touch, that the carer has to interpret and which give reasonable evidence of the growth of faith and hope. These acts of care become themselves rituals that directly affirm life meaning between those involved. Most importantly such collaborative work can help all concerned to know that they are 'addressing spiritual needs as they accomplish their daily routine duties' (Schurter, 298). The same one-to-one and group work can be used in support of the patient experiencing a crisis. This approach stresses the importance of any spiritual meaning emerging in the context of practice and empathic presence.

Stage one
This is characterised by intuitive-projective faith – seen in a normal child between two and six years of age. As noted in earlier chapters, this stage sees a development of thought and language but no cognitive operations such as perceiving cause and effect. Thinking tends to be fluid and magical, not logical. The perspective is ego-centred, making it difficult to see the other's view. Authority is clearly external. Perceptions of reality are made up of 'clusters of images', not logical associations or stories. The person may listen to narrative but cannot retell it. For those who remain in this stage throughout their life it is then precisely the images and the body language which become important for spirituality. This spirituality focuses especially on integrity and the way in which any embodiment of care remains congruent with the underlying attitude of care. This is true for both one-to-one work and shared community events.

At one 'mentally handicapped hospital', some years ago, one of the major events in the week for the children was the assembly. It took most of one afternoon and was felt to be important for staff as well as patients. The chaplaincy team, including one of the authors, spent a lot of time preparing 'interesting' assemblies, full of 'significant' symbols. A good deal of the input was purely Christian and very cognitive. Some chaplains, for instance, read from the Bible. Others told stories about the Bible, but stories that presupposed that the listeners might know something about Jesus.

It took a while for the team to realise that the ones who were 'different', on the margins, were the chaplains themselves. They had attempted to engage:

- from the premise that the patients would develop some theological understanding as if they had intellectual capacities;
- with a set of symbols and actions which were not related to the persons themselves. The team was trying to put across a set of ideas, rooting them in symbols. Hence the cross became the symbol of God's love. This is of little use to the learning disabled in that it asks them to relate to the idea of a being through a symbol that requires a great deal of background knowledge. More important than the idea is the attitude and how this is communicated;
- on the assumption that spirituality was primarily about religion and that, as a result, any assembly was primarily didactic, getting across to the other the meaning of the religion.

The result had been that the weekly event had focused strongly on the staff rather than the patients. It was the staff who responded to the words and actions of the chaplains and who tried to get the patients to respond.

Despite all this, a review of the practice with all members of staff noted that the occasion was important. It was a different context for staff and patients to come together and, as such, could primarily be seen as a ritual of celebration of the community of those involved.

The assembly then changed. First, it changed its name to 'the party'. Secondly, it began to engage with the spirituality of the whole community. Symbols were developed from the life of the community, and from direct expressions of care, with sharing of focused play, food and expressions of security and belonging. Thirdly, individual stories were shared as part of the weekly celebration, including all birthdays or events. Each had to be accompanied by a symbol, especially a cake. Fourthly, the event became more tactile, with a lot of hugging, and more emphasis on music that enabled participation and encouraged a sense of solidarity.

In all this the ritual of the event was stressed. The order remained the same and certain key images. At the same time, within the order, items would be very different each week with the aim of stimulating the imagination of the patients. The staff was insistent that the symbols of religion should not be simply forgotten. A cross remained at the front of the room, for instance, and the patients handled this on occasions. However, the cross then became a multi-layered symbol. For all, it represented the community together, for some it was an image that was simply anchored in a feeling of support, for others it made a link into a wider spirituality of the church. Families also felt the need for such symbols, alongside many others. All those who were able to reflect cognitively on the symbols used in the celebrations were quite clear that their major function was to reflect love.

An important part of this celebration ritual was that it provided a context of meaning for one-to-one care. The central symbols and images of care included a cross, cake and even a tennis ball. Throwing and catching a tennis ball became an early part of the party, aiming to include all, to heighten awareness of the other, and to inject humour.

At times of crisis for the patient such symbols could be used as part of the care. One patient who lost his father asked to touch the party cross. The image of the cross was anchored both in the service and in the care given and he was given a small cross to keep. At times of anxiety he would reach for the cross and touch it. This cross, like the tennis ball or the cake or flowers was not a symbol of some more profound conceptual meaning. It was rather associated with and thus embodied the feeling generated in the community – warmth, belonging, excitement, security, faith, hope and love. There are parallels in this with neuro-linguistic programming and the practice of anchoring a good feeling with a particular symbol or action (Bandler and Grinder 1979).

Such objects then could become part of a network of faith for the patient. In all this, the celebration provided an experience of transcendence, taking the patients beyond themselves, seeing themselves in the context of others and how they were valued, and feeling a sense of the other through many different kinds of story. The story might involve:

- *Individuals.* A teacher bringing in her baby and talking about it, a patient sharing her experience on holiday.
- *The community.* This may be about celebrating a past event or some ongoing project such as fundraising for another cause.
- *Beyond the community.* Visitors from local groups or different religious stories.

This reflects the fact that no community is uniform, but is rather made up of many different others, groups or individuals. The other point about ritual celebrations such as these is precisely that it can operate on different levels, and speak to persons with very different levels of faith. Staff and families spoke of how it affected their view of spirituality. The teaching and nursing staff became more a part of the whole expression of community. They had valued the first attempts at an assembly because it gave them a little time off. They valued the second because it was a celebration of the whole community and the different relationships within.

Stage two
Stage two involves mythic-literal faith. As previously discussed, in this stage reality is organised into narrative form (hence mythic) without discerning intellectual meaning in that narrative (hence literal understanding).

There is more logical thinking in this stage, and the capacity to form a narrative and respond to a narrative of the community enables the person to give unity and continuity to the images developed in stage one. Story in this becomes the 'medium for organisational reality' and the meaning of the story itself is not reflected on. Along with this is a capacity to see the perspective of the other, enabling the possibility of developing a concept of fairness and ethics of reciprocity. The person with moderate learning disability may well reach stage two or parts of it. Schurter sums up the major faith matters in this stage as 'affiliation, belonging, being cherished; learning the lore, legends and language of the religious groups; sorting out fact and fantasy' (Schurter 1992, 301). 'Religious groups' is used in a broad sense of communities with shared meaning. The person can use imagination and enter into the stories of the community without drawing conceptual meaning from them. It becomes important for the patient in this context to repeat and learn the stories. When learned in the context of celebration they can sum up the affective well-being felt there.

For someone in this stage the community element of care then becomes all the more important. It is through the development of the celebration and ritual that the person can strongly feel a sense of belonging. The celebration can also act as a focus for people who come with different life meanings and who have spiritualities expressed in very different ways. It also provides the place within which the different narratives can be shared, and in which the person can begin to contribute to the community but also present and relate to other communities.

Vanier notes how ritual can grow out of regular meal times (Vanier

1979, 241). After one meal one member of the community threw his orange peel at another in fun. This soon caught on and became a ritual part of the meal expressing fun, openness and a sense of belonging. Vanier goes on to describe how a visiting bishop shared lunch and without warning was pelted with orange peel. He soon understood that this was a complement signifying his inclusion in the community, and that there was no need to spend time analysing or justifying what made sense in and through the shared action.

Celebrations that are part of the calendar can build in preparation and repetition for months before. In one community, 'Christmas' began at the end of September, building up to events which included families, local community and churches. Such events provide opportunity for reflective sharing on a somatic and affective level. This enables others to feel part of the care and also enriches them. As one family member put it about the Christmas celebrations, ' My Christmas is here. I experience far more joy and awe as part of this community than in any church'.

This same dynamic exists for the learning disabled who are part of other communities. This can be part of the normalisation process. Such a process, however, can go beyond 'normalisation' and greatly enrich the communities. Norris, for example, went to a local Christian church. He participated through being on the sidesperson's rota, giving out books and taking collections. The directness of his behaviour in worship had a dramatic effect on the whole congregation. This was exemplified in 'the peace'. The peace comes at the centre of the Holy Communion. It is a chance to move to other people in the congregation, to shake hands and exchange a greeting such as 'peace be with you'. It is meant to reflect and embody the forgiveness and reconciliation that should be at the heart of all religious experience. For the most part this had been a very polite and brief interlude, until the arrival of Norris. He went round to everyone, and hugged everyone, turning what had been a semi-formal activity into an experience that brought affective and somatic meaning to the whole service. One member of the community commented, 'now I look forward most of all to the peace'. Another noted that until Norris had arrived he had not really understood what the Communion was about. It was for him purely about intellectual concepts, and Norris had enabled him to feel the Communion and so develop a much broader spirituality. In the past, churches have often not given communion to children and to the learning disabled. At this church Norris received Communion not least because the congregation felt that he embodied so much of the central experience of this service and had taught them how to access a level of spiritual meaning that they had not, hitherto, been aware of.

Far from the learning disabled being unable to access the spiritual experience then they have a clear and immediate awareness of the other. This is both genuinely spiritual and can also enable others to develop levels of awareness not often practised. Enabling that spirituality as part of care demands the perspective of community, in addition to any individual care needs, and the provision of discipline, ritual and celebration which give security and a sense of belonging. Such provision is not about 'achieving' so much as finding ways of 'being with' and responding to the other, something which becomes the end in itself.

Conclusion

Spirituality is at the heart of care for the learning disabled. Whilst normalisation is important this takes care one stage further enabling meaning to be developed through tasks, personal relationships and community networks. Rather than seeing all these as exclusive it is important to facilitate connection between all these different areas, leading to further enrichment of meaning.

Working with the learning disabled is a very particular vocation. For the nurse it means a great deal of effort and attention without any cognitive appreciation or feedback, and in certain cases having to deal with negative feedback. This raises important questions, relevant to all areas of healthcare, about the need for professional support that will enable the nurse to nurture and explore her spirituality. These will be looked at more carefully in the final chapter.

On the other side of the reckoning the learning disabled often teach their carers about a level of awareness and meaning which is not constrained by conventional views of illness and health, a meaning which is found in the here and now of the personal encounter, very much in the context of community, and underlining the mutuality at the centre of spirituality.

Questions and exercises

1. What do the learning disabled have to teach us about spirituality?

2. How would you develop weekly rituals that could develop and sustain life meaning for the learning disabled?
3. With a colleague, attempt to express your spirituality, first with concepts and then without the help of concepts.

References

Bandler, R. and Grinder, J. (1979) *Frogs into Princes* (Moab: Real People Press).

Bannerman, M. and Lindscy, M. (1993) 'Evolution of Services', in E. Shanley and T. Starrs (eds) *Learning Disabilities: A Handbook of Care* (London: Churchill Livingstone), 19-40.

Benner, D. (1998) *Care of Souls* (Grand Rapids: Baker Books).

Birchenall, P. and Birchenall, M. (1986) 'Caring for Mentally Handicapped People: The Community and the Church', *The Professional Nurse*, **1**, 6, March.

Birchenall, M. (1997) *Learning Disability and the Social Context of Caring* (London: Churchill Livingstone).

Emerson, E. (1992) 'What is Normalisation?' in H. Brown and H. Smith (eds) *Normalisation: A reader for the Nineties* (London: Routledge).

Fitchett, G. (1993) *Assessing Spiritual Needs: A Guide for Caregivers* (Minnesota: Augsburg).

Hauerwas, S. (1986) *Suffering Presence* (Edinburgh: T. and T, Clark).

Kant, I. (1949 [1788]) *Critique of Practical Reason*, trans. L. Beck (Chicago: Chicago University Press).

O'Leary, D. (1986) 'Signs of Contradiction – People like Joseph'. In Kelly, D. and McGinley, P. (eds) *Mental Handicap: Challenge to the Church* (Chorley: Lisieux Hall), 131–42.

McCue, M. (1993) 'Helping with behavioural problems', in E. Shanley and T. Starrs (eds) *Learning Disabilities: A Handbook of Care* (London: Churchill Livingstone).

McGinley, P. (1991) *Mental Handicap: Challenge to the Church* (Chorley: Lisieux Hall)

Montgomery, C. 'The care giving relationships: paradoxical and transcendent aspects' *Journal of Transpersonal Psychology*, **23**, 2, 91–105.

Narayanasamy, A. (1997) 'Spiritual Dimensions of Learning Disability', in B. Gates and C. Beacock (eds) *Dimensions of Learning Disabilities* (London: Bailliere Tindal).

Narayanasamy, A. and Owen, J. (2001) 'A critical incident study of nurses' responses to the spiritual needs of learning disabled clients', *Advanced Journal of Nursing*, **33**, 4, 274-85.

Pailin, D.A. (1992) *A Gentle Touch* (London: SPCK).

Parish, A. (1987) *Mental Handicap* (London: Macmillan Education – now Palgrave Macmillan).

Pattison, S. (1989) *Alive and Kicking* (London: SCM).

Schurter, D.D. (1992) 'Fowler's Faith Stages as a Guide for Ministry to the Mentally Retarded' in J. Astley and L. Francis, *Christian Perspectives in Faith Development* (Leominster: Gracewing), 297–304.

Swinton, J. (1999) *Building a Church for Strangers* (Edinburgh: Contact).

Thomson, M. (1998) *The Problem of Mental Deficiency* (Oxford: Clarendon Press).

Vanier, J. (1999) *Becoming Human* (London: Darton, Longman and Todd).

Vanier, J. (1979) *Community and Growth* (London: Darton, Longman and Todd).

Wolfensberger, W. (1972) *Normalization* (Toronto: National Institute of Mental Retardation).

10

Spirituality and the Professions

'Scandal of NHS "Death factories"'

Patients in NHS hospitals are dying unnecessarily, because of unbearable pressure on overworked nurses, according to the leader of Britain's nurses.

The claim comes after a West Midlands hospital last week admitted it was responsible for the death of elderly Frederick Thomas, who died of dehydration after lying in a hospital ward for 12 days without water.

Beverly Malone, the general secretary of the Royal College of Nursing, said Thomas's death was symptomatic of a system where stretched resources and staff led to nurses picking and choosing which patients they gave full attention to.

. . .

Malone said that the huge pressure of working in the NHS meant individual nurses could not be blamed for deaths like that of Thomas. Rather it was the whole system and its manpower shortage that was at fault.

. . .

Michele Baker, the daughter of Thomas fought to get Walsall Manor Hospital to admit they in effect starved the 86-year old grandfather to death over almost a fortnight after he had undergone a successful hip replacement operation.

A doctor's order that Thomas be given a saline drip was never carried out and he died on the 6th June, his sixtieth wedding anniversary. 'I can't blame one person, one nurse and I don't want to, it's a breakdown in the system and my father was seen by two doctors and half a dozen nurses,' said Baker.

'But I still want to know why, if I, with no medical knowledge at all, could see this man deteriorating before my eyes, then why on earth the professionals could not? I go over it again and again,' she said.

'It was a factory ward, a death ward. As one old person goes out, whether in a box or not, another is filed into the bed. The staff were clearly over stressed. My dad was a quiet man who would not make any fuss, the only thing he said to us was to whisper "get me out of here". I wish we had.' (*The Observer*, 11 August, 2002).

It is all too easy to comment on a case when you haven't been directly involved, but Beverly Malone's claim doesn't ring wholly true. How can anyone die in a hospital ward, apparently as a result of dehydration, when hydration and nutrition are two of the mainstay's of nursing care? How can it be that someone can die in such a way, almost unnoticed? It may well be that nursing and medical staff are overburdened, working in frantic conditions, but every healthcare worker, whatever their profession and mode of work, has a responsibility for their actions and omissions.

As the opening of the 1992 edition of the United Kingdom Central Council (UKCC) for Nursing, Midwifery and Health Visiting Code of Professional Conduct pointed out:

> Each registered nurse, midwife and health visitor shall act, at all times, in such manner as to:
>
> • safeguard and promote the interests of individual patients and clients;
> • serve the interests of society;
> • justify public trust and confidence and
> • uphold and enhance the good standing and reputation of the professions.
>
> As a registered nurse midwife or health visitor, you are personally accountable for your practice (Nursing and Midwifery Council 1992)

Responsibility and accountability are important themes in today's health services. But it is also helpful for healthcare workers to ask why they are there in the first place for, without the patient, there is no reason to be there at all. We hear much of the 'modernisation agenda'. Clearly, it is good to acknowledge the good practices and bad influences of the past, and to look forward in ways which challenge our thinking and which positively influence practice. It would be wrong though if the 'modernisation agenda' is merely chanted as a mantra, as though everything which has gone before is of no account. Many who grew up in the fifties and sixties have brought with them a sense of service or self-giving. Old fashioned a term as it might seem, the nature of professional vocation should not be discounted. Campbell (1984, 70) asks whether, 'it is possible for a whole group to profess "love of neighbour" in activities which are also a means of livelihood and a source of status and influence'? No doubt in today's society there is a mix of inter-related altruistic and egotistic motives in such professional relationships, but we shouldn't allow this to negate the loving relationship which is possible, one to another, between patient and staff, and also in terms of working relationships, between staff. A hospital is a community of people who have to find the best ways of working with each other for the good of those whom they are there to serve.

This book has focused on the practice of spiritual care for the person who is facing an experience of illness. Spiritual care was defined as enabling the patient to maintain or develop spiritual meaning in their life thereby enabling, where possible, a positive meaningful relationship to that illness. Sometimes this involves clear focus on the already developed spiritual meaning of the person's life. At other times this involves a development or sharpening of extant spirituality. At others it is simply about the professional providing a care which is more than simply a task – focusing the whole presence on the patient. This is very much about the quality of care, a focusing on the whole person and the need to find meaning in the whole experience, as much as any simple aspect of care. All this may involve direct work from the nurse, or referral to or collaboration with staff and or family.

This chapter broadens the perspective to look at the spirituality of the healthcare professions, and by extension the spirituality of the carer. What is the spiritual identity of the nursing profession *per se*? How does the professional concern for competence in health management relate to the concern for spirituality? What are qualities which go towards enabling spiritual care? What are the spiritual needs of the carer? How can the work organisation, including training, enable these qualities to be developed and sustained and these needs fulfilled?

The nursing profession

The opening statements of the UKCC Code (Nursing and Midwifery Council 1992) provide a framework within which the spirituality of the profession can be explored. In the preamble it sets the tone and focus of the code. Firstly, the healthcare professional is primarily there in the interest of others. None of this is to discount the interest of the professional herself, not least in earning money for herself and any dependants. Nonetheless, the underlying raison d'être is to serve. The idea and use of the principle of service has, rightly, received some severe blows from the feminist movement. This has been mostly because patriarchal society has stressed the view of women as there to serve, service being equated purely with self-sacrifice.

Secondly, those whom the professional serves or whom the profession relates to are clearly set out: the client or patient; the wider society; and the profession itself. The professional then is not relating to society as an individual but rather as a member of a profession whose values and identity she shares. Hence, how the professional relates to others affects not just her own relationship with the client but also the relationship of the whole profession to the wider society. The profession relies upon its members to maintain the bond of trust with society, something based in turn on the integrity of the profession. Significantly, some other professions use that exact word. The American Accreditation Board for Engineering and Technology code, for instance, states that 'Engineers should advance the integrity, honour and dignity of the profession' (quoted in Robinson and Dixon 1997, 339). Each of these are qualities or characteristics which are used of individual practitioners and which look to the integration, constancy, commitment, belief and value systems of the professions – all asserting the service of the profession. Ultimately, any relationship with society, clients, patient or profession is based upon trust.

The identity and thus the purpose of the professional nurse is about how he responds to the different relationships he is involved in. This in turn requires an awareness of their needs, and the capacity to respond to the claims and call of all the different groups. The claims have to be held in tension. Hence, the professional is not at the service of only one of these groups, nor an employee who has to do what he is told. He has to determine how his service will be worked out in every different situation. Like other professions, then, he has the independence on the ground, within constraints such as safety, to work out the best way to respond in the situation.

The later sections of the Code (1992) begin to detail what the relationships might involve in practice, spelling out:

- certain key principles such as respect, safety and beneficence.
- the limitations and constraints of relating to the other.
- instrumental principles, such as confidentiality.
- ways of resolving conflicts, including whistle blowing. This is more than simply an ethical dilemma; it is important for the integrity of the whole profession, and the importance of transparency is emphasised.
- continual development. Intellectual development is stressed along with the lengthy period of training.
- basic needs of the client, including the spiritual   and holistic concern for the patient.

The most recent edition of the Code (Nursing and Midwifery Council 2002) includes many of these concerns in the preamble, including respect, confidentiality and consent. In the Introduction it stresses that the nurse must protect and support the health of the wider community as well as that of the individual patient. The personal accountability of the nurse, stresses a responsibility which is prior to and does not depend upon the advice or directions of other professionals. The nurse, moreover, is seen as responsible for the development of public trust and, with this, for upholding and enhancing the reputation of the profession as a whole.

Spirituality is at the heart of all this, with awareness of the self and others, and the concern to respond to the needs of the other. This sets nursing down then as a vocation, a calling. This is not simply a religious concept. It can be seen as a calling from the different groups for whom the profession has responsibility. It also has this sense of calling *to* a high ideal, not least that of care. A critical part of that calling is to develop and maintain faith in all the different clients and through this to enable hope.

In response to these claims, different identities have been formed of the nurse and her profession. At one extreme is the image of the angel, the de-sexed, ultimate carer (Campbell 1984, ch. 3). At the other extreme is the image of technician, whose task is to save lives. The first is all care, the second is all competence. Neither is human and neither reflects the complex and rich spirituality of the nurse who has to hold together both care and competence, something reflected in the concepts of covenant and contract.

Covenant and contract

The spirituality of any profession and in particular the caring professions tends to be based upon covenant rather than a contract. May, basing his observations on Old Testament writings (May 1987) sums up the covenant as:

- *gift* based. The caring professions offer care to society based upon need, not upon ability to pay. If need arises beyond the contracted hours then there is a duty to respond. Titmuss take this whole spiritual identity further with the concept of caring for strangers, an inclusive and unconditional offer (Titmuss 1970). In this sense, the action of the carer can be seen as sacramental, as a sign which points to this broader view of care, taken beyond simply individual response. Thus, the health service as a whole can be viewed as a sacrament of care.

- offering a *promise*. The profession remains available whatever the response of the patient or client. Just as the lawyer will stand for the criminal, the nurse will treat whoever is in need.
- *open*. The commitment of the caring professions defies precise specification. In this sense, the precise responsibility of the profession can only be worked out in the particular situation through further dialogue. This can be contrasted with the more exclusive view that professions have their responsibility predetermined. This openness to the situation enables space for creative response.
- *community* based. The profession forms part of a wider community and group of communities which share interlocking aims, and which work together to achieve those. For all the problems in delivery, the National Health Service is a good example of promise, openness and community.

By the side of the covenant of care is what May describes as its 'first cousin', the contract. Contract is specific, calculative and limits relationships. It can be put to one side if the terms of the agreement are broken. It would be very easy to polarise the two approaches to agreements and lead to a battle between covenant and contract. Titmuss, for instance, saw the two as mutually exclusive foundations to any national health service and advocated the gift relationship based upon 'ultra obligations', obligations which were more than simply family or tribal ties. Hence, for him, the contribution to any health service had to be anonymous, genuine stranger giving, as in blood-donorship (Titmuss 1970).

However, important though this theme is to the profession, it runs the danger of obscuring the important part that contract can play in professional spirituality. The covenant emphasises the unconditional 'being there', and the attempt to be aware of the network of different relationships involved in the caring relationship. The contract emphasises the specific activity and outcome of the healing relationship, and thus stresses a spirituality of doing. A contract enables expectations to be clear and boundaries drawn, so that the professional is able to remain in role. This enables freedom for the patient. The limitations of care can be focused on, and therefore the best stewardship of resources. In focusing on the specific, the contract can also focus on professional competence, the capacity to maintain standards of care.

Any spirituality of the profession needs both of these elements, encompassing, on the one hand, an all-embracing concern and a practical organisation on the other, which take into account the realities and standards. The two in fact involve the twin axes of spirituality; *sameness*, which is based upon the recognition of common humanity and *difference*, which takes account of the particularity of a person and of her situation and need. Of course, the openness of the covenant will never be fully 'achieved' but that is not a reason for not continuously working towards it. Without covenant there is the danger of a professional identity that is task orientated, which stresses expertise and encourages the dependency of others, and which treats the patient as a 'case' rather than a 'patient or client' (Campbell 1985). Without contract it is hard to see how care can be delivered efficiently.

Training and professional development

The focus of virtues in spirituality raises the question of how these can become a part of the training and professional development. Some argue that virtues cannot be taught, they are either inherited or 'caught'. Others argue that virtues are identified and developed through living in communities and through the reiteration of and reflection on the community stories. These stories, such as the Icelandic sagas, illustrate or embody the virtues (McIntyre 1985). Indeed, such stories which focus on practice are the only way of actually understanding the virtues. They cannot be understood apart from the action. However, even this approach runs the danger of imposing a view of the good or a view of the spiritual. In this view the virtues are transmitted or infused, a predetermined spirituality that is passed across.

However, virtue development in the light of the spirituality noted thus far is a little different. The virtues which are the fruit of spiritual development are critically developed through what Rogers (1983) refers to as the person–centred approach, enabling the individual to learn for herself and with others. Narayanasamy (1999) suggests that the learning process should focus on self-awareness, spirituality and the spiritual dimensions of nursing, the outcomes of which are noted in Table 10.1. Developing such learning will involve the following:

1. Providing a learning environment that is safe and enables students to reflect on and begin to articulate their view of spirituality and how it works in any practical decision-making. This enables the first stage of articulation.
2. Enabling students to reflect on the meaning of this drawing out of the purpose and values that are involved. It is precisely at this stage

Table 10.1   Spirituality and the learning process

Structure/Content	Process	Outcome
Self awareness Spirituality	Experiential learning related to: value clarification holism perspectives of spirituality broad aspects of spirituality	Value clarification Sensitivity and tolerance Knowledgeable practitioner in spiritual dimensions of nursing
	Assessment	Competence in assessment of spiritual care needs
	Planning	Planning spiritual needs-based care
Spiritual dimensions of nursing	Implementation	Competence in counselling Positive nurse- patient relationship
	Evaluation	Competence in making judgement about effective spiritual dimensions of nursing Enhancing quality of care Spiritual integrity Healing and relief from spiritual pain

that the process of meaning and value clarification begins. Hence the importance of an environment that can reflect back their thoughts to them. This also involves any spiritual world views that the students may have. The dynamic up to this stage is entirely about how the learning process enables the person to work out their spirituality in the light of the shared practical experience. When we come to the sharing of spiritual perspectives this is not approached suddenly or covertly, so that spiritual values are sprung on the student. On the contrary, the values and life-meaning emerge from reflection on practice and experience.

3. The third stage is to work through the part the nurse and others play in the situation, and what their responsibilities might be. This

leads to the rehearsal of negotiating responsibility with others, and the importance of developing negotiating skills. Such skills also begin to increase data about the other groups involved, both professional and non-professional. In this stage, the resources and constraints for any response begin to emerge.

4. Planning. This involves developing agreement on how spiritual distress can be recognised and responded to, and how the spirituality of the patient can be enabled. In this light, assessment and planned care is possible which enables the patient to articulate her spiritual narrative.

This approach enables:

- practice and theory to come together, and thus the development of holistic thinking.
- respect for other perspectives to be fostered. One can listen to them and begin to understand how the different ideas and resources might be used. This in turn fosters empathy.
- talking about spiritual perspectives to be accepted as a reasonable part of the professional development. There is permission to talk about values and life meaning. As part of this process the sameness and difference in the different views and meanings is brought out.
- the clarification of values and life meaning. At one level the person clarifies his values as he articulates them. At another the values are tested and worked through as part of a dialogue with other views in the light of the praxis, the practical context. Practice enables the spirituality to become 'real', enabling a development or strengthening of both corporate and personal spirituality. Areas of agreement are made clear and areas of difference are accepted. A common values system and life meaning can begin to emerge which also accept diversity, and which are built around the shared project of care.
- respect for the freedom of the students and their own views. It also enables the development of critical thinking with respect to life meaning. In all this it allows the student to be authentic, and allows them empowered responsibility of action.

The learner-centred dynamic is critical to the development of virtues, enabling the student to practice different virtues, such as empathy, and integrity and to reflect upon them (Robinson and Dixon 1997). Integrity is developed, for instance, through reflection on the different ethical and spiritual narratives: personal, professional, and public. Such reflection enables the student to look at contradiction and ambiguities and develop consistency in life meaning. Encouraging students to develop their own methodology also assists the development of integrity. Method enables a focus on practice, and establishes connections between principles and practice (Robinson and Dixon 1997).

The ultimate outcome in question is whether the nurse is able to assess spiritual needs and to enable the patient to develop faith, hope, purpose and, where appropriate, to move to forgiveness and reconciliation.

Other learning examples

1. *Student-centred learning.* It is clear from the example given above that the dimension of spirituality can emerge naturally from modules that focus on particular areas; ethical, psychological, sociological, and professional development. An example of this is given below.

In a seminar on professional ethics the class began with reflection on a particular case. The students were asked to develop a methodology of ethical decision-making. What were the stages in making an ethical decision in healthcare practice?

At the class feedback the students began to develop a shared method which began with data gathering and analysing the different values involved in the situation.

The next stage was a reflection on values and the tutor asked what else might be included. From the back of the seminar room came the shout 'Doctrine!'. This was a Muslim student. He explained that this referred to his life meaning, and that his view of the end of life when faced by judgement meant that he had to carefully review any situation for aspects which did not please his God. He expanded further on the sanctity of life. Very quickly an evangelical Christian student responded by saying how his doctrine also valued the sanctity of life, and that there were some important differences. A humanist student then expressed concern about this religious talk. He was quickly followed by another humanist who politely argued that there was nothing wrong with hearing these different views. She too had a 'doctrine' which majored on the ultimate value of human life and a strong sense of the 'other' both in nature and in humanity.

The role of the tutor throughout this was simply to ensure that all was kept focused on practice and that respect was given to all the different views.

Reporting back he noted that, 'there was no need to motivate. It was as if the group had been waiting for some time to talk about such things. The biggest problem was to effect closure of this stage and move on to the next'. The different views were tested and worked through in practice so that it could be shown how the underlying life meaning affected the moral meaning. He also injected into the dialogue different narratives about the meaning and purpose of nursing and invited the students to test these and clarify them in the light of the other narratives.

Once more this points to a student-centred approach. Many other approaches can be used singly or in combination, including:

2. *A one-day or two-day event.* This might be a professional development conference. Firstly, it provides a good context for building community awareness, team building and so on, and therefore a most effective trust base. Secondly, it stresses holism and can include spirituality along with the outward-bound activities, simulation, role play and other reflective exercises. Thirdly, it provides an easy context for other professionals and professional groups to become involved. The involvement of different professional groups provides opportunities for different professional narratives to be articulated and thus furthers the dialogic process. Such an event is still very much about the practical focus and the idea of drawing spirituality from the practice.

3. *The learning journal.* The learning journal enables the student to reflect on all aspects of experience, be that practical or educational. The major function of the learning journal is to reflect on the immediate learning experience and to begin to make connections with life meaning, both personal and professional. Key elements of this approach are:

• dividing the journal into data gathering and critique (about the learning experience), meaning clarification and spiritual development (making connections with different ideas and experience). This enables the development of critical thinking, and spiritual awareness.
• providing a benchmark for the developing reflection (Bush 1999). This might involve initially establishing the person's understanding of spirituality, to see how this develops. One way of doing this is to encourage life mapping – setting out in linear form the person's life, with highs and lows and some reflection on their meaning.

- the use of frequent interrogative and confidential feedback from the tutor. The tutor's role is simply to encourage the student to reflect and make the connections, not to direct.

The nature of all the training above is that it does actually develop the virtues (Robinson and Dixon 1997, Megone and Robinson 2002). Role-play and the subsequent debriefing, for instance, helps develop empathy and prudence. Importantly, the virtue can then be reflected on explicitly in much the same way as strengths and weaknesses. This can involve identifying the virtues, seeing how they compare with general human virtues, and seeing how they have been developed in the past and might be developed in the future.

The spirituality of the nurse

All of this reinforces the point that the nurse and student nurse have spiritual needs in relation to their work and the work environment which include:

- opportunity for articulation of narrative.
- space to be alone, and to reflect.
- ritual that enables a sense of identity and reflection.
- awareness of the wider care community, and shared meaning.

Articulation of narrative can be part of training and professional development. Space and time to be alone need to be developed as part of the ethos of the workplace. One hospital had a quiet room available to staff, but it was not well used. The reason was because the ethos of the organisation was so pressurised that if anybody did take a short time away from the ward they were made to feel guilty when they got back. Ironically, those who went for a smoke break did not receive the same negative reaction. Hence, such facilities have to be carefully introduced and the message from the management has to be congruent with their use.

One way of signalling the seriousness of such space creation is through the provision of retreats or quiet days, as part of professional development, or services offered to staff. This can be a service available to staff in terms of spiritual needs, or more in the mode of spirituality development/learning experience. Recent example of work retreats involve work with meditation, the possibility of massage, and work on the development of affective awareness, through, for instance, art therapy. Such retreats can range from half days to longer sessions, and can meet the needs of any or all spiritual backgrounds.

Ritual for the staff can range round the development of pre- and post-shift debriefing sessions to major spiritual rituals such as memorial services. The importance of debriefing sessions is not just that the staff as a whole can ensure good communication, but that the nurse can begin to articulate the contradiction and ambiguities that may be on her mind from a shift. As Wilcock notes, there may be incidents or relationships which cause the spiritual meaning of the nurse to be questioned (Wilcock 1996). Wilcock cites the example of those with different sexualities from the nurse, or people living with HIV/Aids. Once again the ethos of the workplace has to enable the nurse to trust staff and procedures enough to be able to work these through. This may include working through any personal wounds which may be at the centre of the nurse's life meaning. Nouwen suggests that it is important to accept that all healers are wounded in some way (Nouwen 1994). This demands ethos and procedures which both encourage the development of high professional skills and competence but also ensure that limitations are accepted, and acceptable.

At the base of this is an often unspoken spirituality of care which sees the purpose and meaning of nursing as involving giving to the other and always caring for their needs. In the light of that, it is all too easy for the nurse to see her own needs as secondary, thus setting up a co-dependent relationship between nurse and patient, and worse still, to see receipt of care, emotional or spiritual, as a sign of failure. As one experienced nurse put it, 'It is my job to care for the patient, not to be cared for. My problems just get in the way of caring.' This in turn can generate a self-secrecy, with staff keeping spiritual and emotional difficulties to the self, and in effect denying the humanity of the self. The self is not given the same care as others. This stress on a spirituality of sacrifice, sacrificing the self for others, has always been one focused on women through the patriarchal society. It can equally be one which focuses on nurses, especially where overtones of Victorian notions of vocation are used, unless there is explicit articulation in policy, procedure and training which seeks to balance self care with other care.

Such provision enables the nurse to develop spiritual integrity and thus develop life meaning in the context of work. For this to happen there is also need for *shalom*, right relationships in the work community, indeed the development of a working community which is not dominated by institutional practice. The work practice of the division of labour tends to alienate the person from the work practices and experiences of others and divide her from the rest of the workforce. This is exacerbated by modern stress on outcomes rather than relationships. The result is distanciation between the different professions within the National Health Service, a lack of awareness of the other professions, and little attention to the building of shalom, right relationships. This can result in rivalry, suspicion, inability to see common aims and in the end adversely affect efficient care (Baggott 1994). Ironically, this is just the atmosphere which the 'modernisation agenda' is working to rectify.

Attention then has to be paid to what Hawkins refers to as the spiritual dimension of the learning organisation (Hawkins 1991). Hawkins argues that beyond the level of operations and strategy the organisation which is developing needs to attend to questions of underlying identity and purpose. At this level, there is the development of 'integrative awareness' which ensures that there is transparency and participation such that all involved recognise shared life meaning and begin to accept mutual responsibility and interdependence. This may be the function of good planning which allows wide participation in reflection on purpose, aims and objectives. It may also enable the learning process to occur in the organisation. One example of this is the provision of whistle-blowing and anti-bullying procedures which enable transparency such that conflict can be dealt with constructively (Armstrong *et al.* 1999, Wright and Sayre-Adams 2000). Readers might be interested to note that in the early working papers for internal NHS purchasers and provider contracts at the beginning of the 1990s, the ability to blow the whistle was given as an issue which should be written into the contract. This was perhaps an ideology too far for many managers, as it was only the most enlightened of NHS organisations that allowed such a clause to be used in their contracts.

Other important ways of enabling empathy, both individual and group, include interdisciplinary training, multidisciplinary projects groups, and the shadowing of staff from different professions, all of which enable increased awareness of other professions. Collaborative work with other professionals can be effectively developed in and through the learning context. The point about the learning context is that it is non-threatening and yet encourages constructive critical thinking. Learning with other professional groups in the core areas of common concern actively enables the development of inter-group spirituality. All of these ideas mean that the professional bodies in the health service need to be in regular dialogue with each other, and be open to different opportunities.

One example of working with other professions, core to the question of spirituality, is the relationship of nursing staff to the chaplain. Even here, there is danger of 'turf wars', with the chaplain claiming the spiritual patch and the nurse adamant that she knows her patients' needs better. Reflection on this relationship can focus on general points about spirituality and teamwork and particular points about the responsibility for spiritual care.

Hospital chaplaincy

How the nursing staff relate to the chaplains is not necessarily a simple matter. As we noted in the first chapter, there can be a real tension between religious and broader spiritual perspectives. The chaplain may easily be viewed as someone who represents the church, and is therefore concerned both to convert and to be pastorally directive. One model of the chaplaincy actually sees the chaplain as providing spiritual care and worship for those in the Christian Church. This is an easily defined role with religious need as the basis for referral. This model has both a consumer element; the fulfilment of particular religious needs, and a church element, about the church reaching out and taking care of its own. In the post modern era, such a model has become increasingly difficult to hold with integrity, not least because spirituality as a human dimension is clearly broader than any particular religion.

At the same time chaplaincy has come under the same pressure as all other healthcare workers to begin to make clear its professional role. In 1992 there was the publication of the guidelines 'Meeting Spiritual Needs' (Department of Health 1992). In 1993 there was the Health Care Chaplaincy standards working party, which established desired outcomes. These gave the impression of the development of a professional or paraprofessional profile, something reinforced by the College of Health Care Chaplains and subsequent developments such as an MA in Health Care Chaplaincy, offered by the University of Leeds.

The NHS training document known as the 'Sails Report' begins to sum up the chaplain's task under several headings:

- *Identify and assess the needs for provision.* This points to an on-going reflection which builds up a spiritual narrative.

- *Manage and develop a chaplaincy service.* Part of this involves the area of publicity and setting up the service and clearly articulating underlying aims, objectives and values.
- *Provide opportunities for worship and religious expression.* This is partly a religious consumer approach, providing services and networking with different religions. It is also about enabling the embodiment and discipline of spirituality, such that any patient can discover ways of finding meaning and handling the experience of illness.
- *Provide pastoral counselling, care and therapy.*
- *Provide an informed resource which enables ethical and spiritual reflection*, be that formal spiritual direction and guidance where requested or helping the person to establish his own spirituality and response to the illness (NHS Training Directorate Project No. 2110193).

What emerges from this and other writings which stress a broader ethical role outside the therapeutic team (Faber 1971, Grainger 1979) is not straightforward and can be summed up in Box 10.1.

Box 10.1   The role of chaplain

- *Pastor.* Pastoral and spiritual care for all, patients and staff.
- *Priest.* Provision and coordination of religious services for all who need them, whatever faith.
- *Prophet.* This may involve acting as advocate for a patient or member of staff, or speaking out to management on matters of justice, such as work conditions (Pattison 1994).

Given the multi-layered role of the chaplain this makes him quite a hard person for other professions to handle. The first of these functions places him securely in the therapeutic team. The second is about religious rights in illness and catering for interest groups. The third sees the chaplain located outside the team and in direct conversation with the institutional hierarchy. None of these functions should be seen individually, but as recurrent strands which bond together, rather like a double helix. The chaplain thus acts as a visible symbol of the institution's commitment to reflection, to a spirituality which is not confined to one area but is there in practice and the institutional organisation (Monfalcone 1990, Dix 1996, Fraser 1996). What enables the chaplain to hold all those functions together with integrity is precisely a primary concern for the other, whether the other is individual or community, accompanied by a clear intention not to impose her spiritual narrative or direct others.

Working together

Thus, working with the chaplain means engaging with all these aspects and making use of them in the way which will most enhance the patient/staff experience. This involves working with the ambiguity of the chaplain's role. The basis for referral was discussed in Chapter 5. Clearly such referral should not be made without the permission of the patient. However, the creative possibilities of such referrals cannot be realised without an awareness of the purpose and skills of the chaplain and how she can contribute to the healing process and the support of the patient and staff. More important then that the formal process of referral is consultation and negotiation. Consultation recognises the chaplain as the appropriate person with whom to think through aspects of spiritual care. This enables a clarification of the problem and reflection on options. This leads naturally on to negotiation of the response. In all this, the spiritual care of the patient remains collaborative. Once the chaplain is called this does not mean that all responsibility for spiritual care then is given to her. On the contrary it continues in the everyday work of the nurse. Within the bounds of confidentiality, chaplain and nurse can ensure that their care complements each other.

At the core of referral then is joint reflection, something which in itself recognises mutual responsibility, enables the development of awareness and trust, and builds up the meaning of spirituality in practice. An important contribution to such teamwork is to have the chaplain involved in staff development and training, both as student and facilitator. Although certain clinical functions will be beyond her scope, the chaplain should have at least a sound understanding of the working practices of the other professions. This will allow her to contribute her own expertise into the staff development process in a meaningful way.

Local and corporate spirituality

Earlier in this book we noted how spirituality, despite the many books about it, is often not a part of practical care in nursing. In the light of the reflections on the profession and training, we would propose that the most effective way of achieving that practice is for each

Healthcare Trust to establish its own definition and practice of spirituality. This might involve three parts:

• The establishing of definition and practice. Given the very different views and agendas about spirituality this cannot be imposed but demands a process of consultation with the staff and with patients, or their representatives, to establish a broad definition with implications for practice.
• Maintaining ongoing reflection and practice through the professional development described above.
• Ensuring a developing spirituality of the professions and the workplace, as briefly described above.

The core of this strategy is the person- and practice-centred consultation. Only with this could all the different groups involved begin to develop confidence in each other and establish ground-rules for working practice. This would enable the Trust staff to begin to own a shared sense of spirituality in practice. It would be the responsibility of the Trust group to work out particular methods of spiritual evaluation and assessment that work most efficiently and effectively in the light of local practice and the different options offered through research.

Consultation could be effected by a small group including a senior nurse, the senior chaplain and an administrator. To ensure that all are included it might take twelve months, involving a mixture of questionnaires, ward and department meetings and larger plenary groups. To ensure consistency between Trusts, there could be a national steering committee focused in the healthcare professions and higher education, which can then link such developments into ongoing research.

Summing up

We began this chapter with a tragic case, one that seems to exemplify an entirely task-centred ethos. Human contact and awareness of the other was secondary to the completion of tasks. Hence, if a critical task was not completed, no-one asked the basic human questions about well-being. Clearly no-one attempted to listen to the patient, to encourage his narrative. Mr. Thomas plainly found it difficult, like many elderly people in hospital, to articulate that narrative, perhaps for fear of being a nuisance, disturbing the very busy doctors and nurses. Not only then was this a task-centred ethos, it was also reactive. The nurses and doctors, we might speculate, would have responded had Mr Thomas been able to articulate, to demonstrate physical or spiritual distress. But he could only whisper this to his family. The tragedy was one of non communication and lack of awareness.

It is plain that stress and overwork of the staff contributed to this, and that this led to a system that was not sensitive to need, not empathic. There is always one more task to be completed before the end of the shift and not enough people to do them all. In general terms, Bauman notes that inextricably linked to this task-centredness is the stress on expertise (Bauman 1989). In reflecting on the Holocaust, and on the profound question of why good people can do bad things, he shows how systems, not least divisions of labour, and expertise will tend to lead to distance, discouraging the professional from seeing the humanity of the other. He gives telling examples of German engineers who modified gas trucks. In so doing, these engineers fulfilled responsibilities to client, community, workforce, family and so on, but simply failed to see the their responsibility to the 'cargo' which was at the centre of their task (Bauman 1989, 197). In referring to Bauman, it is not our intention to draw an exact parallel between the Holocaust and modern healthcare. It is, however, a powerful example of how any system or organisation will tend to lead to task orientation and human distance if it is not *explicitly* human centred. A critical part of that human centredness is the life meaning of patient and profession; their spirituality. Hence, spirituality is not a bolt-on extra, something that can be looked at if you have that kind of 'bent', a theme for optional modules.

The nurse, along with the wider community of care, is in a unique position to enable the patient and family to grasp, develop and maintain spirituality in their experience of illness, suffering and loss. This does not mean that the nurse has to develop even more expertise, such that she can fulfil a 'specialism'. On the contrary, the qualities and skills which both enable and are the products of spirituality are central to our humanity. They are fundamental to finding meaning in relationships, and thus finding meaning in the experience of illness and healing.

The pressures to achieve targets in the twenty-first century are immense, not least because of increased demand on the National Health Service, and expectations of healthcare which remain massively high and often unrealistic. Such expectations can easily be grounded in a spirituality of magic, which seeks to solve everything for the patient, without ever attempting to engage the responsibility of the patient for life meaning and the embodiment of that meaning. Any government which seeks to demonstrate its achievements, through quantifiable outcomes, runs the risk of encouraging such a spirituality, and thus of destroying the fragile balance between care and competence. This raises questions about the spirituality of government which are beyond the bounds of this book.

Nonetheless, this reinforces the sense of spirituality as being the responsibility of more than the individual. Any organisation is responsible for the articulation, development and maintenance of its own life meaning. It also influences the spirituality of those who are part of it. Hence, the nursing profession and health organisations need to ensure structural empathy which both gives support to the nurse and is able to challenge her. This should provide both the space for reflection and the framework of discipline which can hold together a spirituality of care and competence. Rules, codes, procedures and the like will all provide a framework, but there can be no substitute for the learning organisation enabling reflection at all levels and encouraging awareness within and beyond all who are involved. Similarly, codes of practice are there for the individual nurse, but can never be a substitute for taking responsibility for the other, for person-centred care. This lies at the heart of the UKCC quote at the beginning of this chapter.

The caring professions are themselves then on a spiritual journey, not least in the constant reflection on their own roles and the constant questioning of their value and how others value them. Hence, matters such as nurses' pay should never be seen as separate from the spirituality of the profession. On the contrary, they are directly relevant and keep to the fore the tension between the nurse as competent professional who deserves proper reward and the nurse as altruistic carer who responds to vocation.

At the same time, as Campbell, and before him R.H. Tawney, suggests, the nursing profession, like others, is not simply focused on working through its own spirituality (Tawney 1964, 113; Campbell 1985). It is also able to contribute to the spiritual meaning of the wider community, by embodying publicly the idea of covenant and social contract that we owe each other. As Campbell writes of the caring professions,

> The end, that is the aim, of professionalism is to maintain the social contract, in a brutal world, by demonstrating the possibility of restoring the stranger to

the community, through the discovery and recovery of the human worth of society's casualties and rejects. Professionalism rejects the idea of a permanently stigmatised group – e.g. the senile, the handicapped, the chronic psychiatric patient – by its consistent effort to understand and communicate humane understanding to the society which finds them dangerous or useless. (Campbell 1985)

Such a spirituality is at the heart of healthcare in general, and nursing in particular.

References

Armstrong, J., Dixon, R. and Robinson, S. (1999) *The Decision Makers* (London: Thomas Telford).

Baggott, R. (1994) *Health and Health Care in Britain* (London: Macmillan Press – now Palgrave Macmillan).

Bauman, Z. (1989) *Modernity and the Holocaust* (London: Polity Press).

Bush, T. (1999) 'Journalling and the teaching of spirituality', *Nurse Education Today*, **19**, 20–8.

Campbell, A. (1984) *Moderated Love* (London: SPCK).

Campbell, A. (1985) 'Professionalism – A Theological Perspective' in *The End of Professionalism?* (Edinburgh: Centre for Theology and Public Issues).

Carter, R. (1985) 'A taxonomy of objectives for professional education', *Studies in Higher Education*, **10**, 2, 135–49.

Department of Health, *Meeting Spiritual Needs.* Health Service Guidelines 1992(2).

Dix, A. (1996) 'Is God Good Value?', *Health Service Journal*, 11 July, 24–7.

Faber, H. (1971) *Pastoral Care in the Modern Hospital* (London: SCM).

Fraser, D. (1996) Blessing in Disguise? *Health Service Journal*, 11 July, 28–9.

Grainger, R. (1979) *Waiting for Wings* (London: Darton, Longman and Todd).

Hawkins, P. (1991) 'The Spiritual Dimension of the Learning Organisation' *Management, Education and Development*, **22**, 3, 172–87.

McIntyre, A. (1981) *After Virtue* (London: Duckworth).

May, W. (1987) 'Code and Covenant, or Philanthropy and Contract?' in S. Lammers and A. Verhey (eds) *On Moral Medicine* (Grand Rapids: Eerdmans), 83–96.

May, M. (1994) 'The virtues in a professional setting' in J. Soskice (ed.) *Medicine and Moral Reasoning* (Cambridge: Cambridge University Press).

Megone, C. and Robinson, S. (2002) (eds) *Case Studies in Business Ethics* (London: Routledge).

Moltmann, J. (1985) *God in Creation* (London: SCM).

Monfalcone, W. (1990) 'General Hospital Chaplaincy' in R. Hunter (ed.) *Dictionary of Pastoral Care and Counselling* (Nashville: Abingdon).

Narayanasamy, A. (1999) 'ASSET: a model for actioning spirituality and spiritual care education and training in nursing', *Nurse Education Today*,19, 274–85.

NHS Training Directorate Project No. 2110193.

Nouwen, H. (1994) *The Wounded Healer* (London: Darton, Longman and Todd).

Pattison, S. (1994) *Pastoral Care and Liberation Theology* (Cambridge: Cambridge University Press).

Nursing and Midwifery Council (1992, 2002) *Code of Professional Conduct.*

Robinson, S. (1992) *Serving Society: The Social Responsibility of Business* (Nottingham: Grove Ethics)

Robinson, S. and Dixon, R. (1997) 'The professional engineer: virtues and learning' in *Science and Engineering Ethics*, **3**, 3, July, 339–49.

Rogers, B. (1983) *Freedom to Learn for the 80s* (Columbus: Merrill).

Schon, D. (1987) *Educating the Reflective Practitioner* (San Francisco: Jossey-Bass).

Solomon, R. (1992) *Ethics and Excellence: Co-operation and Integrity in Business* (Oxford: Oxford University Press).

Tangney, J. (Spring 2000) 'Humility: theoretical perspectives, empirical findings and directions for future research', *Journal of Social and Clinical Psychology*, **19**, 1, 35–48.

Tawney, R.H. (1964) *The Radical Tradition* (London: Allen and Unwin).

Titmuss, R. (1970) *The Gift Relationship* (London: Penguin).

Tracy, D. (1996) 'Can Virtue be Taught? Education, Virtue and the Soul' in J. Astley and C. Crowder (eds) *Theological Perspective and Christian Formation* (Grand Rapids; Grace wing).

Wilcock, P. (1996) *Spiritual Care of Dying and Bereaved People* (London: SPCK).

Wright, S. and Sayre-Adams, J. (2000) *Sacred Space* (London: Churchill Livingstone).

Index